SLAVERY'S DESCENDANTS

SLAVERY'S DESCENDANTS

Shared Legacies of Race
and Reconciliation

EDITED BY

DIONNE FORD AND JILL STRAUSS

FOREWORD BY

LUCIAN K. TRUSCOTT IV

RUTGERS UNIVERSITY PRESS
New Brunswick, Camden, and Newark, New Jersey, and London

Library of Congress Cataloging-in-Publication Data

Names: Ford, Dionne, 1969- editor. | Strauss, Jill, 1965- editor. | Truscott,
    Lucian K., 1947- author of foreword.
Title: Slavery's descendants : shared legacies of race and reconciliation /
    edited by Dionne Ford and Jill Strauss ; foreword by Lucian K. Truscott IV.
Description: New Brunswick, New Jersey : Rutgers University Press, [2019] |
    Includes bibliographical references.
Identifiers: LCCN 2018046485 | ISBN 9781978800762 (hardcover)
Subjects: LCSH: African Americans—Race identity. | Slavery—United
    States—Psychological aspects. | Racism—United States—History. | United
    States—Race relations. | Slaves—United States—Social conditions. |
    Slaveholders—United States—History. | African American families. |
    African Americans—Biography. | Whites—United States—Biography. |
    Reconciliation—Social aspects—United States.
Classification: LCC E185.625 .S58 2019 | DDC 305.800973—dc23
LC record available at https://lccn.loc.gov/2018046485

A British Cataloging-in-Publication record for this book is available from the
British Library.

www.rutgersuniversitypress.org

Manufactured in the United States of America

For our families

CONTENTS

FOREWORD
COMING TO THE TABLE

I remember my Great-Aunt Aggie telling my brother Frank and me, "Just because you're related to Thomas Jefferson doesn't make you any better than anyone else, so you just keep your mouths shut about it."

I followed that rule for almost fifty years. In all the times we studied the founding fathers in school, from elementary right through high school, I never raised my hand and said I was related to one of them. I went to West Point, which Jefferson founded, and I never breathed a word to anyone that I was the sixth great-grandson of the founder.

Then came 1998. A DNA study was done on the descendants of Jefferson's grandchildren through his long-time relationship with enslaved Sally Hemings, and the results were about to be announced. I called the op-ed editor of the *New York Times* and asked if he wanted an article about the controversy that was sure to come. What was remarkable about this is that I had written for the *Times* op-ed page for almost thirty years without telling anyone that I was a descendent of Jefferson. But when I told the editor at the *Times* that I would be writing my next piece as a sixth great-grandson of the man, all he said was, "We'd love that piece, Lucian." No questions about the legitimacy of my claim. No demand to see documentation. They just took me at my word.

Well, I wrote the story for the *Times*, and the DNA results were announced, shocking the world of Jefferson biographers and historians: at least one, and probably all, of the descendants of Sally Hemings were also descendants of Thomas Jefferson.

A couple of months went by, and the *Oprah Winfrey Show* called from Chicago, asking if my sister Mary and I would be willing to go on the show with several of our Hemings cousins. It would be the first time we met each other. After we agreed, there were extensive pre-interviews done by Oprah staffers before the show. We were informed that we would be put up in a hotel separate from our cousins. The way they were treating the whole thing gave us the impression that the show would be controversial, even explosive. The descendants of what was perhaps America's most famous slaveowner would be meeting the descendants of his most famous slave, and sparks would fly!

The show was something else altogether. Mary and I appeared on stage with Shay Banks-Young and her son Douglas, a preacher from Columbus, Ohio. In the front rows of the audience were perhaps ten more descendants of Hemings and Jefferson. Mary and I were on the show alone with Oprah for the first segment. After the commercial break, Oprah brought out Shay and Doug. We embraced and took our seats. There wasn't a confrontation. In fact, it was something more akin to a reunion. The meeting of Thomas Jefferson's two families was way more matter-of-fact than anyone, including Oprah herself, could have predicted.

We were all Jefferson's great-grandchildren, after all.

Toward the end of the show, Oprah whispered to me during a commercial break that she would be asking me the first question when we came back, and it would be a good one. Sure enough, it was. "So, Lucian, now that you've met your cousins, what are you going to do?"

The truth was, I had no idea. I looked over at Shay and Doug and the rest of my Hemings cousins. It was evident, even from the brief time we had spent together—and despite the fact that that time was on the biggest daytime television show in the nation—that we had far more in common than any of us could have predicted. Although we didn't know each other at all, the way that we had all been raised was almost unnervingly similar. All of our parents had made the same point to us again and again: just because we were related to Thomas Jefferson didn't make us any better than anyone else—and man, we were not to forget that!

We had also been told not to talk about being descendants of Jefferson at school, albeit for different reasons. Mary and I were told it would be unseemly, like we were bragging; however, Shay and Doug and our other cousins had been told that people either would not believe them or would make fun of them. Unfortunately, that was exactly what happened to several of our Hemings cousins who broke their family rules and spoke out not only in school but later in life, as adults. Their experiences were quite a contrast to mine with the *New York Times*.

So, I thought for a second about Oprah's question, and I said, "Why don't all of you come to the family reunion at Monticello with me next May." They didn't accept on the spot, but I could tell they were thinking about it. Later, all of the cousins on the Oprah show and about fifty more would go to the reunion of Jefferson descendants at Monticello as my guests. They attended the family meeting of the Monticello Association, which took place during the reunion, and I made a motion that we members of the association welcome them into the family. The motion was defeated on procedural grounds, but the die was cast.

I would go on to invite my Hemings cousins to the Monticello Reunion for three more years, until finally the Monticello Association took a formal vote on whether to admit the Hemings into the family. The vote was ninety-five to six against admitting them. Five of those voting in favor of the Hemings were Truscotts: my brother, my three sisters, and me. The sixth vote was from our cousin Marla R. Stevens.

We stopped going to the Monticello Association reunions after that. Instead, we now regularly attend Hemings family reunions and events for the descendants of slaves, put on by the Getting Word Project and Coming to the Table.

The Monticello Foundation recently removed the qualifying words, "most likely" from its description of Jefferson's paternity of Hemings's children, and the foundation has fully acknowledged that the history of enslaved people at Monticello as just as important as the history of Jefferson himself.

My cousins Susan Hutchison and Shannon LaNier were instrumental with Coming to the Table in this transformation of Monticello and the way history looks at Jefferson as a founding father and as a man. I'm also proud of the role I played in revealing the story of slavery at Monticello to the world, and I'm proud to be a part of Coming to the Table.

We have come a long way.

In fact, little did I know on that day when I embraced my Sally Hemings cousins and invited them to Monticello, how far we still had to go.

A turning point on the road to reconciliation came in the year 2000, when several of my Hemings cousins, including Shay Banks-Young, and I were invited to the annual convention of the Congress of Racial Equality (CORE) in New York. We were to be presented with humanitarian awards for our work on racial reconciliation. The main speaker that night was George W. Bush, who was then running for president. The CORE convention was a campaign stop for him.

Right after Bush spoke, I was invited to the podium. There to my right were Bush, Mayor Rudolph Giuliani, and New York Governor George Pataki. To my left were my cousins from the Hemings family. In front of me was a crowd of people who looked to be half from Harlem and half from Wall Street. Suffice it to say, it was something of an out-of-body experience.

Following the speech I had written down, I briefly outlined what my Hemings cousins and I had done to try to break the ice with my white Jefferson cousins and with Monticello itself, which was still treating Jefferson's relationship with Hemings like it was radioactive. But then I quickly pivoted to why I was there that night: I was there because my mother and father had raised me right. I told the crowd that people asked me all the time why I was standing up for my Hemings cousins, and they frequently remarked that it "must take a lot of courage." But I responded to these people the same way: I told them it didn't take any courage at all. Plus, although my parents had both died by then, I knew that if I hadn't taken a stand, my mother would have reached down from heaven, snatched me up by my short hairs, and asked why not.

After the convention, we were invited to a reception in a suite atop the New York Hilton, where we were all staying. Finally, around 2:00 a.m., I left the reception and went back to my room. I was in a Hilton bathrobe getting ready for bed when I heard a knock. I opened the door to find Shay standing in the hall, also wearing a bathrobe. I invited her in, but she demurred, saying that she would only take a minute. So we stood there in the hallway of the Hilton in our bathrobes.

Shay told me that she and the rest of the Hemings descendants hadn't been able to figure me out until tonight. She said that they had thought I might have some kind of agenda in inviting them to the Monticello reunions. A few of them thought I might have plans to write about it in a book.

I didn't, but now I find myself writing the foreword to this collection of stories from Coming to the Table, a much better way to talk about the legacy of slavery than one story alone. The stories told and the connections made through Coming to the Table have waited far too long to be shared, but they are here now. This painful and disgraceful part of our nation's history is finally being brought out in the open by the descendants of slaves and slaveowners both.

But this story has always been bigger than one man having children with one slave, even if his name was Thomas Jefferson and hers was Sally Hemings. It's about the stain that slavery has left on this country and the legacy with which we must live even today. Coming to the Table has helped to extend that story beyond two families in Virginia to the experiences of slaves and slaveowners throughout the nation. Moreover, Coming to the Table has helped to begin the process of reconciliation between the descendants of slaves and the descendants of slaveowners that will be necessary if this country is to move forward.

On that night in the hallway of the Hilton Hotel, Shay told me that they finally understood why I had taken the stand I took on behalf of the Hemings family. It was because of the legacy left to me by my mother and father. She took me around the shoulders in a big hug and said right into my ear, "Welcome to the family."

You have to hope, don't you, that one day everyone, the sons and daughters of slaves and slaveowners alike, will be like Shay and me in our bathrobes, embracing as family.

Lucian K. Truscott IV

SLAVERY'S DESCENDANTS

INTRODUCTION

DIONNE FORD AND JILL STRAUSS

S*LAVERY'S DESCENDANTS: Shared Legacies of Race and Recon-ciliation* addresses the legacy of racism and slavery in the United States through a collection of stories told by descendants of both enslaved people and enslavers who are members of the national organization Coming to the Table (CTTT).

Though legalized slavery ended more than a hundred and fifty years ago and civil rights laws were passed more than fifty years ago, we know that the United States is still very much divided along racial lines. Whether it's the shooting of unarmed black and brown people by police, the mass incarceration of people of color, or the 2016 presidential election in which the Ku Klux Klan endorsed the winning candidate, present-day racism is an outgrowth of the legacy of slavery.

Many Americans were introduced to the inextricable connection of US history to slavery through *The Oprah Winfrey Show* in 1998. It was there, after DNA evidence concluded that Thomas Jefferson fathered at least one child with his slave Sally Hemings, that our third president's descendants, both black and white, met for the first time. After the show, descendants from both family branches grew to know each other personally. The first ever family reunion of Hemings descendants was held at Monticello in 2003. At the reunion, Susan Hutchinson, one of the white cousins invited, learned about Will Hairston, the descendant of another slaveholding family in Virginia. For years, Hairston had attended the family reunions of descendants of his family's former enslaved people. Hairston worked at Eastern Mennonite University (EMU), a liberal arts college in Virginia known for its Center for Justice and Peacebuilding (CJP) that fosters positive deep-rooted sustainable change. Hutchinson eventually met Hairston, and her acquaintance with him and her Hemings cousins planted the seeds for Coming to the Table, founded in 2006. As Dr. Martin Luther King, Jr. had hoped and dreamed, "the sons of former slaves and the sons of former slaveowners" were coming together at the table of brotherhood.

Anthology co-editor Jill Strauss first learned about Coming to the Table while attending training sessions at CJP. She had been following CTTT's formation and joined in 2014 when an open invitation was made to all who recognized the injustice of slavery and racism, both past and present, and wanted to work for racial healing and social change. She joined Coming to the Table because she wanted to learn how to engage in the difficult conversations surrounding the legacies of slavery, racism, and white supremacy. She hoped that by learning from people who had forged relationships across racial lines, she could bridge contradictions in her own European-Jewish American identity.

Regardless of ethnic and racial background, in the United States, we are all affected by the legacies of slavery and deep-seated racial prejudice. As the anthology contributors demonstrate, we are all slavery's descendants. However, there are still those who think that discussing a family's connections to slavery is somehow disloyal or shameful or that we should not be held accountable for what our ancestors did. Nonetheless, the conversations continue. The language of the legacy is shifting to center on the humanity of the people forced to work in bondage rather than the status imposed upon them. Slaves, slaveholders, and masters are ceding to enslaved, enslavers, and slaveholders. The latter is the terminology we use here as editors. Our authors employ a variety of descriptors depending on context and perspective. Likewise, the term "reconciliation" is sometimes questioned because it implies that there was some kind of positive relationship in the past. And in the context of righting historical wrongs, how can there be reconciliation between people who have never met? We use "reconciliation" to describe the development of trust, empathy, and positive relationships. An anthology of narratives by descendants of both enslaved and enslavers seemed like one way to take on the challenging conversations that must happen to bridge these disparate beliefs.

The seeds for the anthology were planted during one of CTTT's monthly dialogues: a conference call in September 2014 that focused on developing a writers' group. This conversation sparked the idea for a collection of nonfiction essays by descendants of enslavers and enslaved, to be published in one volume. There are many commendable books on slavery in the United States,[1] but none takes a multiple-perspective approach the way one by Coming to the Table members could in keeping with the organization's mission to challenge and transform the nation's legacy of slavery and racism.

Most Coming to the Table efforts are co-led by an African American and a European American, so journalist Dionne Ford, a descendant of both enslavers and enslaved, joined Jill to co-edit the anthology.

Dionne had found Coming to the Table in 2010 when, in researching her family history, she discovered descendants of the family that had enslaved her great-great-grandmother. Susan responded to Dionne's petition for help, and thereafter, from their homes on opposite coasts, they emailed frequently, finally meeting in person at Coming to the Table's first national gathering. They later partnered to represent CTTT at a genealogy conference in 2016. The conference was in Susan's hometown of Seattle. As a guest in Susan's home, Dionne was given a room of honor—the newly decorated room where Susan had spent her time recovering from cancer. From the serene colors to the beautiful tapestry on the wall, the "healing room," as Dionne called it, exuded peace. Susan died the following year, but not before she got to see the fruits of her labor with Coming to the Table, and not before she had heard about the plans for this anthology—a physical manifestation of the Coming to the Table dream.

CTTT's vision for the United States is of a just and truthful society that acknowledges and seeks to heal from the racial wounds of the past—namely, from slavery and from the many forms of racism it spawned. Its approach is grounded in the theories and practices of Strategies for Trauma Awareness & Resilience (STAR), with a focus on transforming historical harms[2] and its generational transmission into racial justice and equity. The CTTT approach involves four interrelated practices:

1. Uncovering History: Researching, acknowledging, and sharing, with openness and honesty, the personal, familial, community, state, and national histories of race.
2. Making Connections: Connecting to others within and across racial lines in order to develop and deepen relationships.
3. Working toward Healing: Exploring how we can heal together through dialogue, reunion, ritual, meditation, prayer, ceremony, the arts, apology, and other methods.
4. Taking Action: Actively seeking ways to dismantle systems of racial inequality, injustice, and oppression, and working toward the transformation of our nation.

The four parts of this book correspond to these Coming to the Table approaches.

In Uncovering History, Shannon LaNier, a descendant of Sally Hemings and Thomas Jefferson, writes that he was always aware of his heritage but learned early on not to speak about it unless he wanted to be ridiculed. His story uncovers history that our nation's conscience has actively tried to suppress. Anne Westrick writes that her Virginia ancestors had a role in racializing slavery, while Bill Sizemore acknowledges the segregation, unequal distribution of resources, and unequal educational opportunities that existed for the black Sizemores enslaved by his family. From a humble family background, Catherine Sasanov recounts being surprised to discover that her Missouri ancestors enslaved people. In Oregon, Gregory Nokes recalls being similarly taken off guard upon learning that his ancestor brought a slave with him to this free state. Still other narratives reframe our assumptions about exactly who was touched by slavery; for example, Rodney Williams recalls discovering that his ancestor was the son of a slave and a Quaker (a member of a religious group typically thought of as pacifist and egalitarian).

Contributors Antoinette Broussard, Leslie Stainton, and Eileen Jackson tell about forging relationships with their linked descendants in Making Connections. Tom DeWolf, a descendant of the largest slave-trading family in the United States, gets reacquainted with an old friend, the only black man to attend the otherwise all-white church of his youth. Seasoned journalist Karen Branan tells of the lynching of four innocent black people by her ancestors, and she shows how uncovering this story has led to new, positive relationships. Fabrice Guerrier both despairs at the violence of racism and rejoices in the community and solidarity he has found at Coming to the Table, which recognizes society's wrongs and works collectively to right them.

In Working toward Healing, Sara Jenkins, and Elisa Pearmain probe another kind of link that was the outgrowth of slavery; they recount their relationships with the black domestic workers who helped raise them and who felt more like family than employees. Debian Marty explores the contradictions borne of being a descendant of slaveholding Quakers, whom we associate today with abolitionism. Likewise, David Terrett Beumée faces his own racism and his enslaver ancestors'. He documents his ancestors' role in slavery and names those whom they enslaved to make amends and promote healing. Tammarrah Lee and Karen Stewart-Ross uncover surprising stories and hope in their research of their enslaved and enslaver ancestors, helping them grapple with the violence in their respective histories.

As many in our country struggle with how to make known and memorialize the legacies of slavery and racism, our authors take the reins in Taking Action. Sarah Kohrs tells about restoring a cemetery for the enslaved in her community. Stephanie Harp reconstructs her family's part in a lynching and works to memorialize the victims. In honor of her ancestors—enslaved, enslavers, and lynching victims alike—Sharon Leslie Morgan documents her development of an online database in which descendants of enslavers can contribute information from family papers, such as deeds and wills, about the people their families enslaved. Joseph McGill recounts sleeping in slave dwellings around the country in hopes of bringing recognition and preservation to these sacred spaces; one slave-dwelling sleepover guest, Grant Hayter-Menzies, writes about the people his family enslaved, whose descendants are also his relatives. Phoebe and Betty Kilby, linked descendants of enslavers and the enslaved, recount their respective journeys to finding each other, their shared history, and activist present.

From published authors to first-time writers, the contributors to *Slavery's Descendants: Shared Legacies of Race and Reconciliation* take action by telling their stories. The essays are uncomfortable and sometimes harrowing, filled with displacement, shame and guilt, silence across generations, rape, and even death. But they also include generosity, gratitude, and love, as they uncover truths that challenge our understanding of history and promise opportunities to engage in the more thoughtful conversations these topics require.

We are grateful to these twenty-five contributors for sharing their descendant stories, which confront the legacy of slavery and reclaim a more complete picture of US history, one cousin at a time.

NOTES

1. See the bibliography.
2. Coming to the Table, "Vision, Mission, Approach, Values & Facebook Community Guideline," https://comingtothetable.org/about-us/vision-mission-values/.

PART I   UNCOVERING HISTORY

1 ⇥ PRESIDENT IN THE FAMILY

SHANNON LaNIER

"SIT DOWN AND stop telling lies!"

Those were the words asserted by my first-grade teacher when I told the class that "President Thomas Jefferson is my great-great-great-great-great-great-grandfather." We were studying U.S. presidents, so I was excited to share the information that I had been hearing in my family my whole life. At seven years old, I didn't understand the complexity of what I was saying or why someone wouldn't believe it. This was not "fake news." It was my family's legacy—the oral history that had been passed down to my brother Shawn and me as a matter of fact. Luckily, my mother, Priscilla, whose family line (on her father's side) makes the Jefferson link, went to my school the next day and told the teacher who had berated me, "My son is a ninth generation descendant of Thomas Jefferson and his slave Sally Hemings, and don't tell him differently!"

From that day on, I think I realized that not everyone would believe the story of my heritage. Not even some of my close friends would believe me at first. Their responses were usually, "Yeah, right, and I'm related to Abraham Lincoln." After so much criticism and disbelief about my connection to Jefferson, I stopped telling people about it. I knew who I was and didn't need to prove it to anyone. As my mom always said, "Be strong in the belief of who you are and don't let other people define you." I still practice that lesson to this day.

Fast forward thirty-one years, and I'm now coauthor (with photojournalist Jane Feldman) of the book *Jefferson's Children: The Story of One American Family*. The Jefferson-Hemings relationship has been validated by researchers like Annette Gordon Reid, with the help of DNA samples, and it has been accepted as fact by countless sources, including the Thomas Jefferson Foundation, which runs Jefferson's home and museum, Monticello. The family was even featured on the *Oprah Winfrey Show*, the *Today Show*, *CBS Sunday Morning*, and the list goes on. There is still a faction, however, that claims that a relative of Jefferson was the one to father some of Sally Hemings's children. I'm pretty sure, that today, my first-grade teacher would not challenge me.

Although my family story is more widely accepted now than ever before, wrapping our minds around all of the complexities in this family, as well as in other families touched by slavery, can be challenging. This is one reason that Jefferson/Hemings family members came together to help start the organization Coming to the Table (CTTT). When my cousin Shay Banks-Young, who we call Mama Shay, told me that the descendants of slaves and the descendants of slaveowners were coming together at the "table of brotherhood" to break bread and to discuss in depth our country's complicated past and its connections to our personal families, I knew I had to be involved. However, I had no idea what to expect. I'm not even sure if the organization had a mission statement at that point or if they just knew they had a novel idea. Either way, the concept was enough to catch my attention. It sounded like Dr. Martin Luther King, Jr.'s dream was being realized, and I wanted a seat at the table.

Not only was I not going to miss the opportunity to participate, but I also didn't want to miss the opportunity to document the experience. So, my wife Chandra and I asked for permission to film the conference for historical documentation and for CTTT to use to inspire others and to uncover future opportunities.

At that first CTTT gathering at Eastern Mennonite University in Virginia, a small and diverse group talked about the pain, anger, and guilt, along with the barrage of other feelings that were surfacing upon our discovery that we were descendants of slaves or slave masters. In some cases, like mine and that of a few of my cousins, we had to deal with the thought of being a descendant of both slave and slave master.

For some, it was the first time they had heard others talk about how they were dealing with the news and what it meant for them. While this may not have been the first time the black people in the room had talked about their views on slavery and its effects on our families, it may have been the first time they shared these thoughts and feelings with white people. It also seemed to be the first time many of the white people faced confronting and sharing their feelings about the issue. I remember thinking that the whole exchange was very brave. It was a vulnerable situation, and it was refreshing to see people willing to have in-depth conversations about a topic that most would never touch but that we all knew needed to be talked about. It was a truly enlightening experience. I often say that in order to let go of the anger, pain, and resentment we feel about slavery, we have to talk about it and go through the healing process, and CTTT allowed that outlet.

One experience especially sticks out in my mind. In one of our sessions with the entire group, my cousin Mama Shay said she wanted to tell everyone a story. She wanted everyone to have a better picture of what African people went through when they took that two- to three-month journey to a new land to be broken into slaves.

"Close your eyes and clear your mind," she said. Then she proceeded to narrate the highlights of that slave voyage to the new land. She led us through the kidnapping, the deplorable living conditions, the murder, rape, physical abuse, and dehumanization. When she finished, there was not a dry eye left in the house. It was an experience many had never even thought about, let alone been "transported" to.

Not only was Mama Shay's slave journey powerful and impactful, but it was also a learning experience. While some appreciated that glimpse into the reality of slavery, some were upset that she had caught them off guard and had subjected them to such a horrible and graphic experience without a warning or disclaimer. Mama Shay used these insights to open up a discussion about how slaves also never got a warning or disclaimer before being ripped from their families and having their lives disrupted and violated.

That discussion is a perfect example of what's great about the CTTT organization. It forces us out of our comfort zones but doesn't leave us faltering in unknown territory. For it is outside our comfort zones where the real work begins—work that can lead to deeper understanding, healing, and, in many cases, reconciliation.

I felt that those who participated in that first year of CTTT opened up and saw the world differently; or, at least, I saw them differently. I saw white people apologize for the injustices of their ancestors, and I saw black people accept those apologies, embracing and reassuring the slaveowners' descendants that what happened more than two hundred years ago wasn't their fault. In fact, we acknowledged that while the people in the room were not to blame for the past, they could be thanked for being part of the solution—by being involved in those important and difficult conversations. It seemed as if we were embarking on a new movement that had the capability of spreading to communities throughout the country.

That first year especially, the ideas behind CTTT really called for people who were open to understanding and accepting others and to extending forgiveness. Today, it still calls for such people. CTTT acts as a catalyst for those hard discussions over race relations, history, and healing, and those willing to go through such uncomfortable conversations and feelings, both personally and communally, grow into better people for a greater cause. After all, the only way we are going to grow and someday be a unified nation, is to start talking about our painful past.

The CTTT organization and conference is one of those deep and life-changing experiences that you may have to go through to truly understand, but once you do, you will not be sorry. And you certainly won't be the same.

2 ❧ SO MANY NAMES

A. B. WESTRICK

IN THE FALL of 2015 while researching Richmond, Virginia, as the setting for a novel, I came across a book by Benjamin Campbell titled *Richmond's Unhealed History*.[1] I was devouring the text, underlining and highlighting passages, totally absorbed in Campbell's presentation, when I hit a section about Virginia's House of Burgesses and stopped cold. I say that "I hit a section," but the effect was more like the section hit me. Here before me was colonial history I hadn't learned. How could I have missed it? How could American textbooks have left it out?

I'm descended from a number of men who served in Virginia's House of Burgesses. Aunt Margaret had played the role of family historian and instilled in all of us—cousins, aunts, uncles, anyone who'd listen—a tremendous sense of pride in our family tree. Textbooks describe our ancestors with words like *courageous,* for having fought off "Indians," and *bold* for having established a government "of the people, by the people, and for the people." Our ancestors forged a nation that would become great by virtue of its principles, such as "all are created equal." They were strong leaders and articulate speakers, greatly respected and admired.

But in *Richmond's Unhealed History*, the author doesn't gush with admiration over these men. Instead, he sheds light on some of the legislative accomplishments of the House of Burgesses—specifically, on laws having to do with slavery. These were laws I hadn't heard about, or if I had, I'd forgotten. They certainly hadn't been emphasized when I was in school.

I blog regularly, and a few years before reading *Richmond's Unhealed History*, I happened to mention in a post that my ancestors had enslaved Africans. Aunt Margaret hadn't ever said as much, but I'd figured it out through deductive reasoning: If textbooks presented Thomas Jefferson as a reluctant participant in the institution of slavery, and if Jefferson was the first cousin of my direct ancestor, then mine had to have been an enslaver too. The blog post in reference was on a different topic (slaveholding was an aside), but the line about slavery clearly hit a nerve.

Three thousand miles away, a close relative read my post and shot me an email with the subject line, "2Much Information!" He wrote that it was inexcusable for me to blog about the family, adding, "I do not think that our family history of owning slaves, if indeed true, as which is very new-news to me, needs to be in the public domain." He thought I should "become more appreciative" of our relatives, and he asked me to take down the post.

While he didn't use the word *shame,* I imagine he felt it. Or he felt embarrassed or wronged or something—I'm not sure what. But I realized that if I was going to put information like this out into the world, I would need proof; deductive reasoning wasn't good enough. But proof would require research, and I was busy, so I turned to Wikipedia. I pulled two names from our family tree—William Randolph, 1650–1711,[2] and Richard Bland, 1710–1776[3]—and in less than a minute, I had at least some measure of proof; that is, both men's wiki pages mentioned their ownership of slaves. Seeing the confirmation in print was simultaneously affirming (it meant my blog post was true) and unsettling (it meant my family's denial ran deep). No one in my family had ever talked about this fact.

Well, wait. I take that back. I have a vague childhood recollection of a day when I managed to get a bit of information out of my parents. I was maybe ten years old, and in my Pennsylvania classroom, I was the only kid whose parents had Southern accents. We were learning about the Civil War, and I was starting to put two and two together. When I got home from school, I asked whether our ancestors had owned slaves, and I remember Dad, in his warm Alabama-Florida drawl saying something like, "Well . . . I don't know, but if they did, I think our ancestors would've been good to their slaves. They'd have taught them to read and write." I pressed for details, but Dad shook his head. He didn't like to talk about the South.

When I asked Mom the same, my memory is that she answered along these lines: "Oh, no, of course not. My grandfather and great-grandfather were Episcopal priests, and you know how it is when you're in the church—you never have much money. And in any case, no, my family wouldn't have owned slaves." Her answer made me feel better than Dad's had, and up until just a few years ago, I never questioned it. I loved the notion that our family's roots and story were quintessentially American: humble beginnings and success through sacrifice, education, and hard work.

But decades later, when I was reasoning things out, it occurred to me that Mom's answer wasn't true. Her family line is full of the Randolphs, Blands, Bollings, and Harrisons of Virginia. That means her answer was a flat-out lie. A *lie!* The truth of it stunned me. Why would my wonderful, well-meaning mother have lied?

At this point, it had been so long since I'd heard her say "Not in our family" that it didn't feel right to bother her with a vague childhood memory. I filed it away but didn't forget, and later, while reading an article about the Noble Lost Cause ideology, I connected the dots. Statements like "We were good to our slaves" and "Not in our family" came straight from the Lost Cause catechism. Both of my parents had simply told me what their parents had told them.

Fast forward a number of years, and I was dealing with the "2Much Information!" email from my relative. I sent him a polite thank-you, saying I'd continue to think about what he'd written, and I've certainly kept that promise. But I've never fulfilled his request to take down the post. Details related to our ancestors had been hidden from us, and I wanted to learn more.

I began digging deeply into Southern history, and learning about white privilege. Growing up, I'd had no awareness of my privilege. I simply hadn't thought about it (which I now understand is itself an element of privilege—that I can walk through the world not thinking about issues related to race). My book group chose to read Michelle Alexander's *The New Jim Crow*[4] and Isabel Wilkerson's *The Warmth of Other Suns*,[5] exposing me to ideas and perspectives already known in African American circles but quite new to me.

I found the books compelling and the discussions lively, but for the most part, the issues raised by these authors seemed to have more to do with society in general than with me in particular. Or perhaps I should put it this way: for years, I kept racial issues framed in a political context—not a personal one.

But in the fall of 2015 when I read *Richmond's Unhealed History*, I could no longer hold racial issues at arm's length. The political was becoming personal. On page 79, Campbell wrote, "By its slave system, Virginia codified, institutionalized, and regulated poverty . . . Virginia's leaders racialized slavery. . . ."

That line was the one that made me look up from the page.

My ancestors were Virginia's leaders.

My ancestors *racialized* slavery.

My ancestors voted on how the institution of slavery would function, justifying the enslavement of Africans with the claim that people of color were inferior to Europeans.

My ancestors established a hierarchy of human value based solely on race.

My ancestors were *responsible* for America's peculiarly horrific institution of slavery. The system was their design. Their plan. Their legacy. And in support of their declarations, they quoted the Bible.

Richmond's Unhealed History rattled me to the core.

When I finished the book, I wanted to meet this author—the Reverend Benjamin Campbell. For many years, Campbell had served as the pastoral director at Richmond Hill, a spiritual community and retreat center twenty minutes from my house. One part of Richmond Hill's mission is to seek healing for the city through racial reconciliation. I'd attended various lectures at the center and had sometimes prayed the prayers that are recited three times daily in their chapel. But I hadn't yet met the reverend.

Online, I saw that Campbell was scheduled to give a talk in late September 2015 as part of a series titled "Finding Grace in Race." I drove to Richmond Hill to hear him, and this time when my car rolled up Broad Street and crept through the opening in the vast brick wall surrounding the center, I knew my visit would be different. This time I wouldn't simply stroll beneath the mature trees, pray in the restored chapel, listen to a thoughtful lecture, and go home. Deep inside me, something was churning, telling me that when it came to issues regarding racial reconciliation, I had a lot of work to do—deep and personal work. Campbell's book had exposed my ancestors and, by extension, he'd exposed me.

On that warm fall evening, I slipped into a crowded pew. I had a spiral notebook and pen at the ready, and when I heard Campbell say, "White guilt is not helpful; it paralyzes us," I scribbled his words and took a deep, cleansing breath. But my sense of guilt didn't go away simply because I wanted it to. I didn't feel clean.

After the lecture I attended a small-group session. We went around the room, introducing ourselves, and I managed to mumble that I was grappling with the realization that I was descended from generations of slaveholders. I didn't mention my horror over learning the extent to which members of the House of Burgesses were responsible for America's racialization of slavery, and none of the other participants mentioned any horrors from their histories, but I imagine if I'd said something more personal, more shame-filled, this group would have understood. They already knew what European Americans had done. I was the ignorant one.

Someone suggested that I might want to look into the work people were doing at Coming to the Table. It was the first I'd heard of CTTT. Within a few months, I'd read numerous CTTT articles and joined CTTT's Richmond chapter. In June 2016, I attended the national CTTT Conference in Harrisonburg, Virginia, and now, here I am, writing this piece.

CTTT encourages its members to uncover hidden history and share their research with openness and honesty, striving to heal the wounds of history by linking the descendants of former slaveholders with the descendants of the formerly enslaved. For me, this meant that knowing the names of my European American ancestors was no longer enough; I also needed to find the names of the people enslaved by my ancestors. I would need to do some serious research.

So I did.

And I found names. So many names.

In estate inventories and in last will and testaments, my ancestors had listed all of the people they'd claimed as property. In some cases, they added the estimated market value of each person. In only two days—at the Library of Virginia in downtown Richmond and online at Ancestry.com—I found one hundred and thirty-eight names. That was too many to include here, so I put them into an addendum, but had to wonder: if I can uncover this many names *in only two days*, how many more must there be?

One bright moment in my research was finding that Patty Woodlief, niece of my ancestor Peter Woodlief, emancipated two young people, Lucy and

Captain. She swore to provide for their care and instruction until they arrived "at full age." In her declaration, witnessed on May 29, 1790, in Prince George County, Virginia,[6] she wrote that "Freedom is the natural Right of all mankind, and that no Law, Moral or Devine hath given me a just right or property in the persons of any of my fellow creatures."

Oh, how I wish that more of my ancestors had possessed Patty's courage and resolve!

Outside of CTTT, when I mention that I'm researching my family's history of enslaving African Americans, invariably someone says, "But you're not responsible for what your ancestors did." I nod and find myself lost for words. A sense of shame resurfaces like an itch I'd like to soothe but can't manage to reach. They don't get it. They don't understand that the wrongs my ancestors committed continue to infect our society, and the historical trauma will keep festering if no one ever talks about it.

But at CTTT, people get it. Instead of shutting me down, they lean in to hear what I have to say. They allow me the time and space to express my shame. They encourage me to dig deeper.

I'm grateful that although my husband hasn't joined me in attending CTTT meetings, he understands my need to get involved. When I told him I'd signed up for the national conference, he nodded and said that for decades, he's seen in me an interest in racial issues. Books, articles, movies about racism—I've sought out all of them. "Put *Twelve Years a Slave* on the Netflix queue? Yeah, okay, honey." He'd like to see our country move past divisiveness, and while racism concerns him, it doesn't plague him the way it plagues me. His ancestors didn't enslave Africans. They were German and immigrated to rural Pennsylvania in the mid-1800s. They could embrace poetic gems such as, "Give me your tired, your poor, your huddled masses yearning to breathe free"[7] in ways my family members could not. None of my ancestors sailed past the Statue of Liberty. Instead, they came up the James River with huddled masses in the hulls of ships. Then they passed laws meant to keep people of color huddled for centuries.

Throughout my life, I've lived in (mostly) white suburbs and have absorbed racial stereotypes and misunderstandings. I'm ignorant about many things having to do with race, and I don't know what to do about white privilege. I feel heavy. Weighted down. And the deeper I dig into history, the more horrific the details I find. For example, books such as Edward Baptist's *The Half Has Never Been Told*[8] shed light on Virginia's role in supplying vast numbers of enslaved people to meet the demand for labor on Southern plantations after the 1807 Act Prohibiting the Importation of Slaves. Our laws permitted white men to rape black girls, get off scot-free, and sell their own offspring for a profit.

The truth is so abominable, it's no wonder the writers of America's history textbooks left the details out. It's no wonder that, after the Civil War, white Southerners conjured up the Noble Lost Cause ideology to put a positive spin on what they'd fought for and what their family members had died for. I get it now. I get why my Southern family and others like mine swept under the rug any talk about the institution of slavery. I get why they came to deny their complicity in it. I get that they needed to find ways to live with themselves, ways to clear their consciences so they could sleep at night.

Sometimes I wonder whether, in my appetite for lectures, books, and movies about racism, I am searching for forgiveness for them and for myself. But I don't feel that I deserve it.

I don't think my ancestors deserve it.

I don't think I'm ready to forgive my ancestors.

This anger and despair and shame—this is what it feels like to be descended from generation upon generation of enslavers.

But when I embrace others at CTTT gatherings, I find a sense of hope—the hope that by acknowledging the truth of our horrific history, European Americans and African Americans might embrace our shared humanity and brokenness, and we might begin to heal.

I hope that someday soon, I'll meet a descendant of one of the many people whom my ancestors claimed as property. Maybe we'll break bread together. Perhaps we'll stand side by side and link arms during a healing ceremony, like the one held at CTTT's national conference. I might get the opportunity to whisper, "I'm sorry. I'm just so very sorry." As emotionally draining as that day might be, I look forward to it. I anticipate that the deeper I'll dig into the history of my ancestors and the African Americans they enslaved, the more pain I'll uncover. But I'll also find truth, and that's the motivation for me.

Recently, I registered to attend an African American genealogy workshop at the Library of Virginia, where I hope to learn how to trace the family trees of the many people held in bondage by my ancestors. Right now, all I have are lists of first names and I don't know how to proceed. The task seems daunting, and if my relatives knew I was setting out to do it, I'm sure some would tell me to let it go—to let bygones be bygones. But to me, that's like leaving deep wounds to fester—wounds stitched shut before they were exposed and cleansed. No, I can't go there.

Instead, I'm lifting up Campbell's vision that Richmond might someday confront its unhealed history. By extension, America might confront hers, too. I'm embracing CTTT's mission to uncover history with openness and honesty; and at the table, I'm celebrating America's promise of equality for all. *Ahhh,* it sounds like a dream, doesn't it? A really good dream.

ADDENDUM

A. B. (Anne Bryan) Westrick's ancestors who served in Virginia's House of Burgesses include Richard Bennett, Archibald Blair, Theodorick Bland, Richard Bland I, Richard Bland II, John Bolling, Robert Bolling, Thomas Harrison, Richard Kennon, and William Randolph.

According to last wills and testaments and inventories of estates, what follows are the names of one hundred and thirty-eight of the many African Americans enslaved by the ancestors of A. B. Westrick.

John Poythress, whose will was proved December 11, 1712, in Prince George County, Virginia,[9] bequeathed to his wife and children the negroes Coffer, Sis, Jack, young Mary, Peter, Beck, Tom, young Sarah, Frank Cook, Amy, Frank Cook at Nattuah, Bess and Nanny and their increase, Ben and Nanny and their increase, Catto, Usse, Sarah, Pegg and her son Tom, Moll, John Cook, the child Shu, [another] Shu, and Jude.

Richard Bland, whose will was proved April 12, 1720, in Prince George County, Virginia,[10] bequeathed to his daughters the woman Scis and the girls Frank, Kate, Judith, Phillis, and little Scis; and to his sons "All my Negro's [sic] not before mentioned."

William Beale,[11] whose will was proved July 6, 1778, in Richmond County, Virginia, bequeathed to his children the negro woman Sue, the girl Priscilla, Nancy (formerly a kitchen scullion), Corinna, Betty, and Phillis. In a codicil, he added Nancy, the daughter of Nell. The inventories of his Richmond County and Culpepper County estates included the names and estimated market values of Bookuy, Toby, Jacob, Siman, David, Ned, Daniel, Jack, Able, Keen, Dick, Joe, Baker, wench Brifs and child Billy, Jane, Winny, George, Ephraim, Tom, Creenor and children, Ben, Jack, Rachel and child

Fanny, Luce, James, Nell and child Jaible, Nann, Nanney, Moll, Sarah, George, Pegg, Sarah, Jury, old Daniel, [another] Moll, boy Harry, man Harry, wench Mary, Glouchester, Jury, Dudley, Tom, Ben, Peter, James, Sie, Randolph, wench Rose and child Daniel, wench Agga and child Fortimore, Vinah, Violet, Fanny, Sarah, Cate, Pegg, girl Judah, Easter, Winny, Nann, and Suck.

Burr Harrison, whose will was proved February 7, 1791, in Prince William County, Virginia,[12] bequeathed to his children the following negroes: a woman Poll and her child Salle, a girl Rachael (daughter of Amy), the boys Will, Sammy, and Gabriel (a child of Aimigo), a man named Big Jerry, a man Frank, a fellow Tom, a wench Rachel, Suck (a child of Ruth), and a child Shartell. The appraisement of his estate[13] included the above-named persons in addition to the wenches Ruth, Anny, and Doll (with child), the boys Davy and Jury, a woman Ginny, and fellows Charles and May.

The 1816 inventory of William H. Parker's estate in Loudoun County, Virginia,[14] included the negro man Juba, woman Winnifred, and boy Peter.

Leroy P. Daingerfield, whose will was proved March 31, 1823, in Frederick County, Virginia,[15] bequeathed to his children the negro men John, Robin, and Henry; boys Ambrose and Danny; girls Lizzy, Patty, and [another] Patty; and the woman Caty, plus [another] Caty and her child Betty.

NOTES

1. Benjamin P. Campbell, *Richmond's Unhealed History* (Richmond: Brandylane Publishers, 2012).

2. "William Randolph," Wikipedia, Wikimedia Foundation, last modified January 31, 2018, en.wikipedia.org/wiki/William_Randolph.

3. "Richard Bland," Wikipedia, Wikimedia Foundation, last modified January 29, 2018, en.wikipedia.org/wiki/Richard_Bland.

4. Michelle Alexander, *The New Jim Crow: Mass Incarceration in the Age of Colorblindness* (New York: The New Press, 2010).

5. Isabel Wilkerson, *The Warmth of Other Suns: The Epic Story of America's Great Migration* (New York: Random House, 2010).

6. *Prince George County Deed Book, 1787–1792*, deed of emancipation of Patty Woodlief's Slaves, recorded June 18, 1790, pp. 368–369, Reel 3, Library of Virginia, Richmond, VA.

7. Emma Lazarus and John Hollander, "The New Colossus," in *Emma Lazarus Selected Poems*, edited by John Hollander (The Library of America, 2005).

8. Edward E. Baptist, *The Half Has Never Been Told: Slavery and the Making of American Capitalism* (New York: Basic Books, 2014).

9. *Prince George County Deed Book B, 1710–1713*, will of John Poythress, proved December 11, 1712, pp.175–177, Reel 13, Library of Virginia, Richmond.

10. *Prince George County Deeds, Etc., 1713–1728*, will of Richard Bland, proved April 12, 1720, pp. 394–396, Reel 1, Library of Virginia, Richmond.

11. *Richmond County Will Book 7, 1767–1787*, will of William Beale, proved July 6, 1778, pp. 308–309; codicil recorded November 2, 1778, p. 334; inventory and appraisal of estates in Richmond and Culpepper Counties, recorded November 8, 1778, pp. 328–331, Reel 24, Library of Virginia, Richmond.

12. *Prince William County Will Book G, 1778–1791*, will of Burr Harrison, proved February 7, 1791, pp. 474–479, Reel 18, Library of Virginia, Richmond.

13. *Prince William County Will Book H, 1792–1803*, appraisement of the estate of Burr Harrison, recorded January 7, 1793, pp. 47–50, Reel 19, Library of Virginia, Richmond.

14. *Loudoun County Will Book M, 1816–1818*, inventory of estate of William H. Parker, recorded September 22, 1817, p. 40, Reel 56, Library of Virginia, Richmond.

15. *Frederick County Will Book 11, 1820–1823*, will of Leroy P. Daingerfield, proved March 31, 1823, pp. 381–383, Reel 55, Library of Virginia, Richmond.

3 ❧ THE WILL, THE WOMAN, AND THE ARCHIVE

CATHERINE SASANOV

For Traci Wilson Kleekamp

For NORTHERNERS, KNOWLEDGE of slaveholding ancestry often happens the same way: a story heard or a stumble-over. In my case, it was both.

In 2005, my elderly cousin, Carolyn, called from California to wax nostalgic over family memorabilia found in a long-sealed box: delicate late-nineteenth-century Halloween cards. A wedding invitation to the shotgun nuptials of our Aunt Maude and Uncle Cory in 1903. Tintypes of young male ancestors, circa 1870. Grandpa Steele's 1857 will with the slaves in it. "What slaves?" I asked, dumbfounded, mind beginning to race: I grew up in northern Illinois, my father in southwest Missouri. The Ozarks. *Hill* country. (*Beverly Hillbillies?*) We weren't rich. We weren't some down-at-the-heels family hanging on to the status of an old, respected name. *How* was that possible? Like most Americans, I'd been *Gone with the Wind* educated. The props swirling through my head—Big House, hoop skirts, rice, cotton, moonlight, magnolias, acre upon acre of manicured plantations—I couldn't place any of them into what little I knew of the Missouri Ozarks.

"What slaves?" though, was all I could get out of my mouth. My cousin had as little idea as I did and could only read off the names in the will: Flora. Ben. Eliza. George. Alex. Edmund. Henderson. Henry. "Easter I wish to live with whichever one of my children she chooses." Nine names. "Negro boy, negro girl," the only other identifiers. But not for Easter. "Perhaps Easter is a horse," my cousin offered weakly.

We stayed on the phone a little longer, mostly with Carolyn explaining and situating for me who this "Grandpa Steele" was. Richard Steele positioned himself three *greats* back in our line of grandfathers. At his death in June 1860, his son, great-great-grandfather John P. Steele, would inherit his father's enslaved man, George. John's daughter, Nannie Steele (born in the thick of the Civil War) and her husband, Joseph William Knox, gave birth to my grandmother, Pearl Steele Knox. Grandma married Henry Baker. In 1914, they brought my father, John Knox Baker, into the world in Springfield, Missouri, a short drive from where Richard Steele, his family, and the people he enslaved once lived. Life in southwest Missouri ended for my father during World War II when he met his future wife, my mother, in Rockford, Illinois, married and settled there.

I thanked my cousin and hung up.

Flora. Ben. Eliza. George. Alex. Edmund. Henderson. Henry. Easter.

I can't say how long I sat up with those names that night, but I had started the clock on the five years I'd spend trying to flesh them out. By evening's end, I would discover that I also had a copy of the will. It was buried in family papers I'd inherited, part of a proof-of-lineage packet my late cousin Marjorie Knox Temple had sent to the DAR. She'd hoped to become a Daughter of the American Revolution, and the will had clinched it: there she found our great-great-grandfather listed among all the rest of Richard Steele's children. For her, the will seemed to have meant nothing more than a *missing link*: it completed our family's connection to two Revolutionary War ancestors. Still attached with a now rusty paperclip was a note to my parents, dated February 5, 1981: "Dear Peggy and John, Lou and I had found a brief form of Richard Steele's will but not the complete one. We knew John P. was the 10th child—now we have all twelve names." The names of the enslaved, paired off in bequeathment to Grandpa Steele's children, hadn't been worth so much as a comment on Marjorie's part. What did my parents think, not think, when they read them? As for myself, I could hardly believe it. The will I'd asked Cousin Carolyn to photocopy and send to me ASAP had already been in my possession for years.

Do the dead choose the time to reveal themselves?

Once you *know*, you can't *unknow*.

For a long time after discovering my family's slaveholding, it was hard for me to articulate to others why it bothered me so much, why I was utterly driven to find out everything I could about the people my family had enslaved. Guilt it wasn't. Guilt has never much motivated me (especially over sins perpetrated by long dead ancestors). Guilt, though, was the only motivation most folks could fathom for why any sane Northerner would make public their ancestors' slaveholding and willingly dive into that mess. In my adopted home of Boston, Massachusetts, in August 2005, no one else I knew had "this problem," so to speak. And for the majority of the people I talked to, it wasn't a problem at all. *It's over* was the implicit/explicit message I received from family and friends. Sadly, anyone in my family who might have known something, including my parents, was either long or freshly dead. So I was on my own. I had enough sense of genealogy (my mother had been an amateur genealogist extraordinaire) to realize that trying to piece together the lineage of human beings who were considered property was going to have its own set of challenges. Bless the internet. Through it, I found Traci Wilson-Kleekamp of Columbia, Missouri, who has worked with descendants of both the enslaved and slaveholders, helping them navigate African American genealogy. With her guidance and enthusiasm, I dove into the Greene County, Missouri, archives (albeit mostly long distance, with photocopied documents being mailed to me). I went to Missouri in 2006, locating and spending time in the physical locations where the people who had taken my great-great-great-grandfather's surname, the black Steeles of Greene County,[1] had survived the hold that my ancestors had had on their lives.

My one early attempt to locate descendants of the black Steeles in Greene County, in hopes of sharing the information I had gathered so far and finding out more about their ancestors, ended up badly timed. I had scheduled my research trip to Missouri for when I could travel—a date way too close to the hundredth anniversary of the lynching of three innocent men in Springfield—the town where I'd be staying. In anticipation of the trip, the Greene County Archives had given me the names of two people in the black community to call who might be able to help me in my search for Steele descendants. Both were polite but suspicious of my motives. Even though I tried to make clear that I wasn't calling regarding the lynching, I was told later that the community was used to whites (especially the white press) trotting out the lynching every April, while ignoring present-day concerns and achievements the rest of the year. How could I take it personally? I was white, an outsider, and an absolute unknown. Not to mention that it could hardly be anyone's version of good news to pick up the phone to some variation of "Hi. I'm a descendant of a family who enslaved ancestors in your community." Until I had something more to offer, until I'd done something to earn people's trust, I'd have to carry out the search on my own.

By late 2006, I had gathered enough information about the lives of the black Steeles and their allied families to publish two articles for the local genealogical journal *Ozar'Kin* (in Fall 2006 and Spring 2007). A series of poems I had also worked on during the research process was published as the book *Had Slaves*. As opposed to my prose, those poems allowed me to bear questions I'd likely never find answers to. They gave me a nonlinear lens through which to consider the lives of the black Steeles, my family, slavery in the Missouri Ozarks, and its aftermath. Poetry gave me a place to set down a grief that grew more profound with every detail I uncovered, every detail I couldn't find, and the shock of how recently so much had been lost. One particular sorrow: Mrs. Elizabeth "Betty" Sharp, who was enslaved as a child and grew up knowing all of the black Steeles, both in slavery and in freedom, had died in 1945. She'd lived only blocks from where my father grew up. When she passed at a hundred and five, my father was thirty. That meant for thirty years, their existence in this world overlapped. They could have met, could have talked, but as far as I know they didn't. I was wild with grief at the missed opportunity. It brought home that slavery's past was hardly a long time ago.

As I look back on those first writings—the genealogical work, but especially the poems—they were my early attempts at trying to flesh out lives while staying within the limits of what the archive had to offer. I didn't want to create generic slave stories, imagine happy endings, or find resolutions where none existed. I didn't want to let my family off the hook. The work that resulted from that time, as I groped around, trying to figure out how to make sense of and use what I had found in the archives, is less than perfect. As the white Steeles had left behind no personal papers, I was left working with bits and pieces I collected from public records regarding my family's slaveholding. I didn't yet know there were ways to wear what I did find in the archives as anything other than a straitjacket and choke chain. And I didn't know how to make the best use of what I *couldn't* find. I felt that I needed to be in the volume of poems about my ancestors' slaveholding, didn't want to duck my part in that bloodline, but found it difficult, at times, to keep out of my own way. Still, I'm glad that I wrote that book. I had written my genealogical articles for the living, but the poems were my letters to the dead— the best I could craft at that time. And while it wasn't my motivation, I hadn't found any other white poet at the time taking on the subject of their family's slaveholding. So *Had Slaves* at least was a start. My hope then is still my hope now: that descendants of the black Steeles will come across the research and writing (my articles, poems, and polished notes are housed in the *Black Families of the Ozarks*[2] section of the Greene County Archives in Springfield, Missouri) and that it will help piece together at least part of their own genealogy. For that matter, I hope that descendants of the white Steeles find the information as well. How can our own history be complete without that knowledge? All of my gathering, trying to create some semblance of a *whole* out of bits and pieces gleaned from wills, land deeds, tax lists, bills of sale, marriage and death certificates, probate files, plat maps, Civil War pension applications, court cases, census records, local histories, even listings for stray horses that had wandered onto private land—all of it was a way to try to give form to individuals whose presence in Richard Steele's will had been stripped down to a business transaction. As it turned out, slaveholding among the Steeles went back as far as the Revolutionary War, taking place in Williamson County, Tennessee, and Rowan County, North Carolina. Giving over some of my life to finding out all that I could about at least some of the people my family held in bondage has been a small price to pay on the debt that I owe to the nine people who furthered my family's life. This isn't even counting the people I know even less about, named and unnamed, outside the will, whom the white Steeles held in bondage during their eighty-four years as enslavers.

It took me awhile, but the poetry and prose finally allowed me to articulate what troubled me most regarding my family's slaveholding: how easily I could have gone to my grave without knowing that it had even taken place. It was only in coming across a will that a cousin had once ordered to help her enter an exclusive club that I even came to know. That's how little the enslavement of nine people, and the toll that enslavement must have taken on each of their lives, haunted my bloodline or was even a concern to the culture at large.

By 2010, I had gone as far as my finances and research skills would take me in regard to investigating my family's slaveholding. I used it as an opportunity to give myself a break from looking at slavery through the emotionally complicated lens of family connections and turned my attention toward my now hometown of Boston and, to some extent, toward New England itself. The region had its own tangled involvement with slavery during the 1600s and 1700s, and much like southwest Missouri, had managed to successfully eradicate or obscure evidence of its thriving existence. Now, instead of residing half a continent away from the people whose lives I was trying to piece together and understand, I lived in the midst of one of slavery's crime scenes. Primary sources no longer arrived in the mail as black-and-white photocopies but were put into my hands as original seventeenth-, eighteenth-, and nineteenth-century documents, full of immediacy and emotional resonance. And carrying on my daily life in the same places where the enslaved once carried on their own allowed me to slowly pick apart and examine the layers of "progress," commerce, cultural amnesia, and American myth-making that bury or disguise New England's slaveholding past. All of this, a luxury I didn't have as I tried to flesh out the lives of the black Steeles back in Missouri.

A couple of years into my New England search, I was online looking for one thing when I came across something else: the digitally reproduced image of a cargo document, a bill of lading where "one negro woman" was being shipped from Barbados to Kittery, Maine, in 1719, to be sold by father and son merchants, the William Pepperrells.[3] I was startled by how pristine it looked for being nearly three hundred years old; the ink so fresh, it might have been written yesterday. I enlarged the image and began reading more closely. The document made clear that it wasn't by asking for her name that the Pepperrells would come to identify the woman, but by searching her body: she'd been branded—"mark^d with a Y on ye right Sholder"—with the initial of a former slaveowner or trader.

I sat back like someone had slapped me. Over the years, I'd developed a strong stomach for the horrors of slavery. But a woman *seared* with one of the twenty-six letters I've given my life to as a poet—*this* I wasn't prepared for. I felt much as I had as when I'd first learned about my ancestors' slaveholding: I wanted to learn more and write a response to what had just set me reeling. But how does one write about someone already injured, both literally and figuratively, by writing? How not to harm her again? The very characters of the alphabet were infected with slavery. This was the challenge, though I realize now it had *always* been the challenge, from the moment I entered the unsettling world of slavery, history, memory, and the archives back in 2005.

Can an existence be salvaged from a handful of words?
Live in the space of fractures.
Make visible the loss.[4]

It was sometime in late 2013 when I found historian and writer Saidiya Hartman's essay "Venus in Two Acts" and her book *Lose Your Mother: A Journey Along the Atlantic Slave Route.*[5] When I did, I discovered someone who gave words to, and deftly exemplified in her own work, what I had been awkwardly groping toward in the writing of *Had Slaves*: That there were ways to "strain against the limitations of the archive," as Hartman elegantly put it, and yet to remain within the boundaries of what the archive held. This didn't mean making up details that couldn't be known but recognizing opportunities in documents where "creative speculation" could occur.

This was hugely important to me as I struggled with how to stay true to what I found in archives that weren't necessarily true to people like the black Steeles and the unnamed woman branded Y. Archives that were focused on what was important to *white* memory were the only places I was finding—when I found anything at all—evidence of their existence. I started looking for ways to use the archive against itself, to work with the materials I found there for purposes other than what they were originally intended. In doing so, I began to recognize opportunities to illustrate (among other things) resistance, comfort, and the better hanging of slaveowners on the petard of their own words than I might have formerly recognized. At the same time, I tried (as Hartman urges) "to make visible the loss"—what was left out, what had never been deemed important enough to record or collect, what can't ever be known. Absence, too, has a shape.

So for the past three years, I have "strained against the limitations of the archive" as I work on my latest book of poems. *Mark^d Y (Archives & Invocations)* is written out of my search through New England archives for further traces of the unnamed woman mark^d Y.[6] Hartman's ideas have helped me make connections between materials that I might not have thought to otherwise. A balsam sachet from Maine and an advertisement for a man called Christmas who had managed to slip away from his enslavers in Barbados. A letter from 1754 to consider what the woman mark[d] Y might have faced in the Pepperrell home in 1719. A 1718 bill of sale to Pepperrell for a man named Seasor, a man who might have still been in the Pepperrell household when the woman mark[d] Y arrived less than a year later. And an article about the 1960s dismantling of a house that Pepperrell had built for his daughter and son-in-law in 1742. These and other materials helped me flesh out in my writing the second appearance of the woman mark[d] Y, this time in a letter's terrible, terse news of how she—and four other enslaved people with her on the brigantine *Sarah*—had died: "June 25, 1719: Sir, I received yours by Captain Morris, with bills of lading for five negroes and one hogshead of rum. One negro woman, marked Y on the left breast, died in about three weeks after her arrival, in spite of medical aid which I procured. All the rest died at sea. I am sorry for your loss. It may have resulted from deficient clothing so early in the spring."[7]

This letter, so full of death, was meant to be read, though, as nothing but business. Penned by William Pepperrell to his agent in Barbados, even the phrase "I am sorry for your loss" has nothing to do with human mourning. Pepperrell just wanted his agent to remember *You're the one taking the financial hit for five dead slaves—not me.*

What follows here, in a prose meditation and poem,[8] are two ways I stayed within the limits of the archive but worked to return *life* to the death of the woman branded Y (and I have not forgotten her companions; their own fate is addressed elsewhere in my writing), a woman whose death Pepperrell's words would otherwise strip down to nothing more than a failed business transaction:

One of my only clues as to what might have greeted the unnamed woman mark[d] Y in 1719 comes from a letter written in 1754.[9] That year, Pepperrell's son-in-law, Nathaniel Sparhawk, sends six enslaved women by ship from Boston to his Kittery home. (Don't bother looking for the scene of that crime; in the 1900s, the owners of Sparhawk Hall began to dismantle the house around themselves. Room after room sold off for its fabulous paneling. In the sixties, Portsmouth's Strawbery Banke Museum bought the colonial mansion, gave it one final gutting, then burned its shell.) Like the unnamed woman, the six women

Sparhawk enslaved were also to be sold. In his November 29 letter, Sparhawk anxiously directs his business associate that:

". . . they must have Cloaths & shoes sufficient, & more shirts & shifts . . . see they have a good fire & good room & an old Sail to lay upon & the Ruggs to cover them . . . Be sure they don't suffer, for wch end see them 2 or 3 times a day . . . pray see they have good care taken of them, & let me know they are well. . . ."

At the Pepperrell home (*that* house still stands), did this same anxious attention greet the unnamed woman as she stepped (was carried?) off the ship? Was she shocked at the care likely lavished on her physical well-being? Warm and dry for the first time in weeks, sufficiently dressed, fed, doctored, and allowed to sleep. Or did she recognize *concern* for what it was: father and son merchants attempting to mend a piece of damaged merchandise.

In Sparhawk's case, his "investments" were already healthy. He just hoped to save money on feeding the women until he could sell them off: "I Hope you will be able to get some Body to take them for their Victualls wch I shall like much. . . ."

Be sure they don't suffer, for wch end see them 2 or 3 times a day . . . pray see they have good care taken of them. When New England slavery is broached in nineteenth- and twentieth-century local histories, it's often lauded as short-lived and benign. But in Sparhawk's exhortation, there's also admission: threat of mistreatment and injury were constants in the lives of the enslaved.

But for the unnamed woman branded Y, finding herself another voyage, another climate, another continent away from home—when it came to *care* (even with the possible care of the Pepperrells' other enslaved people), was it all too little, too late, for all the wrong reasons?

MAINE HISTORICAL SOCIETY, PORTLAND, ME
In Collection 420, Box 8/36

this: 26th Day of May
Anno Domini Thous. Seven hundred & Eightteen

what passes for hope

that you didn't die
alone—

One Negro Man Aged about Thirty five years;
called by ye name of Seasor;
Given, Granted, Bargained & Sold
Signed, Sealed & Delivered   **I'm yours**
unto Willm Pepperrell his heirs & Assigns
To have & to Hold   **till death do us part**
for Ever
for Ever
for Ever a hope

so fragile
it can no longer be
touched,

was Xeroxed once, what's
in my hands now:

a copy of
a copy of
a copy of
a copy . . .

To have
a faint hope   **till death does its part**
& to Hold

that in a house that still stands,
under at least one set of eyes,

you weren't seen
as a piece

of dying merchandise.

Perhaps *this time*, when I have gone as far as my research and writing skills
take me, as I try to document the second life the unnamed woman mark^d Y
has been forced to live out in the archives, I will return to Richard Steele's

will and the nine people I imperfectly tried to loosen from its grip through poetry and prose between 2005 and 2010. I wish that I'd been better able to see the possibilities of the archive back then, been more skilled in my writing and more distanced emotionally. (Grief over what I was finding and not finding had me, at times, too much in my own way). But I am glad for what I wrote and that I put the work out there. I don't think I could have arrived where I am now if I had not done it; if I had waited until the work was somehow perfect; or worse, if I been too afraid of what other people might think to have attempted the writing at all. Attempting perfection while wrestling demons in the minefield of our nation's slaveholding past (part of our "afterlife of slavery," as Saidiya Hartman calls it) is a killer. As a perfectionist, that's not easy for me to say.

To find Grandpa Steele's will was to have him come back from the dead and tell me it was my turn to inherit the people he was bequeathing: Flora, Ben, Eliza, George, Alex, Edmund, Henderson, Henry, and Easter. To have ignored his words, to have shoved those nine people locked in his will, locked in his words, back in a drawer, would have been my tacit agreement to accept.

Here's what becoming that slaveholder would have meant: never finding out, much less making public, that Flora had managed for thirty-four years to keep Richard Steele from selling her children, Ben and Eliza; that she had kept her family intact until the machinery of the will, on September 15, 1860, finally creaked into motion and separated them. It would have meant leaving George and Henderson Steele frozen in enslavement when, in fact, by 1864, both had become soldiers in Company B, 68th Regiment, U.S. Colored Troops, taking part in the Civil War. It would have meant abandoning the youngest enslaved Steele, three-year-old Henry, to the whims of his new ten-year-old master, Richard Steele Young. Henry, who survived the Civil War and, by 1876, returned to Eliza—living in *her* home, on *her* 50 acres of land, adjacent to the 40 acres owned by Alex Steele. Only four years earlier, Easter Steele, then age thirty-six, had been living with Eliza too. Now Henry Steele shared the house with Eliza and his eleven-year-old cousin, Francis, the youngest child of his Uncle George's six children. On November 4, 1871, that war veteran's death from pneumonia had shattered his family. Had George Steele asked his sister Eliza to take Francis in? Did Henry try to comfort the orphan, telling her how he, as a child, withstood his own trials and assuring Francis she'd get through hers too? Did he keep to his nineteen-year-old self how he had watched, as a toddler, nineteen-year-old Edmund taken away to Tennessee by Richard

Steele's eldest son, *also* named Richard Steele? Did it seem at that time like there'd be no end to Richard Steeles, even with the old master dead?

All this—so little but still so much—would have been buried away in ignoring the will.

In the "afterlife of slavery," one *can* still be a slaveholder.

Grandpa, I don't want to accept.

NOTES

1. For more on the black Steeles and their allied families, in slavery and in freedom, see Catherine Baker, "The Slaves of Richard Steele of Greene County, Missouri," *Ozar'Kin*, Fall 2006, and Catherine Sasanov Baker, "The Steeles, Their Slaves, and the Civil War," *Ozar'Kin*, Spring 2007.

2. An indispensable genealogical guide for people seeking their black ancestors in southwest Missouri is the multivolume *Black Families of the Ozarks*, compiled by the Greene County Archives and Records Center in Springfield, Missouri, https://thelibrary.org/lochist/blfamilies/index.html.

3. The 1719 bill of lading for the woman branded Y can be viewed online at the Maine Historical Society and on their Maine Memory Network website, https://www.mainememory.net/artifact/7372. It can also be viewed at https://pooryorickjournal.com/markdy-archives-and-invocations/.

4. Saidiya Hartman, "Archaeologies of Black Memory" symposium, University of Miami, June 2007.

5. See Saidiya V. Hartman, "Venus in Two Acts," *Small Axe: A Caribbean Journal of Criticism* 12, no. 2 (2008), 1–14, and Saidiya V. Hartman, *Lose Your Mother: A Journey Along the Atlantic Slave Route* (New York: Farrar, Straus and Giroux, 2007). The books by Michel-Rolph Trouillot, *Silencing the Past: Power and the Production of History* (Boston: Beacon Press, 1995) and by M. NourbeSe Philip, *Zong!* (Middletown, CT: Wesleyan University Press, 2008) are also incredibly useful in thinking about black history and the archive, and straining against its limitations.

6. Other work from *Mark^d Y* (*Archives & Invocations*) can be found, accompanied by an interview about the project, in the online journal at https://pooryorickjournal.com.

7. At this point, William Pepperrell's June 25, 1719, letter to his agent Benjamin Bullard in Barbados can only be found in secondary sources. Its first appearance was in Usher Parsons' *Life of Sir William Pepperrell* (Boston: Little, Brown, and Company, 1856), 28.

8. The two prose passages and the poem in this essay, regarding the death of the woman branded Y and her companions, are part of *In Search of the Woman Markd Y* by Catherine Sasanov, first published in the *Poetic Research* column of the online journal at common-place.org (vol. 15, no. 2 [Winter], 2015).

9. Nathaniel Sparhawk's 1754 letter can be read in full in Reverend Henry S. Burrage, *Colonel Nathaniel Sparhawk of Kittery* (Portland, ME: Maine Historical Society, 1898).

4 ⟩ OVERCOMING AMNESIA

How I Learned the Forgotten History of Two Families Linked by Slavery

BILL SIZEMORE

⎜ SPENT SIXTY years on this earth before I had a clue that I was descended from slaveowners.[1]

For someone who spent his entire professional life as a journalist—much of that time as an investigative reporter—it's a little embarrassing to make that admission. But there it is.

Why did it take me so long to figure it out? I don't know. I suppose some of the reasons are mundane: I was busy making a living and raising a family. But more than that, I think I was infected by a sort of historical amnesia—self-induced, perhaps—that has long held sway in my native South.

Never once during my growing-up years in the 1950s and 1960s did my parents mention any history of slaveholding in my family. While researching a book on the topic, I surveyed my cousins, and in every case the response was the same: the subject never came up in their families either.

Did our parents not know, or did they know but choose not to talk about it? The consensus of my cousins is that they didn't know. I retain some skepticism on that point. But if my cousins are right, it means that by the time our parents' generation came along—barely half a century after slavery was abolished—it had already been erased from the family's collective memory.

My discovery of my family's slave-owning past is burned into my mind.

I was in Utah on a reporting assignment for my newspaper *The Virginian-Pilot* in 2009. I had a couple of hours to kill before boarding my flight home and decided to visit the world headquarters of the Mormon church in Salt Lake City, which includes the world's largest genealogical library.

I strolled in and was greeted by a friendly volunteer, who asked what I'd like to know about my family history. I said I wondered if any of my ancestors owned slaves. I've never bought into the old adage that ignorance is bliss. On the contrary, I believe knowledge is power. If my family participated in America's original sin, I wanted to know about it—for better or worse.

Within minutes, there was the answer on a computer screen in front of me: a slave schedule from the 1860 U.S. Census showing my great-great-great-grandfather Daniel Sizemore as the owner of sixteen people. I felt like I'd been punched in the gut.

From that moment forward, I couldn't get it out of my head. I was full of questions. Who were these people? What were their lives like? Who were their descendants? Where are they now? What scars do they bear from their ancestors' enslavement?

My curiosity led me on a years-long odyssey.

Uncovering the story has been a little like trying to piece together a jigsaw puzzle with a blindfold on. My ancestors were simple country folk. In contrast to large planters who left voluminous paper trails, the Sizemores left no written records. So I had to rely on public records.

Deeds in the county courthouse show that my ancestor Daniel gradually acquired nearly five hundred acres along the Dan River in Mecklenburg County, Virginia, near the town of Clarksville, in the first half of the nineteenth century.[2]

He also acquired slaves. According to census records, he owned four by 1840.[3] He was typical of the nearly 400,000 slaveholders across the South. Nearly nine out of ten had fewer than twenty slaves.

By far, the biggest money crop grown by Virginia's slave-owning planters was tobacco, which was extremely labor-intensive. In a society dominated by the tobacco economy, my ancestors were no exception. They used slaves to grow a highly addictive product that has killed millions of people all over the world. What a legacy!

Daniel Sizemore's homestead, a modest clapboard house with a stone foundation, two rooms downstairs, and an upstairs loft, still stands today, surrounded by rolling pastureland along a centuries-old thoroughfare three miles west of Clarksville. Daniel, his wife, and his son Harvel are buried in a family graveyard nearby.

According to the 1860 census, Daniel's slaves lived in three cabins on the farm. As far as I have been able to determine, there is no trace left of them, and no sign of where their inhabitants are buried.

What was life like for Daniel Sizemore's slaves? In a word, I don't know. I have been unable to find any historical accounts that shed light on how they were treated.

But there are dozens of firsthand narratives from other Virginian slaves, most of them collected by interviewers from the Federal Writers' Project in the 1930s, that tell of egregious cruelty.

Those accounts include frequent references to slaveowners' most common method of discipline: flogging slaves' bare backs with a cowhide whip, sometimes for transgressions as small as stealing a candy cane or cutting a tobacco leaf before it was ripe.

Another common theme in the narratives was the breakup of slave families by owners who sold spouses, siblings, and children to slave traders, who in turn sold them to cotton and sugar planters in the Deep South. The narratives contain wrenching accounts of young children being torn from their sobbing mothers' arms. Most never reconnected with their kin again.

Many slaves turned to religion as a refuge, yearning for release from their earthly woes in the afterlife. But slaveowners did their best to extinguish the religious gatherings of slaves, fearing they would be breeding grounds for insurrection.

White preachers sometimes ministered to slave congregations but, more often than not, exhorted them to accept their place and obey their masters.

The slave narratives contain many accounts of female slaves being forced to have sex with their masters, often resulting in the birth of a child who then became the master's property. By law, slave children were classified as the property of their mothers' owners.

The sexual exploitation of female slaves was described in haunting detail by Harriet Jacobs, whose autobiography was first published in 1861. She was enslaved in Edenton, North Carolina, a hundred and fifty miles southeast of Daniel Sizemore's farm.

I would, of course, like to think my ancestor treated his slaves humanely. But Jacobs' story gives me little reason to hope.

After a particularly gruesome litany of slaveowner cruelty—including the torture of a runaway slave who was locked inside a cotton gin and left to die— Jacobs wrote: "I could tell of more slaveholders as cruel as those I have described. They are not exceptions to the general rule. I do not say there are no humane slaveholders. Such characters do exist, notwithstanding the hardening influences around them. But they are 'like angels' visits—few and far between.'"[4]

Uncovering the humanity of the Sizemore slaves is as difficult as judging the character of their master.

The census records, which provided the first confirmation of my family's slave-owning past, took me only so far. Through 1860, slaves are listed by age, race, and gender—but not by name.

It's not until the 1870 census, after emancipation, that the names start to show up. I found more than a dozen African American heads of households living in Mecklenburg County between 1870 and 1900 with the surname Sizemore. It's well known that freed slaves sometimes took the last name of their former owners, and since my ancestor was the only slaveowner in Virginia named Sizemore, there's nowhere else that name would have come from.

So, at least, I can attach some shred of humanity to the enslaved Sizemores by reciting their names: Alex. Alice. Andrew. Ben. Berta. Booker. Daniel. Dennis. Henderson. Henry. Isham. Martha. Peter. Stephen. Wilkins.

Most of them married and had families. But many had disappeared from the Mecklenburg census records by 1900, so with just a few exceptions, that's all I know about them.

A surviving court document provides a glimpse of one of them—and a rare record of my slave-owning ancestor's spoken words.

In 1854, a dispute over two slaves sold by the administrator of an estate came to the Mecklenburg court. One of the witnesses was my great-great-great-grandfather, Daniel Sizemore.

He testified that he had purchased "a Negro boy named Wilkins" from one George Avory in January 1841 for $675.00 in cash. The boy had been sold the previous year at a public auction in Clarksville, in settlement of an estate.

"I was present at the sale and heard of no objection to the sale," my ancestor testified. "If I had heard of any objections to the sale I would not afterwards have purchased the boy."[5]

It was a profound moment for me when I first encountered that passage in the longhand script of a court stenographer from a century and a half ago: my ancestor describing matter-of-factly, in his own words, how he bought a fellow human being.

Wilkins Sizemore, a freedman, turns up in the 1870 census as a head of a family of six. He was forty-four then, so he would have been about fifteen when my ancestor bought him.[6]

Another surviving public record from the pre-Civil War era, a slave birth register, records the birth of a slave boy, Peter, on May 12, 1853, and lists his owner as Daniel Sizemore. Neither of the child's parents is listed.[7]

That is the only slave birth recorded under Daniel Sizemore's name. But there could well have been others that went unrecorded. Documentation of Virginia's slave population was sometimes less than complete. Consider this notation by the Mecklenburg commissioner of revenue in an 1860 slave birth register: "Wm. Townes had six negro children born at his plantation. Names and sex not recollected and I am compelled to close. I have no time to ascertain the particulars."[8]

There is no further record of Peter, the slave boy born on Daniel Sizemore's farm. But that is not surprising in light of the astronomical mortality rate among slave children, which one historian has conservatively estimated at 40 to 45 percent.[9] Little Peter probably never made it to adulthood.

Since the 1950s, my extended Sizemore family has held a reunion every August in the rural community near Clarksville where my father and his five siblings grew up. Dozens of my relatives across multiple generations show up every year, some traveling from as far away as the West Coast.

Sitting at my computer a few days before our 2010 gathering, I idly typed in a Google search for "Sizemore family reunion" and made a startling discovery. There was a rather elaborate website dedicated to another annual gathering of Sizemores—not of my kin, but of an African American family.

Their reunion is held on the same weekend each year as ours. Theirs migrates from year to year all over the Eastern seaboard, but every few years, it returns to the place of their roots: Mecklenburg County, Virginia.

When I was growing up there, every aspect of life was strictly segregated—schools, churches, clubs, public accommodations. I had virtually no contact with African Americans, and I had only the vaguest awareness that there were any who shared my surname.

My discovery of the simultaneous reunions came shortly after I had begun exploring my family's slave-owning past. Intrigued, I began seeking out African American Sizemores, asking who could tell me about their family history. I was quickly steered to George Sizemore.

Uncle George, as everyone in the family calls him, lives in the same weathered farmhouse where he has lived since he was one month old in 1919, about five miles from where my ancestor Daniel Sizemore lived. He has been alone since Laura Mae, his wife of fifty-eight years, died in 2007.

When I first met him, Uncle George was a very vigorous ninety-one-year-old—a towering figure at six feet four and two hundred forty pounds, with a toothy smile and immense hands. When we shook hands, mine disappeared inside his.

He was happy to discuss his family history. One of the first things he told me was, "My daddy was born a slave."[10]

I had to let that sink in for a moment. How was that even possible in 2010?

His father, Ben Sizemore, had been born in 1858. He had fathered six children with his first wife and, after she died, five more with his second wife. Uncle George was the next to last of the later set of children, born when his father was sixty-one.

Ben and his brother Stephen were the sons of a slave named Daniel, Uncle George told me—the same name as my slave-owning ancestor. That sent me scurrying back to the census records.

In the 1870 census, I found documentation of Uncle George's ancestors along with an unmistakable link to my own. There, listed in Clarksville Township, were Daniel Sizemore, a thirty-six-year-old black farmworker, and his young sons Ben and Stephen. The listing appears immediately after that of my ancestor Daniel Sizemore, an eighty-one-year-old white farmer, and his four unmarried adult children. That means black Daniel and his sons lived next door to white Daniel, most likely in the same cabin they inhabited as slaves.[11]

How did the black and white Daniel Sizemores come to have the same name? We can only guess. One question that naturally arises is whether there was any blood connection between the two. For the answer, we turned to DNA testing.

Uncle George and I took a test focusing on the Y chromosome, which occurs only in males and is passed from father to son. Uncle George's niece, Eugene Watkins, and I took an autosomal DNA test, which reveals blood relationships stretching out to distant cousins. No kinship was found in either case.

The autosomal test also reveals ethnic makeup. Mine was found to be 100 percent European. Eugene's is 85 percent African, 12 percent European, and 3 percent Native American.

Traces of European ancestry are common among African Americans, reflecting the widespread reality of slaveowners mating with their female slaves. Uncle George is no exception.

He has white blood on his mother's side, he told me in one of our early conversations. When he was a boy, he'd noticed a curious bond between his mother, Ella Jamieson Sizemore, and two white brothers who ran a funeral business. There were no black undertakers in Mecklenburg County in those days. Whenever there was a funeral in the neighborhood, the two white undertakers "would always hug my mama," Uncle George told me.

"I'd say, 'Mama, why are those white people always hugging you?' Finally, when I was a teenager, she told me, 'We're cousins.'"[12] Ella's mother, Uncle George's grandmother born in 1857, had had a white father.

The DNA tests, of course, tell us only about the two Daniel Sizemores and their progeny. There were more than a dozen other Sizemore slaves, and I have been unable to locate any of their descendants for testing.

But one thing is crystal clear from the census records: for decades after emancipation, the lives of the black and white Sizemores were tightly inter-twined. Up through 1900, they lived in close proximity. In all likelihood, the black Sizemores were sharecroppers working the same farmland on which they had toiled as slaves.

Over the decades, the South's Jim Crow laws circumscribed African Americans' lives at every turn. Uncle George remembers many bus rides when he and his kin were relegated to the back of the bus, closest to the exhaust fumes. On trains, the arrangement was just the opposite: blacks were herded into the front car, which got the most coal smoke from the steam engine.

Like other African American children, Uncle George and his siblings were coached by their parents to hold a mindset of constant vigilance, as a shield against the racial prejudice around them. "My mother always used to tell us to be careful when we went out—to watch what you do and what you say," he told me.[13]

The indignities of Jim Crow, the lack of economic opportunity, and the ever-present fear of racial violence propelled a mass exodus of 6 million African Americans from the South to the North during the first half of the twentieth century. Over the decades, most of Mecklenburg's black Sizemores joined what has come to be known as the Great Migration.

Looking back on my youth in Southside Virginia in the 1950s and 1960s, I can count on one hand the opportunities I had to interact with African Americans.

There was a series of black women whom my parents employed as maids. Then there was Charlie Williams, the kindly man who delivered groceries to the house from the small store he ran across town and who always had a lollypop or stick of bubble gum in his pocket for me. And in the summer, black children showed up at our door selling fresh blackberries that they had picked in the wild.

In May 1954, a year before I started first grade, the U.S. Supreme Court ruled in the landmark case *Brown v. Board of Education* that racially segregated public schools were unconstitutional. Nevertheless, it would be more than a decade before Virginia fully complied. Well into high school, my classes continued to be lily white.

In 1958, Governor Lindsay Almond closed schools in Charlottesville, Norfolk, and Warren County rather than let them be integrated, locking nearly 13,000 pupils out of their classrooms. The state offered publicly funded tuition grants to white parents who enrolled their children in segregated private schools. Black families were left to fend for themselves.

The closed schools were reopened in 1959 under court order, but in one Southside Virginia county, the defiance continued unabated. Prince Edward

County, where one of the *Brown* cases originated, closed its public schools for five years, denying a generation of African American children education.

By 1965, Virginia school systems had established what was euphemistically called a "freedom of choice" policy that allowed black children to be admitted to white schools if their parents chose to send them. The result was token integration by a handful of brave African American families.

There were two black girls in my graduating class of one hundred at Bluestone High School. Looking back on it, I imagine that daily life for them was a living hell. When they were not being ostracized, they were being humiliated as the butt of racist jokes and pranks. I recall white boys on my school bus singing "Bye-Bye Blackbird" when the bus dropped off a black student at the end of the day.

Some teachers were participants in the persecution as well. My senior English teacher mercilessly embarrassed the single black girl in the class in front of her peers when she couldn't come up with the answer to a question.

I didn't actively participate in the pervasive racist behavior, but I'm ashamed to say I didn't actively resist it either.

It wasn't until after I graduated in 1967 that full integration was finally achieved by the wholesale reassignment of students. Uncle George's all-black alma mater became the junior high school for the entire town, black and white.

Integration was similarly slow to occur in Virginia's public colleges and universities. In the fall of 1967, my freshman class of a thousand or so students, at the College of William and Mary, included the school's first residential African American students: three young women who roomed together in a dormitory basement. When I joined the college marching band my freshman year, "Dixie" was still a standard part of the repertoire at football games. It was finally eliminated from our playlist in 1969.

As I glided through my segregated childhood in Clarksville, Daffodil Graham was growing up twenty-five miles away in Roxboro, North Carolina—across the state line and the color line. Neither of us was aware of the other's existence or of the historical connection between our families.

Daffodil's mother Bertha was a daughter of Jordan Sizemore, the second child of ex-slave Ben Sizemore's first marriage.

Daffodil's full name is Margaret Daffodil Graham. She long ago embraced her whimsical middle name, and that's how she is now known by everyone in her family. Jovial and straight-talking, she hands out business cards featuring a drawing of a daffodil blossom.

On a crystal-clear spring day in 2013, I visited her home in Winston-Salem, North Carolina, where she retired after two careers as a teacher and social worker. Dressed in a navy-blue running suit, a yellow T-shirt, and a colorful do-rag wrapped around her gray curls, she minced no words as she recalled her life in the waning days of Jim Crow.

She went to school during the "separate but unequal" era, she told me. She could see the white high school from her back porch, but had to walk across town to all-black Person County High School. Whenever she passed the white elementary school, she would cross to the other side of the street, trying to get out of earshot of the racial epithets being hurled from the playground.

Daffodil told me she has nothing but admiration for those African American children who first broke the color barrier by attending white schools during the "freedom of choice" era—but she wouldn't have wanted to be one of them.

"I praise God for them," she said. "But there's no way I would go through that. I'm not that good. I'm not a trailblazer. All that stress! A lot of high school is socialization. For those kids, their socialization was zero."[14]

Daffodil's father, whom she described as "the original deadbeat dad," was largely absent from her life. She was raised by her mother and a great-aunt.

Daffodil's mother worked in a chicken-processing plant in Roxboro. After putting in a full shift, she would come home for a few hours of sleep and then go back at night to catch chickens in the brooder house where young chicks were raised. She also did housework and cooking for white families, setting aside part of her earnings in a college fund for Daffodil.

"She told me from the time I was a little girl, 'You will never walk in the back door of a white person's house,'" Daffodil said. "She was dead set that I would be a teacher. In that day, the highest pinnacle of success for an African American was to teach."

Daffodil's mother acquired a set of encyclopedias, one volume at a time, as a premium for buying groceries at the local A&P, stimulating a lifelong love of books in her daughter.

Like everything else in Roxboro, the public libraries were segregated. "The black library was a tiny, one-room log cabin on the other side of town with a few raggedy books," Daffodil told me. "But the white library was just down the street from our house. I would send my white friend Bill Short with his Radio Flyer wagon, and he'd fill it up with books. We'd split them up, and when we'd finished them, we'd trade off.

"You had to be inventive."

One hundred miles from Clarksville, in 1960, a sit-in by four black college students at a whites-only lunch counter in Greensboro, North Carolina, spurred similar protests around the country. Those actions—and the some-times violent reaction by white authorities in the Deep South—paved the way for a series of federal laws in the mid-1960s banning racial discrimina-tion and assuring voting rights for African Americans.

The legal underpinnings of Jim Crow have been dismantled; however, its legacy remains. In many areas, our schools, neighborhoods, and churches are as segregated as ever. By virtually any measurable social indicator, there is a vast chasm between the life prospects of black and white Americans.

As a beneficiary of white privilege, I stand on the backs of my African American namesakes and the millions of others who played an integral part in building this nation with no compensation for their labor, often under the most inhumane conditions. I believe I owe it to their descendants to break out of the historical amnesia that has isolated us from each other. Belated as it was, learning my family's history compelled me to do something positive with the knowledge.

In 2013, with the two simultaneous family reunions going on ten miles apart, I invited the black Sizemores to stop by our gathering for a get-acquainted visit. To my delight, a convoy of about a dozen—led by Uncle George—showed up. About the same number of my relatives had arrived at the church social hall where we always meet, which is within sight of the cemetery where my grandparents and other forebears are buried. The two families mingled pleasantly for an hour or so. I have the pictures to prove it!

As our visitors drove off late that afternoon, my cousin Dan leaned over to me and said: "That sound you hear is my father rolling over in his grave."

In 2015, when the black Sizemore reunion returned to Mecklenburg County, I asked Evella Hutcheson, one of the hosts, to put me on the pro-gram for the banquet. I gave the family a progress report on my research and said I hoped that telling our story would contribute in some small way toward healing the country's racial wounds.

"White Americans have a lot to atone for, and we need to say it plainly," I told them. "My family stole your family's liberty, their labor, and their human dignity. And I'm sorry."

We have much more hard work ahead of us, confronting our shared legacy and seeking ways to redress the persistent inequities that slavery spawned.

But we have made a start.

NOTES

1. Bill Sizemore, *Uncle George and Me: Two Southern Families Confront a Shared Legacy of Slavery* (Richmond, VA: Brandylane Publishers, Inc., 2018).

2. Mecklenburg County, Virginia deed books.

3. U.S. Census slave schedules, Mecklenburg County, VA, 1840–1860.

4. Harriet A. Jacobs, *Incidents in the Life of a Slave Girl: Written by Herself* (Cambridge: Harvard University Press, 1987).

5. *Avory v. Avory* court records, Mecklenburg County, VA, 1854. Library of Virginia.

6. U.S. Census, Clarksville Township, Mecklenburg County, VA, 1870.

7. Slave birth register, Mecklenburg County, VA, 1853. Library of Virginia.

8. Slave birth register, Mecklenburg County, VA, 1860. Library of Virginia.

9. Brenda E. Stevenson, *Life in Black and White: Family and Community in the Slave South.* (New York: Oxford University Press, 1997).

10. George Sizemore, interview with author, September 2010.

11. U.S. Census, Clarksville Township, Mecklenburg County, VA, 1870.

12. George Sizemore, interview with author, August 2011.

13. George Sizemore, interview with author, August 2011.

14. Daffodil Graham, interview with author, April 2013.

5 ❧ OREGON'S SLAVE HISTORY

R. GREGORY NOKES

BORN, RAISED, AND educated in the northern provinces of the Left Coast—I'm speaking of Oregon—I would never have believed there were African American slaves here, let alone that my family had any connection to slavery.

Bear in mind that most Oregonians pride ourselves on living in a largely liberal state. The nation's ugly slave history belonged in the South, not here. Not anywhere near here. No Civil War battles were fought in Oregon. Moreover, I most certainly had never heard or read anything in school about slaves in Oregon.

Indeed, slavery has been unlawful from the earliest days of Oregon's provisional government in 1843. Hasn't it?

This myth of a region with clean hands was shattered for me beginning with a conversation I had with my younger brother, Bill, a few years ago. I had invited Bill to discuss my ideas for a new book. He steered me away from my ideas, then offered a suggestion of his own. The conversation went like this:

BILL: Why don't you write about Reuben Shipley?
ME: Who is Reuben Shipley?
BILL: He was a black slave brought to Oregon by one of our ancestors.

It took me some moments to absorb this before asking the obvious: how did he know this, when I, the older brother, had never heard of it? Bill referred me to a family genealogy written in the 1960s by my late grandparents, Minnie and Will Junkin.

"They wrote about Reuben Shipley," Bill said. "Look on page 359."

I'd been given a copy of the fourteen-hundred-page *Henckel Genealogy*[1] when it first came out, and carried it with me on my various postings to Salt Lake City, New York, Puerto Rico, Buenos Aires, Cambridge, Massachusetts, Washington, D.C., and back to Oregon. But I'd barely even opened the cover. The arcane listing of names, births, and deaths of members of the Jacob Henckel family, dating back to Germany in the 1600s, held zero interest for me. About all I knew of Jacob was that he led a family wagon train from Iowa to Oregon in 1853.

But my brother was interested, and in retrospect, I should have been too. Returning to my West Linn home in suburban Portland, I wiped the dust off the red cover of the three-inch-thick volume, turned to page 359, and read the following:

Robert Shipley, a white farmer in Miller County, Missouri emigrated to Oregon with his family in 1853, bringing with him a black slave, Reuben Shipley. The black Shipley was said to be a trusted slave, who was overseer for the white Shipley in Missouri. Given his freedom some years later in Oregon, Reuben became a successful farmer and donated land for a cemetery, where he was buried following his death in 1872 from smallpox.[2]

I was to learn elsewhere that Reuben was given a choice by his owner— go to Oregon to help develop the owner's new farm and eventually gain his freedom, or remain in Missouri as a slave.

At first glance, it would seem an easy call for Reuben, as there was little chance he could ever gain his freedom in Missouri. However, going to Oregon meant leaving his wife and two sons behind; they belonged to different owners. Reuben chose Oregon, believing that once he gained his freedom, he could buy his family and have them join him, although that was not to be.

The white Shipley made the same offer to two female slaves, both of whom would also have to leave families behind. But they chose to remain slaves in Missouri, close to their families.

I had shared the smugness of many in Oregon that we had been above all that, but now I was learning we were not. Yes, I had been a journalist and author long enough to not be surprised by much of anything; but this was a surprise, and a most unwelcome one. I found myself rethinking our entire history, and not just that of my family, but that of Oregon generally.

I was to learn that there had possibly been as many as one hundred slaves in Oregon, most brought over the Oregon Trail by early settlers from Missouri between 1843 and 1853. The actual number of slaves will never be known, as no one kept track. The 1860 U.S. Slave Census did not include Oregon, overlooking that two settlers in Oregon's Linn County freely acknowledged owning slaves to census-takers.

The number of slaves in Oregon, of course, paled beside the 114,965 slaves in Missouri in 1860 and beside the nearly 4 million slaves nationally.

However, I shouldn't have been so surprised. I knew about the history of real estate red-lining in Portland; I knew blacks had been unwelcome in many public arenas—the singers Paul Robeson and Marian Anderson were refused decent hotel accommodations after performing in Salem, the state capitol, in 1953; I recalled hearing about unwritten sundown laws in smaller communities around the state; and I recalled hearing that Oregon once had an exclusion clause written into its constitution. As I pursued this story, I was to be reminded of these things with a new awareness that racism ran deep in the currents that shaped Oregon during its early history.

My reaction was to write about it and expose it, and to bring this knowledge out of the shadows of the past into Oregon's remembered history.

In my ensuing research, I was to learn that pro-slavery sentiment was so strong that Oregon actually voted in 1857 on whether to become a slave state, although the proposal was defeated by a three-to-one margin. I was to learn, too, that Oregon had exclusion clauses against African Americans during most of its early history. And I was to learn that most of Oregon's early leaders—governors, senators, judges—were pro-slavery, or, at least, Southern sympathizers.

It is true that Oregon's earliest white inhabitants—missionaries, fur trappers, and a handful of settlers—voted in May 1843 to prohibit slavery. However, when the first major influx of white settlers arrived from Missouri later that year, attitudes quickly shifted. The ban on slavery was modified in 1844 to allow slaveholders up to three years to free their slaves. The law was also amended to prohibit African Americans from settling in Oregon—the first of Oregon's three exclusion laws.

A newly freed slave was required to leave Oregon within a prescribed period of time—two years for adult males, three years for females—or face a severe whipping of up to thirty-nine lashes. The lash law was soon abolished and probably never enforced, but that it was enacted in the first place reflects the attitudes of the time. From 1845 on, slavery was again ostensibly unlawful in Oregon. But there was no enforcement, and nearly every wagon train that came to Oregon in this period included at least a few slaves.

Oregon's second exclusion law lasted from 1849 to 1854. The third was the clause in Oregon's 1857 constitution, which wasn't removed by voters until 1926. It is a scar on Oregon's history that Oregon was the only free state admitted into the union with an exclusion clause in its constitution. Although the exclusion laws were not generally enforced, they accomplished their purpose, which was to discourage black immigrants. Portland today is considered the whitest large city in the country, with a 76 percent white population.

Other bits and pieces of Oregon's slave history were to emerge during my research of old newspaper clippings and journals by early settlers, which I garnered from historical societies and museums. The result was my book *Breaking Chains: Slavery on Trial in the Oregon Territory*, a finalist for the 2014 Oregon Book Award for nonfiction.

One account I read told about a Missouri emigrant who was so intent on bringing a slave named Rose to Oregon in 1849 that he was said to have smuggled her in a box, letting her out only at night. When I first heard this story, I considered it so improbable that I declined to include it in my book.

But I shouldn't have been quite so skeptical. I was recently contacted by a near-neighbor, David Hedges, who after reading my book, sought me out to tell me his great-grandfather William Allen, a physician, had indeed brought Rose to Oregon in a box. Hedges had with him a book that said as much and included a photograph of Rose, her husband John Jackson, also a former slave, and two of their children. They lived near Oregon City.

Rose had been a valued slave in the Allen household who eventually gained her freedom. Evidently, Dr. Allen had been concerned about Oregon's exclusion laws and hid her in a large box so that authorities wouldn't know he was transporting a slave—although it's doubtful anyone would have cared. No doubt there is more to the story, as it's highly improbable Rose could have survived the entire two-thousand-mile journey from Missouri in a box, even with nighttime relief. But Hedges didn't know more than the basics of the story.

Most important to my research, and the book that followed, was an account of a little-known slavery trial, *Holmes v. Ford*, in 1852. I read the account in a 1922 journal of the Oregon Historical Society, which led me to the original handwritten trial record in the Polk County Courthouse in Dallas, Oregon. The trial held unintended consequences for Reuben Shipley.

Robin Holmes, one of six slaves brought to Oregon by Nathaniel Ford in 1844, filed a *habeas corpus* suit against Ford in Oregon's Polk County in 1852, seeking freedom for three of his children who were still being held as slaves. Ford freed Holmes and his wife Polly in 1850, but kept their children, arguing in court that he felt entitled to some of the children's labor as repayment for his feeding and caring for them when they had been too young to work.

Ford was a heavy hitter in both Missouri and Oregon politics. He had been a four-term sheriff in Missouri's Howard County. He also served in the Missouri legislature and had just completed the first of five terms in Oregon's territorial legislature.

Although Holmes was illiterate and lived in a region generally hostile to blacks, he prevailed in his suit, which played out over fifteen months before four different judges. The suit was finally decided by the fourth judge, George Williams, the newly appointed chief justice of Oregon's territorial supreme court. Williams, then a district judge in Iowa and a future U.S. attorney general, had not set foot in Oregon until his appointment by President Franklin Pierce. In his ruling on July 13, 1853, issued only weeks after his arrival, Williams said that while Ford had owned the slave family in Missouri, "as soon as the laws of Oregon touched the parties, the relation of master and slave was dissolved."[3]

While the significance of Williams' ruling was largely overlooked at the time, Williams himself later underscored its importance for Oregon. In a speech to the Oregon Legislature in 1899, Williams said the following:

> Whether or not slaveholders could carry their slaves into the territories and hold them there as property had become a burning question, and my predecessors in office, for reasons best known to themselves, had declined to hear the case. This was among the first cases I was called upon to decide. Mr. Ford contended that these colored people were his property in Missouri from which he emigrated, and he had as much right to bring that kind of property into Oregon and hold it here as much as he had to bring his cattle or other property here and hold it as such; but my opinion was, and I so held, that without some positive legislative enactment establishing slavery here, it did not and could not exist in Oregon, and I awarded the colored people their freedom. . . . So far as I know this was the last effort made to hold slaves in Oregon by force of law. There were a great many virulent pro-slavery men in the territory and this decision, of course, was very distasteful to them.[4]

The outcome determined that slavery was indeed unlawful in Oregon, although few people I talked with were aware of the case. Moreover, the ruling was not enforced and at least one of the Ford slaves, Mary Jane Holmes, remained in the Ford household—sold, or given, to his married daughter's family.

At the time of William's ruling, Robert Shipley was en route to Oregon with Reuben Shipley to put him to work on the white Shipley's new farm in Benton County. Within the next few years—we don't know when—Reuben was allowed to go free, and he went to work for another farmer, this time for pay. He soon had enough money to purchase a one-hundred-acre farm of his own. But his goal of bringing his wife and children to Oregon was not to be realized. His wife had died in Missouri, and, for whatever reason, he didn't connect with his sons.

Completing a circle of coincidences, Reuben met Mary Jane Holmes, and they married in 1857. However, there were complications. Although the facts surrounding what happened are fuzzy, Nathaniel Ford apparently insisted that Reuben owed him seven hundred dollars, which was Mary Jane's value as a slave. Reuben paid some part of this, until white friends convinced him he didn't owe anything. This version of events is disputed by Ford's descendants, who said Ford had no contact with the Holmes children after the trial.

Reuben and Mary Jane would have six children. Their farm straddled a gently sloping hilltop on Mt. Union, overlooking a picturesque valley near the town of Philomath. They probably grew wheat and corn, the crops of the region, and kept some cattle—Reuben's brand was registered with Benton County in 1875. They were sufficiently successful to donate three acres of their farm for a cemetery in 1861, stipulating that blacks as well as whites could be buried there.

Still active today, the much-expanded Mt. Union Cemetery has special meaning for me, even though I had never once visited it until I went in search of Reuben Shipley's grave. I found it among a cluster of the oldest gravesites, where names on many crumbling markers were no longer legible. However, a relatively new block of polished pink granite marked the Shipley grave. It bore the names of Reuben, Mary Jane, and four of their children, along with names of other relatives. I was told the Shipleys' last surviving son arranged for the marker sometime before his death in 1946.

I stood by Shipley's grave a long time and then walked to the graves of some of my ancestors buried nearby, a poignant reminder of the mingling of our family with Oregon's slave history.

NOTES

1. William Sumner Junkin and Minnie Wyatt Junkin. *The Henckel Genealogy, 1500–1960: Ancestry and Descendants of Anthony Jacob Henckel, 1668–1728, Pioneer Evangelical Lutheran Minister, Emigrant from the German Palatinate to America in 1717* (New Market, VA: Henckel Family Association, 1964).
2. Junkin, *The Henckel Genealogy.*
3. "The Negro Case," *Oregon Statesman* (Salem, OR), July 26, 1853, 2 (no byline).
4. George Williams, "Political History of Oregon, 1853–1864," *Oregon Historical Quarterly*, March 1901, Oregon Historical Society, Portland, OR.

6 ➣ SEED OF THE FANCY MAID

RODNEY G. WILLIAMS

I N A HUNDRED years, who will care?

That's what my college physics professor used to say to our class before every exam, an effort to help us put our anxiety in perspective. I've forgotten most of what I learned in college physics, but I never forgot that question.

Twenty years after that class, I took up genealogy as a hobby. Uncovering and unfolding the lives of my long-dead ancestors has made me a better man in countless ways, but I'm most profoundly impressed by the way genealogy reminds me of—keeps asking me—that old question. Genealogy taught me a lesson that is dangerously easy to miss: that a long-forgotten nineteenth-century Quaker has as much to do with my life today as what I had for breakfast this morning.

John Armfield was an ambitious North Carolina farm boy who was born in 1797 to a family of Quakers.[1] Four generations before, his ancestors had come from Northern England to the American colonies to escape religious persecution and help William Penn to help settle and cultivate land in Pennsylvania.

In time, their neighbors, threatened by the Quakers' peculiar dress and outside-the-mainstream political stances, forced the Quakers to leave town. This would become just one in a series of similar moves made by Quakers over time.

In 1812, John Armfield made his own move, leaving Guilford County at age fifteen and vowing not to return until he'd amassed more wealth than Nathan, his father. The source of the seemingly contentious relationship between John and his father is missing from the historical record, but I get it.

People had always told me I looked and acted just like my father. Although he was a success by most accounts—at least at first—I hated hearing those words. In fact, it was my father's success that made his one main flaw, his alcoholism, stand out, leaking poison into all of the other parts of his life. It was likely my father's alcoholism that kept him from fulfilling his potential—and it was this unfulfilled potential that terrified me—the boy, they said, who had so much potential.

For my father's eight great-grandparents who were all born enslaved, there was, for all intents and purposes, no such thing as potential. Their worth was measured only by the amount of physical labor they provided against their will and without pay. At that point in my life, I could not begin to fathom that my ancestors' potential could be realized only through my success as their descendant. My father didn't seem to understand that either. When I graduated from college and accepted a job offer in Chattanooga, his parting words to me were, "You will always be the low man on the totem pole, no matter what those white men tell you." When I left, setting off toward what seemed would be a bright future, there was no way to appreciate how unprecedented the possibilities for my life were.

The practice of moving, either en masse or alone, from places we don't feel welcome to places we think might finally embrace us, only to discover we're still outsiders, is as old as human civilization. It's what caused my distant cousin Jesse McCrary to run North from a lynch mob in rural Georgia in 1910; it's what caused 6 million African Americans to attempt an escape from Southern segregation and Jim Crow laws during the Great Migration; and it's what caused me, nearly twenty years after the Great Migration ended, to run away from home, like John Armfield, to remake myself in another land.

In Chattanooga, I built a decent career as an actuary in the health insurance industry. Although my job was lucrative, I took little pride in my career path. Health insurance wasn't considered the noblest of industries, as it often involved denying care to sick patients and reasonable compensation to doctors and hospitals. You might think it's a bit of a stretch to say that health insurance in the 1990s was as morally repugnant as slave-trading in the 1830s, but my current stance is that we won't really know until we've had a hundred years to look back.

A few years later, at the age of twenty-four, I found myself in the bedroom of my Chattanooga apartment staring at the screen of a clunky computer that had a dial-up connection to a fledgling internet. It was then and there that I made the decision to leave my job at the stodgy health insurer and accept a consulting job across the country, in Newport Beach.

It had started when my busybody coworker Karen had gotten an unsolicited call from a headhunter.

"I hope you don't mind. I gave a recruiter your phone number," she teased, standing behind me as I sat at my desk, a hand on her hip. "I told him your socks match your tie, your headboard is a hundred-gallon saltwater aquarium, and you belong in the city."

Backhanded compliments aside, Karen was right. Chattanooga wasn't quite my speed. But it wasn't true that I longed for just any city. I had my sights set on getting back to Atlanta. Not because I'd grown up there or because my family was still there, but because in my last year of college, I'd finally found a community there that felt like home—nightclub-hopping, young, gay, and black.

But the position the headhunter was calling about wasn't in Atlanta. I nodded with disinterest while he gave his sales pitch, until he said something that got my attention: "This firm is the most prestigious in the industry. They're picky about who they hire. 'SWANS' is what they're looking for, which means you need to show them you're **S**mart, that you **W**ork hard, that you're **A**mbitious, and that you're **N**ice."

And there it was—the line that hooked me. You see, my tendency has always been to lean slightly forward, to always anticipate the next project, the next big "thing." Here was another chance to prove that I belonged among the best and brightest, that I was exemplary, that I wasn't one of *those* black men.

They flew me out to Newport Beach, California, twice for grueling all-day interview sessions and a psychological evaluation. Then they offered me the position there, teasing me with the possibility of a transfer to the Atlanta office in a couple years. I didn't know much about California, and what I thought I knew, I didn't like. The few people I'd known from there struck me as odd, oblivious, and narcissistic. But something called me to wander west. I took the job.

On John Armfield's journey west, while working as a stagecoach driver in Louisiana, he had met a father figure: a man named Isaac Franklin. Franklin owned several large plantations across the South. Angola, his prize property, was a notoriously brutal cotton plantation in West Feliciana Parish, Louisiana. It was named for the homeland of most of its slaves, and it would keep its nickname and violent reputation well after it became the largest maximum-security prison in the United States.

Isaac Franklin had already gotten a taste of the enterprise that would later make him and John very wealthy: slave-trading. When the U.S. Congress banned the transatlantic slave trade in 1808, the demand for a domestic trade boomed. A surplus of slaves in the mid-Atlantic states coincided with a shortage in the burgeoning Southern cotton industry, providing a unique opportunity for two enterprising men with a lot of ambition and a lot to prove. The Franklin and Armfield office opened in 1828, and it quickly became the largest and most successful trading firm in the United States.

As the poster boy for the domestic slave trade, John Armfield often received visits from abolitionists looking to expose the deep inhumanity of the institution of slavery. John didn't mind the visits. He liked to proudly show his slave pens, the slave yard, his offices, whatever the abolitionists were curious to see. He was proud of what he had accomplished: an impressive operation, complete with its own fleet of ships. It transported human cargo from Alexandria to the firm's Natchez, Mississippi office to be sold to an eager market of Southern planters. Every summer, Armfield and his men would make the same trip along the Natchez Trace on horseback, adult slaves on foot behind them in manacles and shackles, with children and injured slaves in wagons. With Franklin and Armfield now buying and selling approximately a thousand slaves every year, John Armfield had finally lived up to his own promise: he'd surpassed his father in wealth and stature, and could finally return home for a father-son reconciliation.

In 1995, when I was twenty-seven, my father ended up in one of those hospitals my industry didn't want to compensate fairly. He was on life support after all his organs had failed. I didn't need to ask my mother why when she called to tell me. We had been waiting for this moment for years.

I flew home to Atlanta as quickly as I could. When I walked into the hospital room, I froze, a haunting image permanently burned into my brain. Breathing tubes, monitors, and a hissing respirator were all crammed into a small, dark room. There was that familiar hospital smell—sickness and death mixed with hope and despair. The man everyone said could be my twin was unrecognizable; he had a shriveled, shrunken body and a gaunt face. Although unconscious, he wore sheer terror and unbearable pain on that face.

My mother said my name out loud to let Daddy know I was there. Before I'd arrived, he had made slight movements or sounds whenever she'd called his other children's names. This time he didn't respond, so Mama started to call my sisters' and brother's names too. Nothing.

Standing there in my khaki Dockers, button-down shirt, sweater vest, and leather slip-ons, I realized I would never get another chance to try to understand the man I'd tried so hard not to become. I wanted to run as fast as I could, out of the room, down the hallway, down the stairs, out the hospital doors, all the way back to California. Instead I stood there, silent, for as long as I could stand it, and,walked slowly and silently back to the waiting room. The next morning we got the call from the hospital. Daddy had died during the night. Mama mumbled that he must have been waiting for me to arrive. Given our always contentious relationship, I wasn't ready to believe that.

After his funeral, after all of the extended family members and polite acquaintances had gone, only a few close relatives were left at my childhood home. That was when Mama told us the story of the events that had led up to Daddy going to the hospital. She had heard him screaming incoherently from the bedroom, and she ran in to find him on the floor. As the paramedics were strapping him into the gurney and rolling him out the door, he kept repeating Mama's name over and over, followed by a half-sentence that he could not seem to complete: "Iris, I want to make . . ." "Iris, I want to make . . ."

As Mama told us the story, which was obviously her way of beginning her grieving process, she wondered out loud about what the end of that sentence should be.

Aunt Phyllis, Mama's sister, began to speculate: "Make peace? Make up? Make love?"

Although I kept it to myself, I wondered if what he had said was all there was. Maybe there wasn't meant to be any more to the sentence. Maybe Daddy's last words, before he was about to lose consciousness forever, were a deceptively simple statement about the creative impulse that drove him. That drives me. Maybe it was even a cryptic warning about getting too caught up in that creative impulse, about setting off on missions to outdo one's father, about dreams that turn to nightmares.

It could be argued that what gave John Armfield's life its longest-lived impact was Franklin and Armfield's so-called Fancy Trade—a booming prostitution venture that involved hiring out fair-skinned, attractive, female, enslaved as sexual commodities. John and his partners had teased each other in letters about their own use of the fancy maids when the women weren't being used in service to the firm.[2] And letters from the fancy maids to the partners attested to the fathering of children by one or more of the partners.

That must be how it happened: my connection to John Armfield. No such letters have been found suggesting that John Armfield fathered children with any of his fancy maids, but my DNA suggests a different story.

Several years into my research, genetic tests started to become available that traced family origins. So, after scraping my cheek with a cotton swab and sending off the envelope to the lab, I waited anxiously for six weeks for my direct paternal DNA results. When the results finally came in, they suggested that I was somehow a direct male descendant of a family of Quakers. A seventeenth- or eighteenth-century male from the staunchly anti-slavery Quaker community, the results suggested, fathered a child with a slave. After looking into this Quaker family a little deeper, I uncovered the boy—my fifth great-grandfather—who ran away from home to find his fortune.

In 1831, John Armfield married Martha Franklin, the niece of his surrogate father Isaac. She was sixteen, about eighteen years younger than John. By 1845, John had retired from slave-trading, sold the firm to an associate, and moved with Martha to central Tennessee. There, he began to invest in Tennessee real estate, soon rising up in respectable wealthy society. No one seemed to care where he'd made his money; only that he'd made it and that he still had it.

In 1850, at age fifty-three, John set out searching again, this time for better health. He suffered from rheumatism, a medical term used at the time to refer to problems affecting the joints and connective tissues. It's likely he suffered from what, today, we could call an autoimmune disease. I know far too much about autoimmune diseases. They run in my family.

John heard about Beersheba Springs, a tiny town in the mountains of Tennessee, fifty miles from Chattanooga where I'd spent my first couple of years after college. The five-square-mile area was known for its mineral waters and health-inducing climate, and John Armfield was enamored. He set out to purchase the lodging establishment that anchored the town and renovate it into a luxury resort to accommodate up to four hundred guests. He brought in French chefs and musical acts from New Orleans to entertain his guests. John and Martha became celebrated innkeepers and consummate hosts, and they supported a wide range of philanthropic causes. They had no biological children, no lineal descendants. "No issue," as a genealogist would say.

I had noticed early on in my research that the white descendants who had studied their Armfield family often stamped "No Issue" after John Armfield's name and said little more. Some made mention of slaves; fewer still mentioned slave-trading. But no one, no one at all, mentioned fancy maids. Other than writing about John's *whos, whats, whens,* and *wheres,* they mostly wrote about his Quaker roots, his days as a stagecoach driver, his connection by marriage to a wealthy family, his philanthropic pursuits, and his days as an innkeeper later in life.

I saw the same thing while researching other branches of my family: after accomplishing the very difficult task of identifying the slaveholder of one of my ancestors, I'd eagerly contacted descendants of the slaveholder only to find no slave schedules, no plantation records, and transcriptions of only the pages in the family Bible that listed white ancestors and descendants.

When I questioned this conspicuous absence of information about the slaves in the family, most of the researchers confessed they'd never thought much about it, even though they'd scoured court, prison, and newspaper records in valiant attempts to uncover all manner of misdeed and scandal.

It turns out that much of a person's story ends up lost and absent from the genealogical records. These records tell the *whos, wheres, whens,* and *whats* of a life. Oral history, passed down and retold repeatedly, can fill in the *whys* and the *hows,* the flesh and skin that layer on top of the factual bones to reveal who a person really was. So much of what we know about people long gone— beyond the basic facts surrounding the times and places of their births, marriages, and deaths—comes only from the stories they told and the letters they wrote.

But for most of us, after a hundred years, very little of that oral history remains.

For example, I know the basic details of John Armfield's life mainly through the documents and records that remain. But the good stuff, the stuff that gives me clues about his hopes, his passions, and his demons, I only know because the people who knew him thought that their impressions of him were worth recording and that his letters were worth saving. No one, it seems, thought this about any of my enslaved ancestors.

A hundred years from now, for instance, a person might be able to find out with very little effort that I was born at the tail end of the civil rights era in the city—and in the very neighborhood where much of it took place. They could discover pretty quickly that I graduated from college with a math degree and moved to Chattanooga, Tennessee, at the age of twenty-two, and that I left Chattanooga two years later to live in various parts of California. But they would find it much harder to uncover the fact that those moves around California were fueled mainly by restlessness and wanderlust. Or to learn that I attempted to quench my restlessness and wanderlust in my thirties via a stint in culinary school and another in the mountains as an innkeeper. They might never know that my innkeeping venture grew partly out of my love for food, which itself grew partly out of biological quirks that gave me a super sense of smell but that also caused my body to attack itself, prompting me to learn how to use food as a tool of healing.

John Armfield died in 1871, his wealth diminished by the Civil War and his health deteriorated by the rheumatism that plagued him. His Alexandria, Virginia, slave pens and the three-story Franklin and Armfield office now form a slavery museum called the Freedom House. And Armfield's stately, elaborate grave sits gated across the street from the intact Beersheba Springs Hotel. But the rest of the story, the *hows* and the *whys*, the meat on the bones, is in danger of fading away with each passing day.

And I am still left with much to wonder. I've wondered many times if John Armfield's wanderlust and ambition were more than just universal tenets of the human condition. Were they genetic traits, passed down seven generations from father, to son, to son? I wonder, too, if John Armfield spins in his grave at the thought of his well-kept secret exposed, or if maybe he would instead take solace in the knowledge that his genes carried on, if not his name. Perhaps he wouldn't have bothered to think too much about it, except to say, "In a hundred years, who will care?"

But most of all, I wonder about the fancy maid, whose name I will probably never know.

For a long time, all of this wondering bothered me. It was caused by the long-standing burial of our shared history, which I felt explained so much of the racial tension and anger that bubbled beneath the surface of our culture. But I didn't know what to do about it.

While standing bored in a long supermarket checkout line, I found an answer in the unlikeliest of places. Thumbing through the latest *People* magazine, I found a surprisingly in-depth piece about the descendants of both slaves and slaveholders coming together to heal old wounds. At the end of the piece, I spotted a short blurb about an organization that aimed to facilitate just such healings. It had the perfect name: Coming to the Table.

As I've gotten to know John Armfield and all of my other ancestors, I'm more convinced each day that we, the descendants of slaves and slaveholders alike, are inextricably connected. And I'm convinced we will never heal this country's wounds and atone for its sins until we look squarely into each other's eyes and claim our ancestors'—and our—stories. We will never feast on the fat of the land until we dare to come to the table.

Otherwise, in a hundred years, who will care about any of us?

NOTES

1. Biographical information on John Armfield came from Isabel Howell, "John Armfield, Slave-Trader," *Tennessee Historical Quarterly* 2, no. 1 (March 1943).
2. Information on "fancy maids" can be found in Edward E. Baptist, "'Cuffy,' 'Fancy Maids,' and 'One-Eyed Men': Rape, Commodification, and the Domestic Slave Trade in the United States," *American Historical Review* 106, no. 5 (Dec. 2001): 1619–1650.

PART II MAKING CONNECTIONS

7 ⤳ STATE LINE

ANTOINETTE BROUSSARD

IN 2003, MY mother was sorting out her personal files while I was visiting her.

"Would you like these papers that belonged to your grandfather?" she asked.

"Of course!" I responded.

Only then, after leafing through the papers, did I realize that my grandfather, Berry Craig, had been a writer. Included with these papers were his writing journals and meticulously typed manuscripts on onion skin paper. I was impressed—and ecstatic that my grandfather's papers had been preserved. They provided me with insight into a man who had died when I was nine.

In 1910, at fifty-six years old, after he'd lost his left leg in a work-related accident, my grandfather took a job as an elevator operator at Oakland's city hall. For the next twenty years, he wrote his stories. One of these stories caught my attention. It was the play he'd written about a Platte County, Missouri, slaveowner and his female slave. As a writer and family historian, I felt it was my duty to determine whether this story was autobiographical. I also hoped to get his work published.

My maternal grandfather was born on a farm in Weston, Platte County, Missouri, on December 4, 1863, more than two years after the commencement of the American Civil War. President Lincoln had signed the Emancipation Proclamation almost a year earlier, freeing all persons held as slaves in the rebel states. However, since Missouri did not secede from the union, it was exempt from the order. It wasn't until December 6, 1865—when the Thirteenth Amendment to the Constitution was adopted and ratified by three-fourths of the states—that slavery was permanently outlawed.

Now, one hundred fifty years later, and ten years after conducting my own genealogical research, I went on my first journey to Platte County, Missouri, situated on the east bank of the Missouri River. On the same trip, I also visited Leavenworth, Kansas, located on the west bank of the river. Leavenworth was where Berry's family lived after they were freed.

During my airplane ride, my mind was racing. I thought about the things my Uncle George had told me. He was Berry's son. When I was a child, Uncle George's stories and the serious inflection in his voice always commanded my attention. He was a handsome light-complexioned black man, around six feet tall and 175 pounds, with a thin mustache and heavy eyebrows. He would stand leaning forward a bit, with a slight bend in his posture, and he sometimes gestured with a half-used cigar between his fingers.

"Her name was Violet, and his name was William P. Wallingford from Platte County, Missouri," Uncle George had said always emphasizing the middle initial P and Platte County. "Wallingford owned Violet. He was your grandfather's father."

The Wallingfords were always on my mind, like a faraway family that seemed impossible to find. I craved any detail that would help me in my search because I thought that if I could just find them, I could breathe better, deal with my anger better. My family's slave history was an injustice, and the responsible people had never been held accountable for it. I needed to bring that past to the present. That history could not be lost or discarded, swept under the rug as though it had not mattered. Truth was power.

But how would Violet feel about my efforts now? My trip here today? Here I was, her great-granddaughter, and I was seeking to get acquainted with her perpetrator's kin. In the only photo I have of Violet, her soft brown eyes mirror a gentle nature, so I imagined that she would say it was okay. That I should let the healing begin.

My flight to Kansas City was delayed two hours, so I called Dixie to let her know. Dixie was one of the descendants of the white Wallingford family who I was going to meet in Missouri.

"Don't worry," Dixie said. "We'll be waiting for you." She sounded intelligent and understanding.

The apprehension resurfaced. I thought, *Are we going to be okay together? Are they more intelligent than me?* Then the voice in my head countered, telling me to believe in myself and my reasons for making this trip.

When my plane landed at the Kansas City Airport that July of 2013, the temperature was in the nineties with a heat index of over a hundred. From my airplane window, I could see flocks of birds, cow pastures, beautiful green rolling hills, and the beginning of a sunset. With its unspoiled countryside, Missouri was unexpectedly beautiful and inviting. I had imagined something uglier, something that would reflect the ugliness of its history, of slavery.

I was on my way to meet two inviting strangers—the white Wallingford's, considered legitimate heirs. I had found them with the help of a genealogist and one of their relatives, Lee Lamar, an avid family researcher. Lee introduced us over the phone and, after a few conversations, they invited me to visit. Despite their openness, I was scared. My grandfather and his siblings, according to white society then, were considered the slaveowner's bastards. They were not recognized as members of the family. Did I need to be recognized? No. Did I need to claim him as my great-grandfather? Not particularly. Did I want a connection with the living Wallingfords? Yes, as long as it was positive. I'd never thought of myself as a part of their family, but I hoped our meeting would at least bring awareness of our existence.

Dixie and her sister Myrna lived in Kansas, a few miles from Kansas City. They were born and raised in Dearborn, Missouri and are descendants of the white Wallingford family from Mason County, Kentucky. Biologically, we share William Payne Wallingford. He was the sisters' great-great-grandfather and my great-grandfather. In 1837, Wallingford had moved from Kentucky and settled on the Platte Purchase in Missouri. He was married three times and fathered seventeen children, including eight by my great-grandmother Violet, his former slave.

Dixie and Myrna's mother lived to be 102 years old, and she shared the same birthday as my mother, except they were born a few years apart. Our mothers also shared longevity. My mother passed at 102 years old as well, shy of her 103rd birthday by only a few weeks. And both women were descendants of William Payne Wallingford. I had never thought of our families as sharing the same lineage, even though we do; I had just wanted to find the people who had enslaved my Violet—but of course, *he* was long gone. Instead, I had found two loving sisters. Until our phone introduction, the Wallingford sisters had been unaware of our biological connection—they'd had no idea my family branch existed. In fact, they had been unaware of the history of slavery in the Wallingford family. Still, Dixie graciously invited me to stay with her while I visited Kansas and Missouri, and I humbly accepted.

When I arrived at Dixie's home, the sisters met me at the front door.

"Welcome, Antoinette," said Dixie. "This is Sis (Myrna), also your cousin."

I was grateful for the warm reception and immediately felt at ease with them. We had cocktails, ate dinner, and enjoyed Myrna's homemade berry pie. We talked about our families as we identified them in family photos. I had printed out all my research material to share with them. They were surprised at the amount of material I had accrued. They were disturbed that our shared predecessor, W.P., as they called him, had enslaved my great-grandmother Violet.

"Can you imagine how terrible it must have been for Violet? To have W.P. coming for you? That she had to submit to his demands?" one of the sisters said. "It was terribly disappointing to realize he committed these sins when he was postured by the family as someone to admire."

"We are really sorry about it," Myrna said.

"Thank you, but it wasn't your fault," I said.

"Lee used the information you provided us regarding W.P.'s land records and mapped out ten farm locations," Myrna said.

I wanted to pinpoint the area where Violet and her children had been kept and learn as much as I could about the local Wallingford history.

Wallingford's farms were spread through three counties, Myrna explained.

"We think Violet lived with her children on one of his farms about an hour from here," she said.

Two days later, Myrna, Dixie, and I drove past Weston into the vicinity of Wallace, Missouri.

"There were four farms in this area," Myrna said. "Violet probably lived on one of them with her children."

I took photos of the lush green rural countryside, trying to reconcile the idea that my family once lived here, enslaved, and apparently isolated. How could someone mistreat people in such a peaceful place?

From the 1850 and 1860 slave schedules, I knew that W.P. had owned a black female slave and several mulatto children. Since there were no names listed on the slave schedules, I used age and description to match them to Violet and her children. Farmers prospered here with slave labor. Slave families were sometimes split up, like a cat or a dog from its litter. The fathers and mothers rarely lived on the same farms and had to get permission from their owners to see their families. Children were rented out to surrounding farmers sometimes for years, alienated from their mothers.

What gives a person the right to own other people?

"The Wallingford men were good business managers. Hard workers. Diligent. They worked six days a week," Myrna said. "Played croquet and went to church on Sunday."

The black soil was productive for corn, soybean, hemp, and tobacco crops, Myrna went on to explain. Nearby Weston had the biggest tobacco warehouses. They had the Missouri River to transport their crops.

In nearby Dearborn, where Myrna and Dixie grew up, we visited the cemetery where many Wallingfords were buried. Myrna pointed to each Wallingford headstone as she explained their relationship to me. We also visited a farm that Myrna and Dixie said had once belonged to their great-uncle, who would have been my grandfather's half-brother. It was difficult to absorb my connection to these people, but I was grateful to the sisters for pointing out that they were my relatives.

I was so happy to be there, discovering and exploring my collective history with Dixie and Myrna. They trusted and appreciated my research and expressed no doubts that we were related. I also met Myrna's children and grandchildren, who embraced me.

My adrenaline was so pumped up that I had a hard time getting to sleep. On the last day of the trip, I rented a car, and ventured out on my own. I wanted to see the areas where Violet, my grandfather, his siblings, and other relatives lived after they were freed. I drove to Leavenworth and through my family's former neighborhoods using the addresses I had found in old city directories. It was a rural town, with lots of trees and green hills, a mile or two from the main part of town that bordered the Missouri River. Though the old buildings were gone and the neighborhoods had changed, I was able to familiarize myself with the town where my family had once gone to school, worked, and lived. Leavenworth was no longer a mystery. Violet and her children had survived here. They were free here.

The "First City of Kansas," Leavenworth was founded in 1854. It is a quaint river town with beautiful Victorian architecture, known for its garrison, Fort Leavenworth, a United States Army installation built in 1827 on the bluffs of the Missouri River. Its river location made it a destination for slaves in pursuit of their freedom from the slave state of Missouri. I was headed toward it when a sign for Platte City, on the right side of the road, caught my eye. Platte County was where my grandfather, Berry, had been born.

Instead of heading toward the fort, I drove across the Centennial Bridge, a medium-blue two-span arch bridge that connects Kansas to Missouri and looks like it was built with a rector set. Just that quickly, I could leave one state for another. Below the bridge were the banks of the Missouri River. This was the same river Violet and her children had to cross when they were freed. She was pregnant with her eighth child, and accompanied by five children, between the ages of one to fourteen. One child was lost or had been sold by his father W.P. Wallingford. Family oral history said Wallingford gave Violet no financial support. He had denied her request for help. Actually, he denied that Violet's children were his and said he did not want them to use his surname. But Violet did not want his name. She chose the name Craig, a name many of her family members had taken when freed and the one she considered her maiden name.

The river held a sense of familiarity. It had a voice, a story to tell. Like Violet's spirit, as strong and resilient as a cypress tree, the river kept pushing forward no matter what it encountered. It was often called the "Big Muddy" or the "Mighty Mo" because, in some places, it had relocated more than two thousand feet of soil.

Once I crossed the bridge, I drove again through the green farmlands of rural Platte County. I took the winding road that led to the small town of Historic Weston, found in the scenic hill country high above the Missouri River. It had once been a significant, mid-nineteenth-century port community. Now it was a favorite destination for antique shoppers. At the Weston Visitor's Bureau, I met historian Brenda Thompson and asked her how people had crossed the Missouri River in 1865 since there had been no bridge then.

"The river was not as deep as it is now," she said. "The Corps of Engineers has changed its depth and width over the years. People used donkeys and mules and looked for a shallow place to cross."

Perhaps someone had helped Violet and her children get to and cross the river after they were freed. When I asked Myrna if the Wallingford farms were within walking distance of the river, she said they were farther than that. I imagined the piercing rhythmic sounds of the cicadas in the Platte country-side matched the constant pounding of Violet's heart. Finally, after thirty-five years of living as a slave, the opportunity for Violet and her children to be free manifested with the passing of the Thirteenth Amendment.

Later that day, before the sun began to set, I returned to Leavenworth. I wondered if the commuters I passed on the bridge, driving cars, motorcy-cles, and trucks at high speeds to their workplaces at the penitentiaries or Fort Leavenworth, realized the importance that crossing the river had to former slaves? Did they ever reflect on or even consider the history of slavery here?

Crossing the Missouri River into Kansas was a slave's road to freedom. One slave, George Washington Jefferson, escaped from his owner and went across the river on foot when it froze in 1862. In contrast, no slave patrol or bloodhounds pursued me as I crossed over into Kansas. It took me all of twenty minutes to drive back to the steel bridge, and cross over the river into Leavenworth. It took Violet at least thirty-five years to make the similar cross-ing to her freedom. She lived so close to it, but yet so far.

The trip gave me a lot of clarity. Being there was almost like experiencing a freedom of my own. I could walk through, drive around, and see the places where my family had once lived. I was also able to do a lot of research on this trip. I now know more about the Wallingfords, past and present, and about the Craigs who settled with Violet when they were all gradually freed. I real-ized that you can't achieve all of the necessary genealogical research online. You have to go there and absorb it and take it all in.

Since that first trip, I have become very close to Dixie and Myrna. They read all of my writing and give me advice and encouragement. I share any new genealogical findings I come across with them. I've returned to Leaven-worth and Missouri numerous times and found more family members, black and white. I've been to family reunions and other events there, and they all call me their cousin.

Fortunately, I did not let fear prevent me from trying the door that opened up my past. Instead, I followed my heart, which furnished me with tremen-dous direction for my future.

Part of that future included joining CTTT in 2011. Its peace-building phi-losophy attracted me, and I found the image of the black and white hands clasped together (on the website's landing page) soothing. It conveyed to me the idea of trying to understand and encouraged me to reach across to the other side to heal. It helped me realize that it wouldn't have been fair for me to make the sisters Dixie and Myrna feel responsible or guilty about the offenses of their forefathers. There was nothing we could do about it but embrace each other and talk about our feelings. Through CTTT, I learned the power of forgiveness. It didn't mean I had to forget what had happened; it meant that I could now write about my family's history effectively, without anger, and be an example for others to heal. Truth is power.

8 ❧ THE PLANTATION CAKE

LESLIE STAINTON

F OR A PERIOD of time in my twenties, my mother and I baked a cake every year at New Year's and served it to friends at an open house brunch. It was more or less a pound cake, with the requisite portions of sugar, butter, flour, and eggs, to which we added a quart of floured berries, blue or black. The recipe, from my great-grandmother, was called "Minnie's Plantation Berry Cake."

I liked the cake. I liked its steep sides, the film of powdered sugar sprinkled across the rigid geometry of its golden top. I liked the plate on which my mother served it. Pink and gold around the edges, white in the middle. That, too, was an inheritance: a decorative piece of china salvaged from my family's old plantation home and passed down, like my great-grandmother's dessert, through the generations.

Before I left home for graduate school, my mother typed up the recipe for me. In a note at the bottom, she reminded me of the time we used frozen berries, and the cake broke apart and the berries streaked. "But remember how good it was?" she wrote.

When you serve Minnie's cake, my mother instructed, cut the slices thin, because otherwise it's too heavy to digest.

I don't know where the name "Plantation Berry Cake" came from. Perhaps my great-grandmother Annie Belle Scarlett—whom everyone called Minnie—acquired the recipe from her mother, the daughter of a nineteenth-century cotton planter near Brunswick, Georgia. Minnie was born one year after the Civil War and died three months before my birth. I grew up hearing about her and about the struggles she faced as a widowed mother of three in the early decades of the twentieth century.

Minnie's was part of a larger narrative of suffering endured by my Scarlett ancestors during and after the war—tales of loss (of land and material goods), of once-rich plantation owners forced to take up farming and shop-keeping, of daughters and wives reduced to nursing or teaching jobs. Minnie herself ran a boarding house and baked cakes for a living. "I see so much that makes my heart ache for young girls who have to work," she wrote to her mother in 1910. "I am old enough to take care of myself and make men treat me right, but you would be surprised to know how some men treat working women."

Her letter is one of scores that has come down to me over the years, most of them collected by my maternal grandmother—Minnie's daughter—in cardboard boxes that now sit on the closet shelves of my house in Michigan. In addition to letters, the boxes hold notebooks, newspaper clippings, autograph books, and a host of family photographs. Dour-faced patriarchs, women veiled in black lace, a uniformed boy holding a French horn. One photo shows Minnie standing beside her parents and daughters in front of the family manse outside Brunswick. Minnie wears a wasp-waist dress with mutton-chop sleeves and a straw boating hat. She holds one child in her arms, while a second—my infant grandmother, born in 1898—sits in a huge wicker carriage at her feet. Bent over my grandmother, a blur of motion as she tends to the baby, is a black woman. A nurse, according to the caption, named Mattie.

Another photograph, circa 1888, shows an African American man drawing water from a well under a grove of live oaks on land that belonged to Minnie's parents. "This faithful old slave at the well died a short while since after [sic] having lived for 98 years," an inscription on the back reads. "He never left after the war."

I knew that my Scarlett ancestors had enslaved people, but I didn't remember my grandmother ever talking about it, at least not in detail. Evidently it was something you didn't discuss—an awkward truth best left out of polite conversation. Or maybe she thought it no use trying to explain such matters to her Pennsylvania-born, irredeemably Yankee granddaughter.

It was only later, more than a decade after my grandmother's death, that I went back to the boxes she'd left me and began to look through their contents. Tucked among the scrapbooks and wedding announcements, I found items that startled: an account of my great-great-great-grandfather Francis Muir Scarlett purchasing an African captive from the illegal slave ship *Wanderer* in 1858 and letters describing the "rebellion"[1] of two-dozen Scarlett "servants" in 1862. The letters explain how the enslaved "servants" broke into Scarlett family trunks and seized provisions for their flight to freedom. The author of the letters, Fanny Scarlett, daughter-in-law to Francis Muir Scarlett, recalls the secrecy with which the group plotted, her own indignation at their betrayal. "I wonder," she writes of one of the leaders of the revolt, "if it is possible that she can be so depraved as to be happy." Fanny names names: Matilda, King, Elias, Dido, little Zach, and pregnant Julia, whose husband placed her in a wheelbarrow and rolled her to freedom.

I found transcripts of letters written to Francis Muir Scarlett in 1812 by a Savannah lawyer named Richard M. Stites. The letters contain strict instructions on how to feed the enslaved people on the cotton plantation my great-great-great-grandfather oversaw. "It will be dangerous to feed the negroes too early on new corn until it is dry," writes Stites, who corresponded with overseers and planters up and down the Georgia coast. "I fear the new corn will make the negroes sickly." Therefore, my great-great-great-grandfather was to find a secure place, "sufficiently dry," in which to store his corn when it was green, letting it mature into a feed his workers could safely ingest.

What are we to make of the ingredients we inherit? The pictures and letters, plates and anecdotes? With its list of luxury items, Minnie's recipe for "Plantation Berry Cake" limns a world far different from one in which human beings are fed dried corn as if they are livestock. How do I reconcile the two?

In 2015, to make way for a new parking lot, archaeologists unearthed the foundations of six slave cabins on former Scarlett property outside Brunswick. They discovered shards of kitchen crockery, slivers of glass, corroded tableware, the charred remains of pigs' heads and feet—evidence of meals cooked and consumed under circumstances I struggle to imagine. I've read reports detailing how my family's enslaved laborers had to supplement the meager rations they were given (corn, bacon, meal) with fish, shellfish, sea turtle, deer, wild fruits, nuts, and berries, for which they foraged in nearby woods and marshes.

Here are the coiled truths buried inside the dense crumb of the family story, the dark fruit of my questioning: When and how did this begin? Did no one protest? With what instruments did my ancestors impose order? Whips? Prods? Branding irons? I've seen the newspaper notice my great-great-great-grandfather posted in 1837, advertising ten dollars each for the return of "two negro fellows,—DICK, a stout black fellow, about six feet high 45 years of age. NED, stout yellow complected about five feet ten inches high 27 years of age." Francis Muir Scarlett advised looking for them near the Brunswick Canal, as they both had relatives in the area, and "it is very likely they may be in that vicinity." His two "fellows," it seemed, were trying to reunite with family.

My mother once told me a story about visiting Minnie when she lay sick in bed late in life. During that visit, for some reason, Minnie confided to my mother—her granddaughter—that there were "lots of dark secrets" in the Scarlett family. She murmured something about wives who didn't fulfill their husbands' needs, and husbands who found other outlets for those needs. "And then she slid back under the covers and giggled," my mother remembered.

I have found proof that Fanny Scarlett's husband Frank fathered at least one child by an enslaved black woman and that his brother-in-law John Parland fathered more. I've been told it's likely my own great-great-grandfather— Minnie's father—did the same. The sour fruit bleeds into the sugared story my grandmother would have had me swallow whole.

When he imagined the sons of former slaves sitting down with the sons of former slaveowners at the table of brotherhood, Martin Luther King, Jr. was envisioning a metaphorical coming to the table. But this work requires a real table gathering as well.

Five years ago, while researching my family's history, I discovered the identity of some of the descendants of the African American "servants" who had fled from the Scarletts in 1862. I got in touch with them and said I had information about their ancestors that I wanted to share, and I asked if I could come to their family reunion in Brunswick that summer. They said yes. I was so nervous, I waited until the last minute to book my flight.

On the first night of the reunion, I walked into a pavilion full of people I didn't know, all black, gathered in small groups, talking excitedly to one another. I was the stranger in their midst. But soon someone led me to a woman in her eighties who sat quietly on a chair in a corner of the room, fanning herself. Her name was Avedell Grant. I introduced myself and told her I was a descendant of the Scarletts. Avedell stood, reached for my hand, and began to cry. "I never thought I'd see a Scarlett again," she exclaimed, as she squeezed my fingers. She had worked for my family as a child, she said, washing dishes and tidying the house. "The Scarletts were always good to the blacks." I didn't know what she meant.

The reunion lasted three days, and most of it took place around food. Lowcountry boil, fried fish, grits, hamburgers, spaghetti, green beans, collards, potato salad, banana pudding, red velvet cake, sweet tea, and lemonade. At the main banquet on Saturday night, we heaped barbecued chicken and ribs onto our plates and sat together at long tables while a Baptist comedian told jokes at the front of the auditorium and family members reminisced about long-gone aunts and uncles and grandparents. Women circulated among the tables with homemade cakes. They slid thick wedges onto my plate, and when I insisted I couldn't eat any more—I was too full—they coaxed me into taking seconds.

On the final morning of the reunion, the extended family gathered for church in a small chapel whose origins dated back to slave times. Midway through the service, I was asked to introduce myself. I stood, gave my name, and said I was a Scarlett. "I stumbled upon your extraordinary family while reading through my own family's papers," I began, heart racing. "You've made me feel so incredibly welcome."

The pastor, a tiny man in a long white robe, with gray hair and aviator glasses, eyed me warily.

"Back in the day," I continued, hunting for vocabulary, "my family was not so welcoming to yours." The wording was clumsy, if not offensive. "Our stories are intertwined in awkward and sad ways, and I am sorry for what my family did."

I told the congregation I'd spoken to my mother by phone the night before, and when I'd described to her the generosity of everyone at the reunion, she'd wept. "She sends her love and hugs," I said. "We love you. God bless you." I sat down, hands slick with sweat.

The room was quiet for a minute and then the service resumed. A group of men in white gloves wheeled in a table draped in a white cloth and positioned it at the front of the sanctuary. The congregation rose. Single file, we circled past the table and each picked up a plastic thimbleful of grape juice and a wafer. We sat back down in our pews, and at a given signal, we ate and drank together. The pastor urged us to remember that this was no ordinary supper; this was *communion*—a reminder, I thought, that difficult conversations can sometimes be made easier if they take place over a meal.

After church, we assembled at a nearby park for a last lunch. Ham, baked chicken, broccoli, corn, peach pie. When the dishes had been cleared and tables put away, a family member announced, "Leslie's got a story about our family, so let's sit down and listen." I took out my copies of Fanny Scarlett's letters and began reading. I described how the ancestors of the people gathered around me had escaped from my ancestors during the war—how they'd seized supplies and commandeered a boat and bravely sailed to freedom on a nearby coastal island then under Union control. I handed out copies of the letters to the descendants. Days later, I received an email from one of them. She and her mother had read through every letter, she said. "We felt proud that my Heroic Great Great Grandfather . . . would risk his life to provide supplies to the Union Army, and help several slaves to freedom."

I don't know whether Minnie ever served her Plantation Berry Cake to any of the black families who lived near her at the turn of the last century, many of them descendants of people her grandparents had enslaved. For all I know, the recipe for the cake *came* from one of those women and was simply adopted by my great-grandmother when she needed delicacies to feed the guests at her boarding house.

A few weeks ago, I tried making Minnie's cake again. It had been nearly forty years since my mother and I had last tackled the recipe. My mother was now dead, and I had only her typewritten instructions to go by. It was a hot July day in Michigan, the sort of weather I imagine Minnie often contended with in Georgia. I set out butter to soften, eggs to warm. I sifted flour and grated nutmeg and measured baking soda and powder.

As I worked, I had the radio on in the background. Fresh Air's Terry Gross was interviewing the author of a book about recent efforts to undermine the Voting Rights Act. As the KitchenAid groaned, I listened to stories about the disenfranchisement of voters, mostly black, in Texas, North Carolina, Mississippi, Florida. It was tempting to think we'd made no progress at all in the century since Minnie last baked her cake.

I floured blueberries and spooned them into the batter and poured everything into a pan and slid it into the oven. The recipe called for the cake to bake for an hour and twenty minutes, but when I pulled it out, the batter wiggled, so I put it back in. When I took it out again, the cake seemed firm, and I set it on a rack to cool. A half-hour later, I unmolded it onto a plate. Within minutes the cake had collapsed into a steaming mass of half-cooked batter. A failure. The only edible parts were the bits around the edges, and they were delicious—laced with nutmeg and redolent of an era when women wore long dresses and prim hats and could count on servants to look after their squirming children.

Who knows what went wrong? Maybe the cake needed more flour, a hotter oven, fewer eggs. It's possible my mother miscopied the recipe. I'm not an intuitive baker, so I don't know how or where to begin to make sense of the recipe, and maybe that's the point—I can't understand my great-grandmother's world any more than she could understand *her* grandparents' world, with its dark secrets and whispered truths. My husband and I spent a day nibbling at the few parts of the cake that had baked through, and then I carried the whole mess outside and dumped it on the ground for the birds to eat.

Once or twice a year, I go down to Brunswick, and when I do, I get together with the descendants of the people who fled from my ancestors and made their way to freedom. We've become friends. I go to their church (the pastor now hugs me), and although I'm still asked to introduce myself, I no longer apologize for my family's actions because I've been told I don't need to. The members of this congregation, at least, want to move on. After church, my friends sometimes invite me to join them for Sunday dinner, or I take them out for a meal. We talk about family and weather and health and church, and from time to time we talk about the past.

One day, I asked Avedell Grant what she'd meant when she'd told me the Scarletts were always good to the blacks.

"Were they really?" I asked.

She was eating a piece of fish, and she chewed thoughtfully for a moment before nodding. Her father had worked for the Scarletts, she said at last. He'd worked for a brother of Minnie's named Robert, and when Robert mentioned that his sisters needed help around the house, her father volunteered Avedell. She was eight or nine years old at the time. She went to work for the Scarletts for a couple of years, washing dishes and cleaning the kitchen.

"They treated me just like one of them," she said. Except for one thing. Whenever Robert and his sisters sat down to eat their noon meal in the dining room, they made Avedell go out onto the front porch to eat her portion by herself. "I didn't understand," she said. "It wasn't like this, you know," and she waved her hand over the table at the Golden Corral where we sat eating.

"Of course," she went on, "later I understood."

Early last spring, I went down to Brunswick with my husband, and we visited Avedell in her home. We talked for a long time at her kitchen table, and just before we left, she gave us a paper bag full of hot peppers from her garden. We then drove down the road to visit with Avedell's cousins. They invited us to pick kumquats and wild plums from the trees in their front yard, and we filled another bag. I carried all of these foods back to Michigan, and for weeks afterward, I cut them into salads and stews.

I have imagined baking Minnie's cake for my friends in Brunswick as a way of sharing the family inheritance, which does, after all, belong to them too, in ways that are complicated and painful and impossible to expunge. But it seems more important to focus on the present, not the past.

I think of the countless people to whom I cannot apologize, the descendants of so many other women and children and men whose names I will never know. You can't slice into this story without leaving someone out or getting something wrong. Often, I fail. I'm tongue-tied, say the wrong thing, misinterpret cues. I can't read the recipe. The cake fails; the berries run. It collapses under its own weight so that we can digest only the smallest fragments. Nevertheless, we keep trying to wrest sweetness from the salt. We keep coming to the table.

NOTE

1. Rather than use the word "escape," Fanny Scarlett preferred the term "rebellion." Like many Southern slaveholders, she also preferred the term "servants" to "slaves."

9 ⇥ AM I BLACK?

EILEEN JACKSON

Even before I knew I had been adopted, whenever I found myself in our garden at night, staring into the night sky, my heart filled with longing and grief; longing to go home to my mother. The pain too deep for tears, crushing my soul, smoldering embers where a fire should be. I had been born from the womb of my birth mother and given away. I knew there was a place I belonged and it wasn't here.

Leo Michael Jackson and Mary (Molly) Bridget O'Sullivan were my adoptive parents, parents trying to make up for not being my "real parents." Dad was born in 1901 to an Irish mother, Agnes O'Connell, in New Zealand and a father of unknown origin. When Leo was around five years old, his mother remarried and gave her son to an uncle to be raised. He stowed away on a merchant marine ship when he was just fourteen and made his way to San Francisco. Molly's mother died from tuberculosis shortly after their crossing from Ireland in 1894. Her father, Joseph O'Sullivan, was an abusive alcoholic who mercilessly beat her brother, Maurice. Molly, rejecting the parental model she knew, turned to Dr. Spock; I was raised by the book.

We weren't rich, but curiously we always seemed to have enough.

Leo and Molly met in the 1930s. During that time they ran the Catholic Boys and Girls Clubs on the East Side of LA. We were Irish Catholic and proud. By the time I was born, my parents were well connected within the Irish Catholic community and were particularly close to the Immaculate Heart of Mary, a community of Catholic nuns who taught in many of the parochial schools in the Los Angeles Diocese. Their mission was the education of girls.

From the day I was baptized on December 7, 1941, I was groomed to be a member of the Immaculate Heart community. Once baptized, Sr. M. Enda Doherty, sister of the Father John Doherty, the priest who baptized me, took me to the altar of our Lady of Grace and dedicated my life to Mary. I attended Cathedral Chapel Grammar School; with me were Jackie Gleason's daughter, Linda; John Wayne's daughter, Melinda; and Robert Mitchum's niece, Vicki. These were children who came to my birthday parties, and I theirs.

In this world, I was not comfortable with my kinky hair and my thick thighs and lips; I was adopted, an only child, and my parents looked like grandparents. I was an outsider, one of the ugly ones, in this world of glamour girls. In grammar school, I was called Thunder Thighs, Nigger Lips, Stalin Jackass, and queer. My mother told me to offer it up for the souls in purgatory, a common Catholic response to pain and suffering. Despite my early experiences of bullying and self-loathing, in high school I learned from the amazing nuns that I was capable of greatness, intellectually, physically, and artistically. I won both the Catholic diocesan and the Southern California science fairs and was a finalist at the National Science Fair in 1957. Two years later, fresh out of high school, I entered the convent and became a teacher.

In 1961 my father died. The boys from my dad's boy's club served as the pallbearers at his funeral. His death was followed by my mother's in 1963. With both parents gone, I was once again without family, and chaos had erupted both within the community and in the world outside. The usual life of active nuns had been fashioned after a strict hierarchical model in which the sisters were deprived of self-responsibility. But the Second Vatican Council admonished nuns to become relevant in the modern world. Now we needed college degrees before being sent out to teach, and we began wearing modified habits and managing our own schedules. Cardinal James

Francis McIntyre, however, later rejected the conclusions of the council and demanded obedience from the Immaculate Heart Sisters.

August 14,1965, I was sent with a partner to the flower market district in South LA to buy flowers for the feast of the Assumption of Mary the next day. For nights, we had watched the fires burning in Watts, and we had prayed. Seeing the tanks looming on a bridge, guns pointed into the heart of Watts, sealed my fate. I had already walked with Caesar Chavez from Modesto to Manteca to unionize farmworkers. I could not stay in a convent in constant contention with the presiding Cardinal of the Los Angeles Diocese when war was going on around me. I took a leave of absence, and in 1969 I officially separated from the community and from the church that had been my second home from birth. Then in 1970, McIntyre fired all community members teaching in the diocesan schools. They were given the choice to obey the edicts of the cardinal or to lose their canonical status as nuns. They chose to follow their principles, and I set off to face the world for the first time. The Immaculate Heart Community remains ecumenical to this day, open to Christians of all genders, races, and orientations.

Torn from my moorings, I set out to discover a new world and a new truth. God was dead, according to Nietzsche, John F. Kennedy, Bobby Kennedy, and Martin Luther King were dead too. Watts had gone up in flames, and the Vietnam War was raging. I enrolled as a student at the University of California, San Diego, and two years later, in 1971, George Winne, a student inspired by a Buddhist monk's self-immolation, set himself on fire on the quad of the Revelle campus to protest the war. The image in my mind of the young man in flames was so vivid, it made my studies in music useless and unimportant. I dropped out of school the next day.

I went to work with the Quakers in opposing the war and met some activists from Chicago; we developed a heart connection that ran deep. I moved from California, my home for twenty-eight years, to Chicago's Hyde Park and graduated from college with a degree in biology and another in nursing. During my last summer of nursing school, I worked at Miles Square Health Center serving Robert Taylor homes. It was there that I learned my first lesson about being black in America. I was a young white nursing student assigned to a team. Two white nurses supervised three black certified nursing assistants. Race and class were the two distinctions between us. We held the formal authority, but they held informal power. They had information that we needed. At the end of each shift, nurse's aides customarily gave reports, but these aides would face away from us, speaking in inaudible tones, in a dialect that we didn't understand. They rejected our authority by forcing us to ask them to speak up and turn around. They only relented after I announced that I had a bad ear and couldn't hear them. One of those nursing assistants was Mildred. She was clearly exasperated by having to accompany me into the projects each day, but after I began working with patients on my own, Mildred and I started talking more. We became fast friends when we organized a Service Employees International Union (SEIU) local chapter at the health center. Mildred taught me the importance of testing the character and trustworthiness of white folk before placing trust in their friendship.

I remained active in antiwar and anti-imperialist activities. I helped open the New World Resource Center, an anti-imperialist bookstore on the north side of Chicago, and I wrote to the Attica Seven and subsequently met one of them at a conference. As a member of the Medical Committee for Human Rights, I joined a caravan to Raleigh, North Carolina, for a rally where Angela Davis was scheduled to speak. There was not enough security personnel, so I was asked to provide personal security for Angela. I made a decision at that moment that Angela's life was more valuable than mine. Angela stood on the steps of the capital, and I stood in front of her watching for any sign of a person with a gun. About a hundred KKK members in white-coned sheets with holes cut for eyes were on the periphery of the demonstration. I couldn't see any weapons, but I imagined them beneath the sheets. That was a critical moment for me that led to some deep soul-searching. I decided that there were only two people worthy of risking my life to save: Angela Davis and Sylvia Woods, a labor organizer and activist, both black women, both lifelong leaders of the movement. This experience gave me a new sense of my own self-worth. I would ever after consider my own life also worth saving.

My friendship with African Americans and my involvement in the civil rights movement inflamed my curiosity about my own roots. I began to pressure my only living relative, my adopted aunt, to divulge my birth mother's identity. She held steadfast. Instead, unbeknownst to me, she wrote to my birth mother about my desire to know who she was. Then, in 1973, I was surprised to receive a phone call.

"Hello, is this Eileen Jackson? This is Maria Stock, your real sister."

All my life, I had felt as though I had been hovering a few inches above the ground. When I heard my sister's words, my feet finally touched the earth.

I met my sister for the first time in the San Francisco Airport. She paged me, and when I picked up the white courtesy telephone, the voice came from behind me—not from the phone. Maria and I were twins separated by ten years. We looked alike and had similar beliefs, life paths, and behaviors. My identity began to shift then. I was the same person, but the play in which I held the lead role had changed as my family was now emerging.

I went on to learn that my mother was Eloise Pierce Humphrey and that her great-great-grandfather was John Rowan, Sr. who built Federal Hill, the plantation in Bardstown, Kentucky known as the Old Kentucky Home (made famous in the song by Steven Foster of the same name, which is sung each year at the Kentucky Derby). With this new piece of information, I suddenly went from being the daughter of impoverished Irish Catholic immigrants to the descendant of slave-owning Southern aristocrats.

With our kinky hair and our thick lips and thighs, it turned out that my sister and I had both wondered if we had black ancestors. Now, I also hoped to identify the slaves who once cared for my family.

That's when I discovered Ida Mae (Rowan) Corley Robert's genealogy of her ancestors, *Rising Above It All: A Tribute to the Rowan Slaves of Federal Hill*. Ida Mae and I exchanged information to learn more about our families. About a year after we met, I got a call from Ida Mae's sister, Pearl Rowan Alexander.

"Hello, Eileen. I'm so happy to have found you," Pearl said, calling me her cousin. Pearl showered me with the love and excitement of a new soul sister.

I began to wonder "What kinds of relationships did the slaves and slave-owners have back when slavery still existed? What was it like during the Civil War and beyond? Were there mixed feelings as slaves left their plantations? I wonder now whether Pearl's great-great-grandmother felt some affection for the Rowan children in her care.

I feel in the depths of my soul the intimacy that existed between the slaves and the women and children in their care. I know that most of the time, it was probably brutal, unrewarding, and unfulfilling. In her book and in person, Ida Mae told me, "Your family was kind." The women and men in my family—musicians, artists, janitors, mothers—are all deeply spiritual, loving, and caring people. I pray with all my heart that this is who we were then too. That our family was as good to Pearl's family as her family was to ours.

In fall 2017, Pearl traveled from her home in Olympia to Whidbey Island, Washington, to visit me and my spouse. When Pearl and I met for the first time, it was as powerful as when I had met my birth sister Maria. It was then that Pearl told me an important story passed down in her family. Her great-grandmother, Mary Lyon, was my great-great-grandfather John Rowan's "mistress." We will never know for sure the relationship between Mary Lyon and John Rowan other than that he was her master. We are waiting to hear whether DNA will confirm the oral history. In her book, Ida Mae writes, "While degradation existed in some parts of Kentucky, in other places such as Bardstown, another side of slavery could be seen. In these places, slaves traveling with their masters were often dressed for show. As property, they were well cared for and were taught to read and write. Just the same, they, like their less fortunate sisters and brothers, were robbed of their human dignity."[1]

While the reality of slavery defines the relations between our ancestral families, it no longer defines us in relation to each other. That is why the deep love that Pearl bestows on me, her capacity to forgive, feels like a reconciliation. It is a gift that I receive with a grateful heart, acknowledging the reality that my great-great-grandfather was the oppressor, robbing her family of their dignity. The bond between Pearl and me is a bond of equals, both nurses of advancing age. It is love and friendship that connects us now. We have come full circle.

NOTE

1. Ida M. Corley Roberts, *Rising Above It All: A Tribute to the Rowan Slaves of Federal Hill* (Louisville: Harmony House Publishers, 1994).

10 ⇻ THE IMMEASURABLE DISTANCE BETWEEN US

THOMAS NORMAN DeWOLF

IN JANUARY 2001, I learned I was related to the largest slave-trading dynasty in U.S. history. They weren't from the South, which is where I'd been told all my life that slavery took place. They were from New England. That summer I joined nine distant cousins to retrace the "triangle trade" route of our ancestors from Rhode Island to Ghana to Cuba and back. Step by step, we learned about the vast complicity of Northern states in slavery and gained an education on issues of race that I never knew existed.

The result was the documentary film *Traces of the Trade: A Story from the Deep North*, which premiered at the Sundance Film Festival and was screened on the PBS series *P.O.V.* My first book, *Inheriting the Trade*, is the story of my experiences making the film and what came after.

Eight days after we returned home from filming, the twin towers of the World Trade Center were destroyed on September 11, 2001.

That November, my parents celebrated their fiftieth wedding anniversary. Preparing to fly from Oregon to Southern California for the festivities, my wife Lindi, our daughter, and I settled into our seats on the plane, when suddenly two security officers approached and removed a man with brown skin who had been sitting two rows ahead of us. They confiscated his carry-on bag. A few minutes later, they came back, checking around, above, and below his seat and in the bathrooms. They instructed our daughter and another passenger who were seated closest to him to go through their bags to make sure nothing had been slipped into them they hadn't packed. They found nothing.

A voice soon announced over the plane's public address system, "We have removed a questionable man from the plane. We checked his bags and the area around his seat and found nothing. He didn't speak English very well, and he made another passenger uncomfortable, so we will not allow him back on board."

The remaining passengers looked around at each other in disbelief. An African American man in the row behind me and across the aisle stood up, grabbed his bag, and said, "I'm outta here. This is bullshit!" He rushed off the plane.

Another man said, "What if the first guy was a decoy? What if the second guy was the one who really left the bomb?" People near his now-empty seat looked above and below where he'd been sitting, including in the seat pockets and the storage area above. Why weren't any airline officials helping them check this second area?

I shook my head, catching myself. I'd bought into the fear surrounding these two men. "What are we becoming?" I thought. The memory of this disturbing event stayed with me all the way to Los Angeles, where we rented a car and drove to our hotel near Pomona—the town of my birth, childhood, and the church I grew up in.

The celebration of my parents' anniversary began Saturday morning in a large room at a college campus where a friend of our family worked. The events of September 11 had discouraged many family and friends who lived in other states from flying there. Even so, over one hundred people showed up. Many of them I did not know, which was no surprise since I had moved away almost thirty years earlier. One person I did know was Mr. Bailey. For many years, he was the only black man who attended our church.

My sister organized a wonderful celebration. Stories were told, gifts were given, laughter was shared, a band played, and food and drink were plentiful.

Sunday morning, the actual date of my parents' anniversary, was an extension of Saturday's celebration. We left the hotel early and I drove through the neighborhoods of my childhood, seeing our old house, remembering how we'd gone to school there, played at that park, shopped at that store, walked along this sidewalk.

Growing up in the 1960s near Los Angeles had been both wonderful and sometimes scary. On television, we watched *Leave it to Beaver* and *Father Knows Best* as well as news reports about racial unrest throughout the United States, including the Watts riots just thirty miles from our house. On my junior high school campus, there were often police in full riot gear, and I remember being afraid a lot. I was particularly afraid of certain black kids; kids who were loud and aggressive and bigger than I was. Fights often broke out between black kids and white kids. I avoided conflict as best I could and tried to make jokes to diffuse tension. But it mostly felt like there was nothing anyone could do that would help. One day, two police officers interrupted my history class and took one of my black classmates away, along with a shoebox from beneath his desk. Rumors flew that the shoebox contained a gun. That kid never returned to school.

I parked outside Pomona First Christian Church, one of the safe places of my young life. We walked up the steps and entered the sanctuary to the sound of bells ringing high above. Mom and Dad had been members of this church since before they exchanged wedding vows here. They were once young parents of a growing family of the future. Now they had become the elders of the congregation, filling roles that people now long-dead once performed.

As we sat in the pew, I looked around. My old Sunday School teacher was sitting nearby, as were a couple of people around my age who I grew up with. A few children were fidgeting in the pews as we once had. After the service, cake and punch were served in honor of my parents. I saw more familiar faces, but long-forgotten names mostly eluded me. Some said hello; others just nodded and smiled, and we let it go at that.

I hadn't had a chance to speak with Mr. Bailey at the party the day before, so I made a point of approaching him. "Hi, Mr. Bailey. Can I talk with you for a few minutes?"

"Why sure, Tom. How are you?" His grip was firm as we shook hands. "It is so good to see you kids in this church again." To Mr. Bailey, who was in his late seventies, I was still a kid, even though I was almost fifty.

"I've spent most of this past year learning about my ancestors on my father's side of the family." I proceeded to tell him about *Traces of the Trade*. Though people were chatting all around us, it felt as though we were the only two in the room. "I learned so much this summer that I never learned before. They just never taught these things in school."

Mr. Bailey smiled as he leaned forward and said to me, almost in a whisper, "You didn't learn that stuff, but we always did. They taught that history in our schools. Tom, I've never understood it. Black people and white people have the most in common in this country. Yet when other races have come here, they always end up somewhere between blacks and whites. Blacks have always remained on the bottom."

Mr. Bailey then shared with me that he had grown up in Texas. As a young man, he had witnessed two white men harassing a black man. They'd had guns and fired their weapons near his feet, forcing him to dance under threat of being shot. They'd laughed and laughed. But when they noticed Jim Bailey, the mood shifted.

"Why aren't you laughing, boy?" one of them said.

"I don't see anything funny," Mr. Bailey replied.

There must have been too many witnesses, because nothing else happened right then. But when Jim returned home that day and told his mother what had occurred, she broke down and said, "You have to leave, son. Those men will kill you. You must leave now."

Jim Bailey left Texas that night. He moved to Portland, Oregon, where he worked for the railroad for a time. Eventually he moved to Los Angeles, and then to Pomona, where he would live the rest of his life.

In early July 1852, Frederick Douglass spoke at an event commemorating the signing of the Declaration of Independence. He told those in attendance, "This Fourth of July is yours, not mine. You may rejoice, I must mourn.

"Your high independence only reveals the immeasurable distance between us," he said. "The blessings in which you, this day, rejoice, are not enjoyed in common."[1]

The immeasurable distance between us. This is what I felt when listening to Mr. Bailey share his story about having to leave his home and family out of fear that two white men might kill him because his skin was dark. I felt it, too, during our family journey to make *Traces of the Trade*. And I felt it when I thought about the two men who'd left the plane before our flight from Oregon. All these men had experienced life in ways I never had. And this immeasurable distance between us had been created due simply to the color of our skin.

The question I asked myself most often after returning from filming *Traces of the Trade* was "Now what?" Now that I know this history, now that I understand more about how our nation was founded on slavery and terror and genocide, and now that I comprehend how the impact of our history continues to resonate so strongly today, what now? What can we do about it? What can I do?

One significant answer for me came when I was invited to participate in a weekend retreat in January 2006. There, some two dozen people gathered on the campus of Eastern Mennonite University in the Shenandoah Valley of Virginia, and Coming to the Table was born.

Black and white descendants of both enslavers and the enslaved had a vision of embracing Rev. Martin Luther King, Jr.'s dream that "the sons of former slaves and the sons of former slave owners will be able to sit down together at the table of brotherhood." Coming to the Table brings together people who are committed to hearing each other's stories; to acknowledging, understanding, and healing the persistent, traumatic wounds of slavery and the racism that remain with us today.

What began with a group of less than thirty of us in 2006 is now a movement of thousands, including dozens of local Coming to the Table affiliate groups around the United States; people with a shared vision of a just and truthful society that acknowledges and seeks to heal from the racial wounds of the past—from slavery and from the many forms of racism it spawned.

"Why do you do it?" I asked Mr. Bailey that Sunday morning. "Why do you stay at this church with all these white people? I don't get it." He shared that he had been raised in a church of the same denomination in Texas, so it was natural that he would seek out a like-minded church in his new community. But still.

"It was easier when you kids were here," he said. "There was a spirit then; a more liberal, welcoming feeling. Now, it's harder. But I need to be here because if it's ever going to change, it must begin in God's house. Where better?" He paused for a moment and then looked deep into my eyes. "You need to tell people, Tom. Once you know the truth, you become responsible for it."

"I know." We held each other's hands.

"That's right, son. You are responsible. You need to tell the truth. I remember when you were going to be a minister. I know your mother was disappointed when you didn't." Then he smiled. "I guess God works in mysterious ways. You will minister to people with this truth after all."

We embraced. I held him tight and felt the warm comfort of his arms wrapped securely around me, here in God's house. Many people stood around us, enjoying cake and punch, but it seemed I was alone with Mr. Bailey. I felt his cheek on mine. I saw the tears in his eyes and felt my own begin to rise as we said farewell. I stood silently as Mr. Bailey smiled, tapped my cheek with his hand, and then turned and walked out through the door of the church.

I love my family and friends, but I have always lived in a world with some degree of boundaries; of separation. I watched a dear man walk away, a man I'd known most of my life and yet had never once shared a meal with; we had never stepped foot in each other's homes. But we had never had a conversation like this before.

As Mr. Bailey disappeared from my view that day, it felt like we had chipped away at that immeasurable distance just a little.

In the years since, Mr. Bailey and I finally shared a meal together at a restaurant in Pomona. We spent time together in his home. And in February 2014, I visited him in the nursing home across the street from the church, not long before he passed away at the age of ninety-one. Walking back to my car that day, I paused and looked up at the church I'd grown up in, remembering the words I wrote in the acknowledgments of *Inheriting the Trade*: "Thanks to Jim Bailey for reminding me of the true meaning of ministry."

NOTE

1. Fredrick Douglass, "What to the Slave Is the Fourth of July?" TeachingAmerican History.org, http://teachingamericanhistory.org/library/document/what-to-the-slave-is-the-fourth-of-july/.

11 ⇥ MAKING CONNECTIONS

KAREN BRANAN

IN 1993, I set out on a journey to find out what happened in the Georgia county of my slave-holding ancestors, the place where I was raised.

Over many agonizing years of trekking to and from Harris County and beyond, I discovered a trail of blood and tears, which included the 1912 lynching of a woman and three men; more than a dozen white-on-white murders among mob members that included cousins on both sides of my family; and what seemed to be a decades-long curse on my male family members who were in the mob, marked by unnatural deaths, freak accidents, drug addiction, alcoholism, and suicides in numbers that were immensely out of proportion to the norm.

Early in my investigation, I met an African American couple who shared my maiden name Williams. The woman also shared my mother's name: Betty Williams. They lived in Harris County and were almost certainly descended from people enslaved by my ancestors.

When the woman asked where my mother lived, I became nervous. *Would she*—the still-cowed child in me wondered—*go to my mother's house to make her acquaintance?* I feared if she did, the meeting would not go well.

My mind flashed to a moment years before, when my mother accused me of being partly responsible for the rape-stranglings of seven white women in her town. The crime had been allegedly done by a black man. She "reasoned" that because I had, while in college, invited a black civil rights organizer into our house and shown sympathy for his cause, I was partially to blame. Such insane twists of logic as this were what I'd grown up with, and they were what had led me back in time to rip the covers off my family's violent, racist past.

But, as my nervous reaction to this woman's question showed me, I was not yet ready to face my history in the flesh. I now know it was because I had not developed the strength of character, the distance from my upbringing, and the insight into my own racism that I needed in order to do so. The old racist warnings and accusations still sat in my cells, dictating too many of my decisions. Deepening that shame was the fact that I still hid from all my Georgia relatives except for my sister and her family, and my mother, that I had a racially mixed granddaughter.

Luckily, my reservations did not stop my research, and I went on to uncover countless African American ancestors in my family tree. Johnie Moore, one of the four people lynched by my white relatives in 1912, was actually a member of a large racially-mixed family spawned by my maternal third great-uncle and a woman he enslaved. Anna Julia Cooper, America's first black feminist and a nationally heralded educator and writer, was the offspring of a distant cousin and his enslaved cook. Alex Manley, the editor of the first African American daily in the country whose presses were smashed, forcing him to leave town during the Wilmington riot of 1898, was a distant cousin as well; and the riot, it turned out, was not so much a riot as it was a coup, which was fomented and funded by members of my extended white family in order to stifle growing black political power in North Carolina.

But the worst of what I discovered was the event that occurred on January 22, 1912, beside the outdoor baptismal font of the black Baptist church in Hamilton. Three men and a woman were lynched by members of my family. One was a preacher. One was the sheriff's cousin. All four were innocent of the crime they were accused of—the murder of a nephew of my great-grandfather, the sheriff.

I yearned to meet at least one of their descendants, and while doing my research—whether at the Georgia Archives, Tuskegee University, the Auburn Avenue Research Library, or the Library of Congress—I found myself glancing across the tables at African Americans, wondering if perhaps they were looking for information on this lynching too, scouring books and articles for the names of the victims: Loduska ("Dusky") Crutchfield, Eugene Harrington, Johnie Moore, and Burrell Hardaway. I also posted queries on genealogy websites to no avail. Once, I came close, but we could not find a fit.

A decade of facing raw truth finally prepared me to meet living relatives of the people my ancestors enslaved; and, on a whim, I posted a query on rootsweb.com: Caucasian Seeking African Americans Descended from Williamses in Harris County.

Within days, I received an email from Deborah Dawkins with an invitation to a family reunion. Filled with both joy and terror, I wondered if there might be a support group for people like myself. I googled variations of "descendants of slave owners seeking descendants of slaves." Up came the website for Coming to the Table. I read through CTTT's four approaches, and I knew immediately that I had found a home.

I'd already embarked upon the first approach—"Uncovering History: researching, acknowledging, and sharing personal, family, and community histories of race with openness and honesty"—but I still struggled with "acknowledging," even to myself, much of the brutality that my law-enforcement family had initiated. I needed the company of other white people undergoing similar excavations. And though I did not fully recognize it then, I needed more connections to African Americans who wanted and needed to hear white people acknowledging these stories. I had begun to find such people among the dozens of elderly black men and women I'd interviewed in Harris County, and I would continue to find them over the years as I became friends and even family with my "linked descendants" (as we in CTTT call those who are connected through slavery).

I began to discover the miraculous ways these relationships pried open my heart and mind as they stiffened my spine, which is probably why the second CTTT approach is "Making Connections."

One of CTTT's founders is Will Hairston, whose large slave-holding family found fascinating ways to stay connected through the decades. I read their story in *The Hairstons: An American Family in Black and White,* by Henry Wiencek, and was further inspired to take steps in that same direction:

making connections and forging bonds that would bring reconciliation and healing.

It wasn't long before I had taken the first of those steps. Within two weeks after Deborah's email had arrived, I was sitting at the reunion, in a black Baptist church less than a mile from my childhood home in Columbus, Georgia. I was surrounded by men, women, and children whose ancestors had been "owned" by mine. It was surreal. Here they were—teachers, nurses, ministers, business people, students, artists, even an accomplished scientist—happy, healthy, and successful. Deborah was handing out her family history books, to which she'd already added photos and genealogy of my white family. Some were singing a family song, a tradition tracing back to the forties. They introduced themselves as "the great-granddaughter of Georgia Ann." Or "the great-great-grandson of Isaac." Many knew their genealogy by heart.

As I looked around, I tried to imagine their great-grandparents toiling for long hours in blazing cotton fields and over wood stoves, baling cotton and clearing forests, fearing the lash and, fearing separation from family if they crossed the "massuh" and got "shipped downriver." I imagined them relegated to the balcony at First Baptist and barred from the church's baptismal pool, sent instead to the muddy Chattahoochee for their own segregated coming-to-Jesus.

I could not help but contemplate the vast difference between these people and my own white family. (Although genetically, these people were possibly also my own family—after all, it was clear from photos of Isaac and Georgia Ann that they bore kinship to Caucasians—this had not yet been established.) Unlike my white Williams family, these Williamses had stayed together in large numbers and, despite far-flung migrations, had gathered and shared their history regularly for seven decades. They'd provided scholarships for their children; wept and prayed together at death and disease; laughed and cheered at graduations, weddings, and anniversaries; and promoted one another's businesses.

Deborah had made it easy for me to be there. "Don't come making apologies," she'd said. "We don't apologize for bad things people in our family do, and neither should you." She added, "We are a rainbow family, so don't worry about being the only white person there." Indeed, there was much admixture of this crazy thing we've been taught to call race, and several women mistook me for a cousin they'd not seen in several years. When one of Deborah's aunts and I discovered we both had O-positive blood, I said, "We might be kin," and she replied, "I was thinking the same thing."

The hard part of that reunion came when I read to them my Uncle Brit Williams's estate listing. There, among the ploughs, the pigs, the peanuts, and the complete works of Shakespeare, were their ancestors. *Isaac. Mike. Mariah.* Dozens upon dozens of human beings. Men, women, children.

I didn't have much information to give for each person, but what I did have—first name, sex, age, and price—was hard to deliver. I did okay until I got to the price, and then my voice began to shake. They sat silently. Mostly just staring into space, thinking thoughts I cannot know. Later Deborah told me some of the elders had said, "We were not slaves." She had thought they meant they were house servants, not field hands. But maybe they meant something even more true: they were much more than slaves. They were men, women, and children with good minds, long memories, strong loves, valuable talents, rich imaginations, powerful dreams, delicious recipes, wise words. Here, a half mile from the house I grew up in, I was learning about a world I had grown up next to and never known.

As it turned out, Deborah had just started Kindergarten when I was about to graduate from high school. She'd grown up in a black, middle-class neighborhood no more than two miles from where I lived, but we might as well have lived in different countries. All of her schools were segregated, as were mine. The only places I'd have ever encountered her would have been a grocery store, a dime store, or perhaps Kirven's department store. At Kirvin's, though, she wouldn't have been allowed to try on clothes before she bought them, as I was able to do. If she'd been one of my father's patients, she'd have had to enter his office through the back door, even though her mother was a registered nurse employed in the "black section" of the city hospital. She could not have even played in the park where I played. We both used to visit our grandparents in Hamilton, but she couldn't visit the splendid Callaway Gardens to swim or water-ski in Robin Lake. She had to go to the more basic Mack Miller Park. Her mother had never even told her about Callaway Gardens.

Growing up, she was protected from a lot of that harsh reality and was taught to respect all people regardless of their color. I, on the other hand, was not taught to respect black people. In "The Case for Reparations," an article in *The Atlantic*, Ta-Nehisi Coates wrote, "The essence of American racism is disrespect."

It has now been ten years since I met Deborah and her family. So far, Deborah's and my DNA have failed to match, but I'm not sure I've put them together in the right place and will keep trying. It doesn't really matter though; we feel like sisters. We are what family therapists call "emotional family." I have had her and her granddaughter Jasmine, a promising young artist, over for visits at my home in DC, and I have enjoyed picnics and horseback-riding with her family at my sister's place outside Atlanta. She paid respects to my late brother-in-law at his memorial service. And we traveled together to Montgomery for the opening day of the new Peace and Justice Memorial, where I tried to explain lynching to her grandson Christopher. I can't recall a time that she didn't show up to watch me speak in Georgia, with her wonderful smile, her ever-present camera, and her kind words of advice on how to improve my presentation.

One night in DC, several years ago, Deborah's cousin Tommy dropped by on his motorcycle to take me to dinner. A vibrant young man in his early forties, he had come all the way from Georgia. Over burritos, Tommy and I talked into the night about our kids, our significant others, our mothers, our values, our childhoods, and racism in Columbus, where we both grew up. Six months later, I learned that this had been his last road trip. Tommy had died of cancer and I was on the phone grieving with his mother Betty. The same woman whose question ten years before, about where my mother lived, had aroused fear in me. Now, remembering that reaction, I could only feel shame, but it came alongside the joyful recognition that I had become increasingly conscientious of the racism I had so long denied.

This journey had brought me new white cousins as well. At a CTTT regional gathering, I met Susan, a distant cousin researching our Magruder-Beall family line. She has since published a magnificent and breathtaking book of epic poetry called *Trafficke*.

Overall, I would spend twenty-five years researching my history and writing my book *The Family Tree: A Lynching in Georgia, A Legacy of Secrets, and My Search for the Truth*. African American cousins have read it and have shown up at my readings. Or they have reached out through email or websites to further enrich our new shared history. It is an exciting time and a wonderful way to "cousin," which I have begun to think of as a verb.

Over time, the initial seeds I'd planted on websites like Afrigeneas, Our Black Ancestors, Rootsweb, Family Tree DNA, and Ancestry began to sprout, and cousins and linked descendants, both black and white, came forth. One linked descendant, another Deborah, told me, by phone, the tragic story of her grandmother who accidentally killed three of her small children by feeding them canned peaches that contained poison. She had lost her mind with grief and had to be put in the state mental asylum. It was my sheriff-grandfather's job, I told her, to drive people to that place, called Milledgeville. He'd have stopped to buy her a Coke. My cousin Buster told me once that our grandfather had always done that, even when taking hardened murderers to the state prison farm.

Another African American woman, out of an audience in my hometown of Columbus, Georgia, put a copy of my book in front of me and said, "Would you write, 'For your great-great-great-grandfather, Mike Williams?'" Chills covered my body as I realized this was Jenny, a woman who had emailed, like so many others, to tell me she was descended from one of my Uncle Britt's enslaved people. Many others like these women brought stories, both tragic and tender. I could help them connect a few dots, send them the slave listings and other documents, and take some pleasure in the fact that we could talk, share stories, and get to know one another a bit.

Another connection was made when a woman who works at the U.S. Holocaust Museum came to one of my book-readings. I talked about getting to know my linked descendants and mentioned that many CTTT members were doing the same thing. The woman said, "I find this so inspiring, so hopeful. It seems that it could make such a difference toward healing the damage done by slavery and racism in this country." I told her that I agreed but that I also knew there was far more to be done to dismantle the systemic racism that continues to stunt our democracy and cripple the lives of millions of African Americans.

The change that has come into my life and heart in the years I have come to know these many descendants of men, women, and children who built my paternal family's wealth and well-being is indescribable. I know for certain that I will never again have the reaction I had that day to Betty's question. She and her family have taught me that we are all one, that we have more in common than we can imagine. Many of us grew up in the same city, at the same time, and we lived in parallel, though unequal, universes. How sad and bizarre that seems to me today, and yet many white friends who still live in my hometown continue to live that segregated life, denying themselves the rich wholeness I have found by desegregating my own.

POSTSCRIPT

For two decades I searched in vain for descendants of the four people lynched by my relatives on Jan. 22, 1912. Somehow, I knew that once my book was out, someone would come forward. Someone has.

On January 22, 2016, two weeks after my book came out, I and members of my family, both black and white, held a memorial service at the library in Hamilton, Georgia, for the four 1912 victims. The room was filled to overflowing with a racially mixed crowd eager to talk about the difficult issues addressed in my book.

"This has never happened in Hamilton," several old-timers told me. I had hoped perhaps to meet a descendant of one of the victims, but none appeared. Four months later, however, descendants of Hamilton's last lynching victim came to hear me speak at the Lagrange library, twenty miles from Hamilton.

Henry "Peg" Gilbert's murder by the town's police chief was not officially labeled as lynching, but that it surely was. My grandfather was sheriff on that day in May 1947, and it was his official duty to protect prisoners in the jail. He failed in that, and an entirely innocent man, a well-known and successful farmer, church deacon, Mason, and father, was savagely beaten by officers and shot dead by the police chief. In Lagrange, where he had lived and was illegally taken to be questioned on suspicion of harboring a felon, I told his story. As I spoke, a small group in the audience exchanged glances and leaned forward in their chairs. Realizing what was going on, I stopped and asked, "Are you Mr. Gilbert's family?" Six African American men and women nodded. I had finally met victims of a lynching that my family bore some responsibility for and was able to express my inexpressible regret. I later learned that a great-uncle on my father's side was a police officer with some involvement in that tragic affair. I have since met more members of this amazing family and am working with them and others in Lagrange to very belatedly memorialize Henry "Peg" Gilbert.

In addition, more recently, Dr. Jackie Jordan Irvine emailed me to say she is related to Johnie Moore, the youngest man lynched that gruesome night, a man I reveal in my book to be my cousin. Her second great-grandfather, Milford Moore, the enslaved son of my third great-uncle James B. Moore, had been wrongfully imprisoned for twenty years. Jackie, who grew up across the Chattahoochee River from me in roughly the same time period (the forties and fifties) was one of the first African American professors hired to teach at

Emory University. In all my time interviewing Emory University history professors and perusing the university's archives for my book research, I had
been totally unaware of this wonderful woman at work just a short distance
away. In our first get-together, we discovered we share much in common. Like
me, Jackie was never told about the 1912 lynching. Together, we are continuing the exploration of some questions left unanswered.

12 ❧ A MILLENNIAL FACING THE LEGACIES OF SLAVERY

FABRICE GUERRIER

M‌Y JOURNEY TO Coming to the Table (CTTT) began at a time when I desperately needed it. Burned out, depressed, angry, famished of hope, lacking any moral imagination. I had accepted with full certainty that no substantial transformation around matters of race could ever happen in the United States.

The murders and killings of people who looked just like me brought whirlwinds of fear that evoked waves of "black nihilism"[1] a term that Cornel West coined to frame the internalized sense of worthlessness and inferiority that exists so deeply in the black community. These murders unearthed thoughts and emotions I had not felt in a very long time. I time-traveled to memories of my fourteen-year-old self, who had just moved with my parents and brothers to the United States from Port-au-Prince, Haiti.

Just like back then, I questioned my self-worth and my intelligence. I questioned a world that inhibited me from dancing and singing to the natural rhythm of my own beat. My black skin seemed to weigh more than the heavy weights I lifted at the school gym.

"What a monstrous world we live in," I proclaimed from the couch in my dorm when I watched Tamir Rice, a twelve-year-old African American boy with a plastic toy pistol, gunned down by the police in a park in Cleveland, Ohio.[2]

In the years from 2012 to 2015, as I walked the campus as an undergraduate at Florida State University, a rigid form of emptiness became my constant companion. I seldom shared what felt like a heavy anchor tied to an endless rope of hopelessness. I kept it hidden behind smiles at passing professors and laughter with friends. The anchor got heavier with the senseless deaths and murders of Michael Brown, Jr., Eric Garner, Akai Gurley, Laquan McDonald, Freddie Gray, Trayvon Martin, and Walter Scott.[3] The brutal images played over and over on my Facebook feed, shared by my passionate millennial friends and activists. I died hundreds of times watching these short clips, spiraling into what seemed a hellish oblivion.

I often entered the fiery realms of anger, clouded by righteousness. I was angry at people I didn't know, angry at the "system," angry at white America for its apathy and ignorance. "More can be done," I would say one day as I awoke. "Nothing can be accomplished," I would say the next. All this bloodshed and the anger that followed drained me. The bitterness was a cancer eating away my American Dream. Just the sight of a police car made my heart race uncontrollably. All I could do was make sure that I didn't do anything wrong. I always felt like I was guilty of something, but I held it all in. I did not know what to say or do. I didn't know how to show my well-meaning white and black friends that these murders threaten who I am and the very soul of this country.

The Haitian struggle for independence was complex, and Haiti was defined by its becoming the first independent black nation in the world. I learned very early on about slavery. I would sit in a small classroom at a private Catholic school in Port-au-Prince, where the warm Caribbean wind flowed through our classroom's open cement windows. As a young boy, I read about Christopher Columbus's "discovery" of this New World in 1492. He'd thought he had arrived in India and deemed the Caribbean the "West Indies." Our popular western history fails to show that he desperately searched for gold. The

Taino and Arawak native people who lived on the island of Hispaniola were enslaved and murdered in his quest. With the natives' complete obliteration, he commissioned the trade of Africans, who were either bought or sold into slavery on the island of Saint Domingue, now home to Haiti and the Dominican Republic.

This is my history. This is how it all began for my ancestors and me. This is where I was born. But it wasn't until I moved to the United States that I realized what it meant to be black. White Americans judged me based on what was taught to them: that blacks weren't as smart, as capable, or as creative as their fellow Americans. And Haitians had to be poor. The victors got to define the narrative, and the result was a slow erasure of my humanity that began the moment I was born.

This narrative was in the movies I saw—*Harry Potter, Spiderman, Superman, Toy Story, Jurassic Park*. It was in the cartoons I loved desperately—*Pokemon, Yu-gi-oh, Dragonball Z, Dexter's Laboratory, The Simpsons*. All of them were dominated by white faces and white bodies, not characters who looked like me. This was the double consciousness that WEB Dubois spoke so much about and that defined me—confused, scared, and full of self-loathing. I lived in two worlds, and neither was mine. One was the world of the past, my Haitian-ness fading away within the oceans of a new culture, my social structure, my friends, and my country left behind.

The other side, my American-ness not fully developed, was entirely defined for me. I was told how I was supposed to behave, what I was supposed to learn, and how I needed to follow certain laws and rules. If I did, I would be okay. I saw the entire world through the lens of this white world and never truly saw myself. I never heard myself either, because my voice was lost in the large, racialized world that consumed every bit of me. It was a balancing act—a very painful one—and it rendered me susceptible to inaction and stagnation. WEB Dubois taught me that one has the power within to emancipate oneself from the daily baggage of life through education and raising conscientiousness. This was an act of revolution, an act that could help me reach new heights.

Yet I faced history every day, right before my eyes. I saw it. All through high school, everyone sat together in the cafeteria in groups that looked like social and racial enclaves, territories that had already been defined. The white kids sat together, the black kids sat together, the Hispanics sat together. Some groups mixed; but as a French-speaking black person from the Caribbean, not from Africa, and not Hispanic, I had no place. I was a floater. I floated to different groups. The world I saw was but a continuation of the legacy of the past. I faced history, and I was living it. I needed a way out, a way to reclaim my sense of self.

Phoebe Kilby was a guest speaker in one of my graduate school Restorative Justice courses at Eastern Mennonite University (EMU). Phoebe is a white woman from North Carolina who worked at EMU and was the president of the board of Coming to the Table at the time. Her blue jacket and blue jeans mixed with the spring blues all around on that sunny day in Harrisonburg, Virginia. She had white-gray hair and spoke with an excited, enthusiastic attitude. It turned out that she was a Zumba instructor.

I was skeptical of this white woman. Why should I listen to her? My entire life, I had listened to a world of whiteness; what more was there for me to hear? What more could I feel than the self-depreciation I had gained and held deep within me after navigating the dominant white spaces in school? The tables were placed together in a large hexagon. Students from America, the Middle East, Africa, Asia, and Latin America all sat together in this panorama of what America could and should look like. It was truly an international classroom, filled with different cultures and backgrounds. We all attentively listened to this white woman, who began sharing her story with great enthusiasm. This was heavy stuff for me. I felt knots in my stomach, old wounds ripping open wide.

This class usually took an international perspective on conflict, but this time, the U.S. was front and center in Phoebe's analysis of the story of slavery. After researching her past through genealogical work, tracing documents and things that her slave-owning ancestors had left, and analyzing details in tax forms and census data, she was able to find Betty Kilby. This African American family's ancestors were buried in the same county as Phoebe's family's old slave plantation. Phoebe connected with Betty Baldwin Kilby through a cold call to see if they could meet. This took guts. Fortunately, Betty was receptive to the notion of their meeting as descendants connected through slavery.

What happened next is a story of magic and healing. Betty and Phoebe cried together, were angry together, laughed together and called each other "cousin." At this point in the story, I was in disbelief. I hadn't really seen or heard of anything that could substantially change America at its core. There was no evidence in practice that America could be transformed by addressing these deep-rooted legacies that no one talked about, these legacies that held the U.S. down. Through Phoebe and her story, I saw a dark corner of racism that I had felt daily in the inner reaches of my body, both during my undergraduate years and when I had first moved to the U.S. Through Phoebe's story, I saw America in her infancy—buck naked and stripped of her attire. All her wounds were tied to slavery and connected directly to what I had felt the moment I moved to this country—a vacuum, a void, an immaturity in dealing head-on with this topic. Through Phoebe's stories, I experienced something I had never felt before, something that I believed could substantially, fundamentally transform this culture. Slavery was this thing from so many years ago, so why did I feel this way?

In our class, we talked about the transmission of intergenerational trauma and how that affected systems, people, culture, and our ability to move forward beyond the cycles of violence that I had seen. For my millennial friends and activists, this transmission was the missing link—the missing piece to all our problems and online debates. But I was still unsure as to how this would look in the practical processes of society.

I had to join Coming to the Table, this organization that had brought Phoebe and Betty together. I had to take part in this movement that was slowly growing. This organization, for me, was the golden thread that tied so much together. It weaved in a new language that gave voice to the pain and isolation pent up inside of me.

Coming to the Table gave me the ability to place my entire life within a context and the legacies of U.S slavery on a continuum. It was fertile ground to build upon. It lifted me out of the depths I was in. It explained why I felt the way that I did; there were finally answers, along with many more questions. Coming to the Table gave me the power to take control of my life. I attended the national gathering of Coming to the Table held on the campus of EMU the following summer, in 2014. It was an eclectic space of people from all walks of life. Artists, mothers, daughters, scientists, blacks, whites, Hispanics, doctors, lawyers, writers, filmmakers, teachers, academics, activists, and genealogists all gathered with a genuine need to speak about race. The conversations I had were not all easy. I was uncomfortable. I had never learned how to have these kinds of conversations. It was new territory for everyone. I didn't know what to expect, but I knew one thing: I was hungry for stories. I was hungry for more of the possibilities I had locked away inside myself.

The conference began in the large EMU chapel, a nondenominational space with double doors that smelled of fresh wood. People welcomed me with the kind of bright smiles that I was not used to; I almost felt they were fake, that they were trying too hard to please me, trying to make sure that, as a black person, I wouldn't remind them how privileged they were. Then what caught my eye was the chance for a session with a genealogist to research my ancestry in Haiti, which I knew nothing about. This session provided me with a refreshing narrative that allowed me to understand how connected we all were; it humanized the bright smiles all around. Later, we all sat in a large circle for the plenary session. A microphone was passed around, and people shared why they had come to the table. We then broke up into groups, during which time I met a descendant of the largest slaveholding and slave-trading family in the United States, which had traded slaves out of the port of Rhode Island. I also met people who told me about their grandmothers' firsthand stories of family members who were born into slavery, bought and sold like products and treated as nothing.

There was a strong level of emotional maturity, for we had acknowledged the traumatic wounds of slavery for what they were. Our approach was not something of myth; it was not something to be studied in a classroom. Neither was this a wishful dream; these were real reparations that were healing the deep, dense energy that had been trapped in America's soul. It was an active and practical process that every attendee had chosen to engage in for America.

I was able to feed deeply on this healing process. For most of my life, when I had brought up the notion of slavery, it had been quickly discarded. Here, it was no laughing matter. Here, everyone could discern that the realities we saw today in the U.S were very much part of the legacies of slavery, and this notion was not up for debate. It was something very real and it was cancerous to thousands of communities across the United States.

I was enthralled by peoples' stories, their family histories, their hopes and their dreams for America, and their personal work to make their communities better across the United States. They left me in awe. I barely noticed that I was the only one at the national gathering who was under the age of twenty-three. In fact, almost everyone there was over the age of forty. I was shocked because I kept thinking how many individuals my age could benefit from the experience. Where was my generation? Why weren't they here? I began to see how important intergenerational spaces would be in creating change for this country and how the lack of such spaces could doom my millennial friends and activists to repeat the mistakes of the past.

Leaving the gathering, I felt that I carried great responsibility, not to be a spokesperson for my generation but to honor the stories I'd heard and the connections I had made. Those sacred stories are deeply imbued in me to this day. They have created in me a new type of consciousness—a realization that I didn't have to cower deep within myself, I wasn't the only one, and I didn't have to face this struggle alone. Because of these stories, I was able to see a different America than the one that had previously left me very numb. And as a result, a greater purpose was born.

I had read in books about the U.S civil rights movement and the U.S anti-abolitionist movement, and now I was at the center of a U.S. reparations movement—a form of reparations that was not necessarily held up by financial promises, but rather one that engaged a national conversation about the legacies of slavery in the United States. Coming to the Table set out to organically push a national conversation that is rooted in people and communities across the U.S., but my role in that conversation began with me—the risks that I took and the choice that I made to be vulnerable and to hear others out.

Now I am part of the dream of the founders, of the black and white descendants of the enslaved and enslavers who want to transform the legacy of slavery in America. And my journey has just begun, as I am set to start a local group in Harrisonburg, Virginia, and later assume the mantle as the president of Coming to the Table.

In the meantime, CTTT remains at the center of a country that has lost its ability to engage in sound discourse. The recent alt-right rallies and the violent events in Charlottesville, Virginia, bring an urgency to the need for meaningful conversations around race. Now, more than ever, what CTTT has to offer is critical, as the U.S. continues to reckon with both its past and its future.

NOTES

1. Cornel West, Race Matters (Boston: Beacon Press, 1993).

2. Shaila Dewan and Richard A. Oppel, Jr., "In Tamir Rice Case, Many Errors by Cleveland Police, Then a Fatal One," New York Times, January 22, 2015, https://www.nytimes.com/2015/01/23/us/in-tamir-rice-shooting-in-cleveland-many-errors-by-police-then-a-fatal-one.html?_r=0.

3. Daniel Funke and Tina Susman, "From Ferguson to Baton Rouge: Deaths of Black Men and Women at the Hands of Police," LA Times, July 12, 2016, http://www.latimes.com/nation/la-na-police-deaths-20160707-snap-htmlstory.html#2014.

PART III WORKING TOWARD HEALING

13 ⇗ STANDING ON THE SHOULDERS OF MY ANCESTORS

TAMMARRAH LEE

I CAME ACROSS the *Ex Slave Narrative of William P. Hogue* (1861–1943) on Juneteenth weekend 2013. Recorded by the Work Progress Administration on January 15, 1941, in Ohio, the narrative was a key to unlocking the hidden history of my enslaved Hogue ancestors.

"I was bawned a slave in Halifax County, Virginia, April 27, 1861," the interview began. "We wuz owned by Dr. P. Hogue. He had two plantations an' a lot of slaves. He had a big fine house settin' in about 14 acres called de home farm. Dey raised a lots of cawn, terbeccer, an wheat, an regular garden stuff an' cattle. . . . Doctor had two sons in de rebel army, an he used to press his slaves to do de hard wuk, an be pu'snal slaves for his boys. Father was pressed in de rebel army, an he died 'fore he came back" (sic).[1]

William P. was not my relative, but he would lead me to the William Hogue who was.

About six years before this discovery, I went searching for my great-grandfather's grave at the Oak Grove Cemetery in Springfield, Massachusetts. At the cemetery office, a staff member recorded the locations of my Hogue ancestors' gravesites on a complimentary map. Still, searching for my great-grandfather's grave was next to impossible because there were no visible markers. A groundskeeper came to my rescue. After a few attempts striking the earth with a shovel, he finally located marker number 1440. I am eternally grateful to the groundskeeper. He had found my ancestor.

To stand on the sacred soil of my great-grandfather's grave at the Oak Grove Cemetery was soul-stirring and left me longing to know more about him. Born around 1858 as Matthew T. Hogue, he was enslaved in Halifax County, Virginia. Shortly before migrating to Massachusetts in the early 1900s, Matthew changed his first name to William. His youngest daughter Alice was my maternal grandmother; in her honor, my mother gave me the middle name Alicia.

As a little girl, I would sit and daydream while looking at Grandma Alice's picture, imagining myself as her. I didn't know much about my grandmother but was captivated by her appearance. She had a mocha-brown complexion and black wavy hair, and in the picture, she wore a long chain necklace with an old coin. People said I resembled her, and looking at her picture, I could see myself. She passed away when my mother was nine, but Mom still has memories of Grandma. Like the time my mother cut her leg on the fire escape, and Grandma Alice carried her from their home to a local hospital on foot. When Alice passed away, my mother recalled, the casket with her remains was placed in the living room of their family home.

Standing at the grave of Grandma Alice's dad, my great-grandfather, I was finally connecting with my Hogue family roots. Here I was, living less than two hours from Springfield, Massachusetts, and through my research I discovered long-lost relatives who still resided there. In the early 1900s, my great-grandparents had migrated to Springfield, Massachusetts with their three children for better opportunity. According to the 1900 U.S. Census, my great-grandfather worked first as a slater and then, in 1910, as a journeyman.

I recall traveling to Springfield with my mother, stepfather, and younger brother to meet some of Grandma Alice's siblings. Her older brother, William E. (known as Uncle Bill) walked with a crutch and gave us tomatoes from the vegetable garden in his backyard. He seemed laid back and easy-going. I remember him referring to his two surviving sisters as boll weevils; it seems they were unstable, likely because of poverty and alcoholism.

Uncle Guy, the youngest sibling, was a sanitation worker who had to get shots on a regular basis because of his job. It was a Sunday evening when we visited him, and his three children were preparing to go to bed. They peered at us from behind a curtain that separated the living room from where they slept.

Aunt Olivia lived in a dark and gloomy rooming house. Aside from appearing intoxicated, she had a beautiful brown complexion just like her younger sister, Grandma Alice, and dark, naturally curly hair.

We couldn't find Aunt Juanita and I'm not sure if Uncle Francis was alive back then. My mother was completely unaware of him until I found information about him through my research. It appears he was incarcerated for a period of time.

Based on newspaper accounts, Olivia and other family members also had run-ins with the law. That might be why my grandfather limited his children's contact with them after Grandma Alice passed. As a result, I had not spoken with the Hogue family in over forty years.

During that period, I was trying to find myself, trying to find my rightful place in society. I went to college, raised a family, and kept my eyes on the prize as a public-school teacher. Half way into thirty years of service, I voiced concerns about racially biased instructional materials and became the target of repeated workplace bullying for the rest of my career. During one of the most trying times of my professional career, I embarked on a mission to retrace my Hogue ancestral roots.

Genealogical research consoled me and helped divert my attention away from toxic work situations. It also provided me with a sense of accomplishment and bolstered my self-esteem. Each discovery about my ancestors inspired me to learn more about their lives and times. After locating my great-grandfather's resting place, the groundskeeper also helped find my great-grandmother's grave. I was able to find the burial sites for two of my great-uncles on my own. Other ancestral gravesites at the cemetery remain to be found.

With the *Ex Slave Narrative of William P. Hogue* as my guide, I searched the web and found the Pruett/Hoge family history blog[2] that corroborated information about my great-great-grandfather's enslaver. Dr. P. Hogue, as

William P. called him in the narrative, was actually Dr. Thomas P. Hoge. (During the Reconstruction, former members of Dr. Hoge's slave community began spelling their surname as Hogue, but the reason is unknown.) Further evidence confirmed my great-grandfather's birth name was Matthew T. Hogue. Why he later changed his name to William remains unknown. While searching online for additional information about Dr. Hoge, I located a marriage record for Matthew T. and Lula (White) Hogue that listed Dr. Thomas P. Hogue and Milly Hogue as the parents of the groom. I recognized the name of the bride. Lula was my great-grandmother. Milly, mother of the groom, was my great-great-grandmother. The 1860 Federal Census slave schedule lists my great-grandfather and two of his three siblings as mulattos. Does this mean that my great-grandfather's enslaver was also his father? It did not come as a surprise that I had a white ancestor. What was a shock was that my great-grandfather had named his former enslaver as his father on his marriage certificate.

Another valuable source of information about Dr. Hoge was discovered in an article featured in a Danville, Virginia, newspaper, the *Danville Bee*, on August 12, 1947. This is what caught my attention:

> Tomorrow Mercy Seat Presbyterian Church will celebrate its hundredth anniversary. . . . The organized communicants were five white and twenty-eight colored persons. The former were Henry Edmunds, Littleton Edmunds, Elizabeth Jennings, Eliza W. White, and Ana V. Wills whose members were increased to six the next day when Dr. Thomas P. Hoge, prominent physician of Halifax County and uncle of Rev. Moses D. Hoge, DD [were] admitted by the session into full membership. The slaves were recorded only by their given names.[3]

I was curious whether the Mercy Seat church records from this period would have more information about the twenty-eight "colored persons" named in the article, and later learned from the Halifax County, Virginia Historical Society that their names were listed in the one-hundred-year anniversary church booklet. I located a copy of the booklet and, amazingly, a young girl by the name of Milly (age seven) was listed as a negro communicant who had been admitted to the church in 1847.[4] I suspected this person was my great-great-grandmother, as it matched the name of my great-grandfather's mother as listed on his marriage and death certificates.

During this process, I found a published book by Dr. Thomas P. Hoge's great-great-grandson—*My Two My Only Sons*, by Edwin "Barney" Lawless.[5] Lawless and the white Hoges could retrace their ancestry back ten generations. In contrast, I have, even now, only partially documented four generations of my Hogue lineage, dating back to the early 1800s. Broken family ties, generational poverty, and other forms of racial oppression prevail within my branch of Hogues, challenging my ability to trace my lineage further.

Although the book is mainly about Dr. Hoge's sons, who died in battle during the Civil War, the author makes reference to his ancestors as well as to the plantation and slave community they were a part of: "Dr. Thomas P. Hoge lived on a small plantation named 'Oakley' in Halifax County with his wife Mary Whitlocke Hoge, a middle-aged couple of comfortable means. The home was shared with three of their six living children. . . . There were also thirty-six slaves on the plantation, and the primary occupation was to ensure the successful planting and harvesting of the crops."[6]

I would like to know more about those who lived in Danville, especially since my great-grandfather and his siblings were mulatto. Interestingly, Lawless also mentioned that most of his other Hoge ancestors were opposed to slavery, and some relocated to Ohio partly because of their views:

> Within the growing nation was the Hoge family, which had established itself in Virginia over the past two centuries. The family already split over the matter of slavery. The venerable patriarch of this branch, Moses Drury Hoge, had voiced his objections to slavery prior to 1800, and two of the clergy's sons relocated to Ohio partly in protest of the peculiar institution. The fourth son had established himself as a slaveholding planter in Halifax County, Virginia.[7]

Dr. Hoge's fourth son was the man who enslaved my great-grandfather and two of his three siblings, among others. I contacted Lawless, who said that his great-great-grandmother Mary had kept a detailed account of those enslaved at Oakley. He confirmed my hunch that it was my great-great-grandmother Milly listed as a "Negro Communicant" of Mercy Seat Presbyterian Church. He also provided me with the names of her mother and older brother, which were noted in his family's slave records: Hannah (circa 1817–1884) and Winston (1821–). Hannah is my oldest known ancestor enslaved on the plantation. Milly was probably born and raised there, since she started attending Mercy Seat Presbyterian at the age of seven.

He noted that at least ten of the adults and all thirteen children were born and raised there, that six weddings occurred in the slave community between 1832 and 1861, and that at least one child was a grandson of an older slave. In addition, he told me that Oakley had previously been owned by Lawless's third great-grandparents Achilles and Agnes Whitlock. Hannah may have been held in bondage by them as well.

While Lawless's help with verifying information and acquiring new knowledge about my enslaved ancestors was invaluable, I had concerns. I was astounded when the first sentence in his initial email referred to my great-great-grandmother as "belonging" to his great-great-grandfather. Then, in the second email, Lawless, using information in his ancestors' records, challenged the validity of information I had given him based on material cited in the *Ex Slave Narrative of William P. Hogue.*

I've noted other discrepancies in our information as well. For example, my great-grandfather and two of his siblings were the third and last generation of ancestors held in bondage at the Oakley Plantation. In his book, Lawless states, "[T]he slaves were generally well treated and cared for and respected. There seems to have been mutual sharing of the effort of daily living with a clear distinction of the difference between owner and slave. . . . [T]here also seems to have been a two-way loyalty between the slave families and Dr. Hoge's family."[8] Yet, in his narrative, William P. Hogue recalls that, while enslaved, he was once scolded for having a book in his possession; someone had told him not to let "them" catch you with a book. This recollection does not seem to exemplify "two-way loyalty."

The discrepancies are upsetting to me, but I hope to muster the courage and strength to reach out to him again in an effort to rectify these differences.

Additionally, two recent developments have emerged in my ongoing research. The first is a connection made with Chenoa Hogue, Uncle Guy's great-granddaughter. We shared our family trees, and she had information about Dr. Thomas P. Hoge's family. The second development is a DNA match for a man who descends from my ancestors' enslaver; it appears we are distant cousins.

These two connections are definitely worth investigating, not only for myself but also, and especially, in honor of William T. For it was William T. who originally passed down the information about all sides of his family, black and white, to his offspring. For me, this journey has given me a purpose and strength to move forward. But for him, it has added more meaning to his life than any unmarked grave could ever give.

NOTES

1. "William P. Hogue: Ex-Slave Narrative." Ohio Historical Center Archives Library, www.ohiohistory.com.

2. Danny Ricketts, "Confederate Soldiers of Halifax County, Va., Pruett/Hoge." History and genealogy blog. http//www.rdricketts.com.

3. https://www.newspapers.com/newspage/12606508/

4. Ruby W. Barnes. *History Mercy Seat Presbyterian Church 1847–1947* (South Boston: Sutherlin, VA, 1967), 28.

5. Larry Redd, Clay Kilby, and Edwin Lawless. *My Two My Only Sons: Two Halifax County Soldiers in Southwest Virginia* (Lynchburg: Warwick House Publishers, 2010).

6. Ibid., 7.

7. Ibid., 7.

8. Ibid., 7.

14 ⇥ SO CLOSE AND SO FAR AWAY

ELISA D. PEARMAIN

I HAD KNOWN Tillie my whole childhood, but it wasn't until I attended her funeral at age eighteen, that I learned her full name was O'Tillia Barnes.

Having grown up white in the late fifties and sixties in a suburban New England town, I learned about prejudice and the civil rights movement first-hand. I attended a Unitarian church, and our minister Rev. Styron was a gentle man with a warm smile, but when he was passionate, his voice would boom from the pulpit. And boom it did when it came to the subject of civil rights. In 1965, after Bloody Sunday, when so many marchers were clubbed to death, Rev. Styron took some of the men from our church down to Selma to march with Dr. King. The stories they told when they came back stunned and moved us. There arose a determination among some of our parishioners that said that if we wanted to respect ourselves, we had to get in there and work for it; we had to work for civil rights for all. But in truth, African Americans weren't in my life—not in school, not in my church or my town, not even among the friends my parents invited home. The only African American person I knew was Tillie—O'Tillia Barnes.

Tillie was the woman who came a few times a year to cook for my grandmother, whom we called Gama. Gama's great-great-grandfather had started a successful grocery business called S. S. Pierce, which prospered for many years in Boston. Her family had two homes, servants, and a driver. Then she married my grandfather, a man whose dream it was to be a farmer. S. S. Pierce was sold, and her wealthy lifestyle changed. The marriage ended when my dad was a teen, but Gama survived in her frugal Yankee fashion on family money. She didn't have servants anymore, but at Christmas and Thanksgiving, and during the summer when the extended family would converge on her home on the beach, she would hire Tillie to come and cook for us.

I didn't know Tillie very well. I only saw her a few days out of the year. I was lucky to get a glimpse of her at Christmas or Thanksgiving when the door between the dining room and kitchen would swing open, and she would come carefully out with a big platter of turkey or a flaming plum pudding. We kids weren't allowed to go near the kitchen when a big production was in session. But the little glimpses of Tillie were enough to make me wonder: Why wasn't she at home with her family for the holiday? Didn't Tillie have children or grandchildren? Don't they miss her? I asked my parents these questions, but the answers I got weren't very satisfying. There was a lot that I didn't know about Tillie.

One thing I did know was where she lived. I remember the first time we picked her up on our way to Gama's Cape Cod house one summer. As we left the highway and started along the city streets of Boston, I saw the faces change from white to brown.

"Roll up your windows and lock your doors, girls," my mother said anxiously from the front seat.

"Why? It's hot out," we argued.

"Just do it quickly!" She ordered.

Looking around, I didn't see anything dangerous. All I noticed was the changing color of people's skin. But my mother's voice told me there was something to be afraid of.

"Tillie lives here?" My younger sister queried as we pulled up in front of several three-story brick buildings, all separated by small areas of concrete. The buildings looked so bleak with their shutterless windows, each one the same. There were no trees, or plants, or lawns, or places to play. It was nothing like my home down the long driveway in the country, where we could make forts in the woods and climb trees. What was it like for her? I wondered. I couldn't imagine growing up there.

But there was Tillie, coming out of the building with my father who was carrying her suitcase. In her late sixties, Tillie was not frail like my grandmother. She was quite round, and her arms were strong. She wore a simple dress with a button-up sweater, even though it was a hot July day. She seemed to tip slightly from side to side as she walked, as if her ankles hurt in those sturdy black lace-up shoes.

When she reached the car, Tillie leaned in through the open front door and gave us a warm smile that seemed to twinkle. "Hello, Miss Puddy. Hello young'uns," she said. Her voice was warm, deeper than what I was used to hearing at home and had a hint of Southern in it. I knew I didn't have to be afraid of Tillie. She was really nice.

Once she had managed to settle herself into the front seat with her black handbag in her lap, my father started the car, and we were off.

"How have you been, Tillie?" asked my Dad.

"Oh, just fine, Mr. Bob."

"And your family, Tillie?" asked my Mom.

"Oh, everyone's just fine, Miss Puddy. It looks like you'll have some nice weather for your vacation."

It was hard to get a lot more conversation going, so things got quiet pretty quickly. Peering out the back-seat window at the bleak cityscape, I wondered what it was like for Tillie to leave her home and come to the Cape with us. Who else lived in her apartment? Would she be lonely at the Cape with us? I wondered if she didn't want to talk to us too much because we were white.

I also wondered why Tillie called my parents Mr. Bob and Miss Puddy. She called my grandmother Mrs. Pearmain. My dad had asked her to call them by their first names, but I guess that was as close as she thought she should get.

When we finally arrived at the Cape house, we went our separate ways. We kids hugged our grandmother and ran upstairs with our cousins to find out if we would be sleeping in the yellow, blue, or green room. It didn't really matter; each one had a view of the ocean. Tillie went to her room, out behind the kitchen.

We kids would mostly see Tillie when we'd parade into the kitchen, hoping for a lick of a bowl or a hint of what she was making for dinner. Tillie wore a pale lime-green dress uniform with a white apron, and her hair was held in place with a hair net. We would surround the white porcelain table in the center of the room, where Tillie's large brown hands might be rolling out dough for one of her famous blueberry pies. Tillie was a wonderful cook. The numbers on the gas oven had long since worn off, but everything she made came out perfectly.

"What's for dinner, Tillie?" We would inquire in our sweetest voices. "Can we lick the bowl? Do you have any children, Tillie? Are you divorced like Gama?" Tillie would gently shoo us out of the kitchen, saying, "Run along now, children. Tillie's got lots of work to do."

One time I came upon Tillie sitting on the side porch in the afternoon sun, with a bowl of peas in her lap. Her eyes were closed, and there was a half-smile on her lips. I wondered what she was thinking about: was she praying, dreaming back to her childhood, or just enjoying the feel of the sun on her skin? I wished that I knew more about her.

I believe that my parents, aunts, and uncles wanted to bridge the gap with Tillie too. My dad was passionate about civil rights. He told me later in his life that he was, "prejudiced in favor of black people." He worked on the housing commission in our town to make it easier for people of color to move in, and he had been blacklisted as a realtor for a time, after renting a house to an African American family.

One night, when Tillie brought a great Baked Alaska to the table for our dessert, my father said, "Tillie won't you sit and have some of this wonderful dessert with us?"

"Oh thank you, Mr. Bob, that's so kind," she said politely, "but I've still got work to be done." And she gave us that twinkling smile and retreated backward through the swinging door to the kitchen.

Later, when I was helping to clear the dishes, I saw Tillie just starting her dinner alone at the wooden table in the corner of the kitchen. I wondered what that was like for her.

Tillie didn't have to work all the time while she was on the Cape. But I noticed that she didn't do things that the other women in my family did on her days off. She didn't swim or sail or collect shells. She didn't lie on the beach to get a tan. Instead, she would go out fishing in the big blue wooden rowboat. She would sit for hours in the peaceful sun, anchor down, line drifting in the lazy water. Often, she would catch bass, which she would bake or fry for us. I wondered how Tillie had learned to fish while living in the city.

This was my experience with Tillie during my childhood: short glimpses and wonderings, but never feeling close or comfortable.

The years went by. JFK was assassinated in l963 and then Martin Luther King, Jr. in l968. Gama and Tillie grew older. Gama moved her bedroom downstairs when her feet had begun to hurt too much. Tillie now rocked side to side so much as she walked that I thought she'd tip over. But still she came to cook for us when she could.

Then, in the summer of l969, we heard that the Apollo 11 was going to land on the moon. I was fifteen. Gama and Tillie were in their mid-seventies. My parents had brought a portable TV to the Cape so that we could watch. We set up the TV in a small room next to the dining room, where the reception was best. We had pulled up the loveseat and arranged several chairs around the set. The *Eagle* had landed, and we were listening to the astronauts talk to NASA when Tillie poked her head in the door. "Mind if I join y'all?"

"We'd love to have you, Tillie," we chorused. A space was made for Tillie next to my grandmother on the loveseat. We sat together, wondering at the images of that far-off place that now looked so close. Then Neil Armstrong came out of the rocket and down the ladder until he was standing on the moon. He planted a flag and began to take those seemingly effortless leaps across the surface. We heard his words, "One small step for man. One giant leap for mankind."

Even to a sullen fifteen-year-old, this was amazing. But somewhere during those moments, I remember looking at our little group huddled around that TV. What was going on in the room was amazing too. The grownups were unusually emotive. My grandmother kept saying, "Isn't it amazing!" My father was clapping his hands together, saying, "Hallelujah" with tears in his eyes. And there was Tillie, sitting right among us. Her face was full of awe. "Oh, my Lord," she kept repeating, "Oh, my Lord, will you look at what they've done."

I distinctly remember being nearly as impressed that Tillie was just sitting there with us and that we were sharing in the experience together, as with the moon landing. It was a big step—for our family at least, if not for mankind. It took putting a man on the moon to bring us together as equals.

Gama died in 1971. She left some money in her will for Tillie's care. Tillie died in 1972. It was at her funeral, in a big brick church in Roxbury, Massachusetts, that I learned her full name. It is telling and sad that I didn't know or think to ask about her name before that. It was also in that overflowing church that I finally got to see just how many people loved her, and to learn about her childhood in the rural south (where she'd learned to fish) and her activeness in her church community.

Many years passed, and I found myself again living in my childhood town, but this time in a neighborhood rich with diversity, including Americans of African, Mexican, Irish, Haitian, Somali, and Asian descent. This was the place where my daughter met her two best friends, who are biracial.

While my daughter was in grade school, I worked on a committee in our church that started in the sixties to help children bussed from Boston in the METCO desegregation program to feel welcomed and to foster friendships between our two communities. Over time, I have developed a few dear friendships with and have become close to colleagues who are African Americans. I still feel amazement and joy when our closeness feels genuine and easy. But I also continue to feel deep sadness, awareness of the divide between us, and frustration at the prospect that ongoing racism and inequality in our country will keep our healing at bay. I still wonder if I am trusted; that is, if I'm as trustworthy as I want to be in this healing process.

Telling stories about and acknowledging my white privilege is a necessary step in closing the trust gap. Tracing the roots of my anxiety, shame, and feelings of disconnection when it comes to relating to African Americans is another step. I can see now that some of my parents' motivations in urging Tillie to join us in a way that she could not was to assuage their own guilt over the legacy of slavery and racism and the vast inequality of wealth between us. I see that I have been guilty of harboring those motivations too. Operating from guilt and shame will not help to build trust. But keeping my heart open to the pain of disconnection motivates me to enter into the deeper conversations and connections that I have so longed for since childhood. I am grateful for the opportunity to come to the table.

15 ⤳ BORN BOTH INNOCENT AND ACCOUNTABLE

A Moral Reckoning

DEBIAN MARTY

FIRST READ this transformative phrase—"I am born both innocent and accountable"—in 1984, as an undergraduate in women's studies at San Francisco State University. The phrase came from a required reading by the award-winning poet and essayist Adrienne Rich. In "Resisting Amnesia: History and Personal Life"[1] she confronts the impact of a whites-only history on her racial identity and race relations. Her conclusion—that she was born both innocent and accountable—resonated immediately with my own struggles to understand the moral contours of being white in a racist society.

This idea of being both innocent and accountable spoke to an internal paradox with which I was deeply concerned: How was I to lead a morally responsible life in a world confounded by immoral "–isms"? Racism, sexism, and classism were the big three discussed by feminists in the early 1980s. Although willing to challenge oppression, my whiteness created an overwhelming culpability that I did not know how to address.[2] Rich's recognition of innocence released me from the presumption of being born bad. It freed me to explore accountability.

In this context, accountability became a liberating invitation, as in the words of Toni Morrison, "the freedom of choosing your responsibility."[3] After dropping in and out of college, I finally chose to major in women's studies. I needed to understand the intersectionality of oppressions, how the "–isms" reinforced each other in everyday life. But even more, I yearned to figure out how to live within this maze, how to navigate the myriad differences of identities and ideas. How could I account for myself in relationships riven by history?

Twenty years after my first encounter with Rich's transformative phrase, I found an opportunity to address its apparent paradox. I had discovered an ancestor who, in his last will and testament, bequeathed enslaved human beings to his heirs. This is the story of the moral reckoning that followed, one both innocent and accountable.

The shock came late at night, during a pajama-clad genealogy session on the computer. I'd just discovered my sixth great-grandfather in colonial North Carolina. There, on the computer screen, was William Arnold's last will and testament, dated 1769. With a "sound mind" and in gratitude to God, he bestowed his "worldly estate" to his wife and nine children. After instructing his just debts to be paid, William Arnold granted to his "loving wife, Mary" permission to reside at their plantation home and "the use of my three Negroes Samson, Joan and Bess for her lifetime."

Moving from the realm of history books to that of my ancestors, slavery became personal.

In his largesse, William Arnold distributed to his children both the people he enslaved and his material goods. He gave his son Thomas, "one Negro boy named Toney and one Negro girl named Hagar" in the same sentence that he allocated to him "all my carpenter tools and two iron wedges." Similarly, the next son received his share of property, both human and mechanical. To Joseph went "my Negro man called Samson and my Negro boy called Sam and my other Cooper's tools."

The third son Asa was promised "my Negro woman called Bess and the next child she brings." Even the youngest, six-year old Rebekah, could anticipate the possession of a "Negro girl called Hannah." Finally, William Arnold stipulated that it was his desire "that if the said Negro woman Bess shall have any more children . . . my daughter Sarah Arnold and my daughter Mary Wood shall have each of them one."[4]

I was stunned. I just sat back and stared at the screen. William Arnold, my direct ancestor, had bequeathed human beings to his heirs. It was too late to wake up my partner to help process this terrible revelation. So, as the academic and lifelong reader that I am, I turned to my bookshelves. I picked up Edward Ball's *Slaves in the Family*, a white man's examination of his family's slave-owning history.

Edward Ball engaged his family's slave-owning legacy dispassionately, as a journalist would. "A person cannot be culpable for the acts of others, long dead, that he or she could not have influenced," Ball wrote. "Rather than responsible, I felt accountable for what had happened, called on to try and explain it."[5] This distinction between responsibility and accountability made sense to me. I particularly appreciated that Ball went beyond "it's not on me" to accept a moral obligation to explain his family's past. So how did I account for William Arnold's actions?

When Arnold wrote his will, eighteenth-century law permitted the enslavement of human beings. Therefore his actions were legal. His final wishes also reflected political norms. With the Revolutionary War still six years in the future, the colonial struggle for independence had not yet crystallized the irony between freedom for some and bondage for others.[6] As a colonist and Southern plantation owner, Arnold's legacy was pragmatic and politic. What then could be expected of William Arnold morally? Answering this question turned out to be more complicated than I initially anticipated.

The moral complexities began to emerge upon finding documentation for William and Mary Arnold's deaths. They died within two days of each other in February 1773, likely claimed by a shared illness. Their deaths were recorded by the Symons Creek Monthly Meeting,[7] of which they were members in good standing. This meant that the Arnold family belonged to the Religious Society of Friends—and that therefore William Arnold was a Quaker. And for over a century, Quakers had been grappling with the moral contradictions inherent in slavery.

When William Arnold's estate was inventoried, the appraisers made note that he owned a copy of George Fox's journal.[8] Fox was the seventeenth-century founder of the Religious Society of Friends. In his journal, he instructed members regarding their moral responsibilities. Without ever condemning the institution of slavery, Fox advocated the humane treatment of "servants"; he also prescribed that they eventually be freed. Fox based these moral duties upon his then-exceptional belief "that Christ died for all people—whites, blacks, and Indians."[9]

Although Fox temporized his views regarding institutional slavery, his sermons on master-slave relations were radical. In the 1670s, he asked his white slave-owning audiences to consider their lives as "if you were in the same condition as the Blacks." He implored them to realize that, if their positions were reversed and they were enslaved, they "would thinke [sic] it hard measure, Yea, and a very great bondage and cruelty." Fox recommended that slaveowners exercise their moral imaginations and "consider seriously of this & doe you for and to them as you would willingly have them or anyone other doe unto you were you in the like slavish condition."[10]

George Fox's invocation of the Golden Rule served as the basis for the earliest Quaker arguments against slavery: Do unto others as you would have them do unto you. This admonition was surely known by William Arnold, who possessed Fox's journal. He also would have been aware of this moral instruction through his personal encounters with leading anti-slavery Quakers. In 1757, one such traveling minister, John Woolman, preached at the Symons Creek meeting where the Arnold family worshipped. Woolman spoke "freely and plainly to [the members] concerning their slaves." He urged them to "act conscientiously" because slavery harmed the slaveowners as well as the enslaved.

> Where slaves are purchased to do our labour, numerous difficulties attend it. To rational creatures bondage is uneasy, and frequently occasions sourness and discontent in them; which affects the family and such as claim the mastery over them. Thus people and their children are many times encompassed with vexations, which arise from their applying to wrong methods to get a living.[11]

Woolman's distress over slaveowners' use of the "wrong methods to get a living" led him to contravene tradition and insist on paying his host families for their hospitality. He pointedly included compensation for slave labor.

"I spoke to the heads of the family privately," he wrote in his journal, "and desired them to accept of pieces of silver, and give them to such of their negroes as they believed would make the best use of them." Some heads of household accepted the payments. When they did not, Woolman noted that "at other times I gave them to the negroes myself...."[12]

As a Quaker in good standing, William Arnold understood that the Golden Rule was emphasized as a guide for developing personal virtue and conducting ethical relationships. He must also have been aware that slave-owning jeopardized a principled Christian practice, for leading Quakers preached that this "wrong method" of securing a livelihood depended on ill-gotten gains and unethical master-servant relations. Though the Religious Society of Friends was not yet consistent on these teachings throughout the colonies, North Carolina Quakers were active proponents of numerous anti-slavery reforms.

The North Carolina Yearly Meeting had oversight of the colony's local congregations, including the Symons Creek meetings attended by the Arnolds. During the 1760s, the yearly meeting began to oppose aspects of institutional slavery. They condemned the slave trade and banned the impor-tation of slaves a full forty years before the British Empire and the incipient United States. Beyond restricting the future acquisition of human chattel, the yearly meeting required members to keep already enslaved families intact and to seek permission from their local meetings to either buy or sell any slaves.[13] Failure to follow these directives, also known as Quaker discipline, could result in loss of membership.

In the midst of these developments, William Arnold remained a slaveo-wner. He did not change his mind in response to Quaker instruction or dis-cipline. He did not free the people he held in bondage. Instead, William Arnold bequeathed human beings enslaved in perpetuity to his heirs. While his choices allowed him to remain in unity with his religious community, the choices of his sons did not.

On April 14, 1776, the Symons Creek Monthly Meeting recorded a com-plaint against Joseph and Asa Arnold for ignoring the yearly meeting's advice regarding "selling negroes." Over the next year, religious elders met with the two brothers, counseling them to renounce their misdeeds. Initially, the older brother Joseph tried to "redeem" the people he'd sold. When unsuccessful in his first attempts to secure their return, he refused to try further. The younger brother's intransigence earned particular censure. His religious elders reported that "Asa Arnold has sold Negroes and upon being gently dealt with and long waited upon, he appears to be "void of sorrow . . . ."[14] The Symons Creek meeting concluded that the brothers would not "make satisfaction" and consequently disowned them. The Arnold men were cast out from Quaker society.

One of the religious elders who likely met with the Arnold family was Moses Bundy. At the time, he was serving on a Quaker committee to help slave-owning members manumit (or free) their bonds people. In this capacity, Bundy and the other committee members traveled throughout the community providing spiritual counsel and offering the yearly meetings economic assistance to conduct emancipation proceedings. While ministering in the Arnold family's vicinity, the committee lamented that their efforts produced only "hard Labour & Travail." Some families, the committee reported, refused to consider freeing their slaves because they were "much Blinded by the gain of Oppression and very unwilling to do as they would be done by.[15] The elders' conclusion might explain why the Arnold brothers refused to make amends with their congregation. Greed prevailed over the common good.

Moses Bundy is also my sixth great-grandfather. He's a direct ancestor who faced the same legal, political, and moral circumstances regarding slavery as did William Arnold and his sons. The Bundy family, however, farmed over a hundred acres without relying on enslaved labor. They also belonged to the same Quaker congregation as the Arnolds, but Moses served as a recognized elder and an anti-slavery advocate. Though living in the same colonial plantation society, Bundy made different choices than the Arnolds regarding slavery.

Like Arnold, Moses Bundy left a legacy for his children. His last will and testament followed the sage advice of the anti-slavery minister John Woolman. Woolman "urged parents to bequeath to their children not worldly treasures earned by a life that encouraged idleness and ease, but the blessing of Providence that came with humble and honest work."[16] Accordingly, Bundy's children inherited feather beds and pewter dishes.[17] He did not bestow upon them human "property" nor any "worldly treasures" derived from "wrong methods."

Shortly after his death, Bundy's adult children joined the Quaker migration north, some in the company of free black neighbors. They relocated first to the free states of Ohio and Indiana and eventually to the wilderness of territorial Michigan. In that latter place, in 1843, Moses Bundy's descendants helped to form the Young's Prairie Anti-Slavery Association. Their collective convictions harkened back to George Fox's exceptional belief in human equality. The Bundy progeny and their anti-slavery allies declared, "Whereas the Most High has made of one blood all the nations of men . . . and hath commanded them to love their neighbors as they love themselves . . . we believe Slaveholding to be a sin against God. . . . [18]

The call of accountability—issued by Adrienne Rich, Toni Morrison, and Edward Ball—begs the question: Why did my Arnold and Bundy ancestors relate so differently to their Quaker faith and to slavery? The colonial record indicates that the Arnolds and the Bundys chose to live on their Southern plantations according to either the "gain of oppression" or the "blessing of Providence." This was the fundamental dividing line—whether they abided by the Golden Rule. Certainly, factors now unknown affected choices made 250 years ago. Yet it was my ancestors' decisions to put that cherished ethic of reciprocity into practice—or not—that shaped the moral legacy they left me. What might their examples mean for how I account for my decisions as a white woman living in a racist society in the twenty-first century?

In 2004, just one month before the discovery of William Arnold's will, I presented, for the first time, my research on my anti-slavery ancestors at an Underground Railroad history conference.[19] When the conference goers broke for lunch, we all headed to the university's dining room. People lined up for the buffet and then headed out to the tables. Slowly but decisively the dining area segregated by race, with white people sitting on the left side and black people on the right. I had never before experienced such intentional public separation. Not wanting to rock the boat, I went to the left side and then, when a few people started to mill about, crossed over after lunch.

During the last decade that I've participated in the Underground Railroad world of academics and community historians, I've witnessed another kind of separation: a moral fault line, straddled by pride and shame in our ancestors' identities. If our ancestors had been abolitionists or freedom-seekers, we could express pride, perhaps even take comfort from such distinguished forebears. But if our descent has derived instead from slaveowners, Southern sympathizers, or even sometimes the enslaved, shame might ensue. In public, such shame produces excuses or judgments, such as, "He was just a man of his time" or "What a wretch!" Most often, though, moral shortcomings are met with strained silence.

Whether in pride or in shame, we who come together to try to understand the past persistently struggle to navigate the moral connections between now and then, between us and them. Our ancestors' lives often move us to wonder aloud, "What would I have done if I'd lived back then?" This consideration is part of our attempt to discern a moral legacy, to think about who we are and how we should live now. It can be challenging, as demonstrated by actor Ben Affleck's embarrassment over his slave-owning ancestor. His attempt to censor the information brought this moral fault line into the national news.[20]

I've been thinking about this moral fault line for a long time. Back in 1999, after Edward Ball published *Slaves in the Family*, a chapter of my dissertation made its way into print. In "White Antiracist Rhetoric as Apologia: Wendell Berry's *The Hidden Wound*,"[21] I explored how Berry—a Kentucky-born novelist, poet, and essayist—wrote about his family's slave-owning past and the moral legacy of racism. He concluded that white people's racism left a self-inflicted "hidden wound" that, over time, grew both more painful and more obscured. Still, "I want to know," he wrote, "as fully and exactly as I can, what the wound is and how much I am suffering from it. And I want to be cured; I want to be free of the wound myself, and I do not want to pass it on to my children."[22]

This sincere motivation was what had originally inspired me to read Berry's work in search of guidance. His collection of autobiographical essays, however, contained its own internal tensions. "Berry's apparent desire," as I wrote then, "to defend himself and his slave-owning ancestors from racist culpability"[23] prevented him from providing an unvarnished account. His claims about his ancestors' historical innocence created an *apologia*—a speech of self-defense—that focused on minimizing or absolving them of wrongdoing.

The Berry family had passed down a story about selling a "rebellious slave." Upon completing the sale, the slave trader "came in the night and knocked the [slave] on the head while he was asleep, and bound him, and led him away with a rope."[24] The violence of the transaction, claimed Wendell Berry, was an unanticipated consequence of his family's actions. "No one could have *wanted* any such thing to happen," he declared. "Far from that, I don't think they even *expected* any such thing to happen."[25] By proclaiming their good intentions, Berry enables his ancestors to evade responsibility. After all, they had "inherited" slavery; the blame should be attributed to the slave trader, who was, according to Berry, an "agent of a horror."[26]

Berry's *apologia* absolved the Berry family of wrongdoing, but at the expense of truly knowing "fully and exactly" their slave-owning roles and responsibilities. As a result, the wound of racism festered. The question of how to account for this immoral legacy remained.

When I wrote the chapter on Berry's admirable yet flawed self-examination, I used Adrienne Rich's transformative phrase as an epigraph. I meant it to express homage to Berry's anti-racist intentions, but also to mark the need for a better way to account for ourselves in a racist society. I believe, then and now, that Rich's phrase powerfully acknowledges humanity's basic goodness: We are born innocent. Yet, a belief in goodness is not the same as actually being good. To live a moral life requires accountability for choices made and consequences wrought.

Now that I know that I have abolitionist and slave-owning ancestors, I find myself confronting these same moral fault lines. Like Ball, Berry, and Affleck before me, I need to discern how to relate to my racial history and its twinned risks of pride and shame. I've often heard white people excuse their slave-owning ancestors or invoke their anti-slavery forebears as moral shields, but I've come to understand these rhetorical options as apologia. Such statements distort historical knowledge as they defend against present responsibilities. I need a more precise moral reckoning, one capable of transforming how I enter into raced relationships, both past and present, both intra- and inter-racial.

If my Arnold and Bundy ancestors have taught me one thing, it is the fact that we have a choice. I can choose how to relate to my family past: I can commit to truthful accounts of their actions. To go "forward though," per Toni Morrison, I must also choose my responsibilities. I must confront racism's legacy in my own life. Here, too, my Quaker ancestors are instructive. Their conflicted embrace of the Golden Rule offers a cautionary tale; the strengths and limitations of their examples underscore the moral imperative to treat others as you wish to be treated.

The Golden Rule offers necessary guidance for a white woman living in a racist society because, as the Quakers taught, oppression harms both the oppressed *and* the oppressor. James Baldwin, a modern sage of conduct and character, opened my eyes further to this ethical boomerang. In "A Talk to

Teachers," he forcefully rejected white stereotypes about black people. I read-ily understood that stereotypes perpetuated falsehoods about what it meant to be black. Baldwin, however, taught me that the lies about black inferior-ity necessarily also falsified white superiority. "Because if I am not what I've been told I am," he said, "then it means that *you're* not what you thought *you* were *either!*"[27]

Here then is another expression of the Golden Rule: What we do to others, we do to ourselves. This reversibility is the underlying law of inter-dependence. My mentor, Josina Makau, taught me in graduate school that academics are obligated to understand other points of view—on their own terms—before offering a response or rebuttal. This is not common practice in academe or, for that matter, in everyday discourse. It's a particu-lar challenge to understand others in the context of their colonial or antebel-lum lives. But it is a moral responsibility when it comes to engaging race relations in the past or present.

In our most recent work on dialogue and deliberation,[28] Josina and I have underscored the profound yearning human beings have to be understood, to be known. Across our diverse identities and varied ideas, people deeply wish to connect and may urgently need to account. However, our commu-nicative skills are too often not up to the task. People get hooked into the cycle of judgment, blame, and defensiveness. Conversations become deeply polarized, relationships torn further asunder.

To support more ethical and effective communication, Josina and I took great care to redefine *civility*. We acknowledged the concept's conflicted past as a vehicle for imposing decorum or manipulating rules of etiquette. We also recognized how civility has been deployed to keep people "in their place."[29] But according to the Golden Rule, this type of civility-as-compliance-and-control is unethical. No one wants to be treated in these ways. And propo-nents of this type of civility, most ironically, embody the very essence of *in*civility.

Rightfully understood, civility functions as communication's Golden Rule. Being civil is actually a "means of communicating respectful regard for each other as human beings . . . to act as if each other matters."[30] In this sense, *civility is communicative conduct*, treating others as we wish to be treated. Every time these needs are unmet because of racism, and all other "–isms," it's a betrayal of human dignity. It is a violation of the Golden Rule. Adrienne Rich, Wendell Berry, James Baldwin, and Josina Makau taught me this. So did my Quaker ancestors. They taught me that I have a choice in how to relate to this wrongdoing.

Their lives and wisdom help guide my journey through the intersection of my family's past and my personal conscience. This necessary self-reflection better prepares me to come to the table, to engage in dialogue across relationships riven by history, to fulfill the need to know and be known. I trust humanity's basic goodness and accept the fundamental reality of interdependence. I seek a truthful accounting of actions taken, past and present, and particularly my own. Finally, I commit to civility, because I know that "if dialogue is the means whereby we know one another as we wish to be known, civility makes the *knowing* possible."[31]

This is my story of a moral reckoning and a journey that continues to unfold.

NOTES

1. Adrienne Cecile Rich, *Blood, Bread, and Poetry: Selected Prose, 1979–1985* (New York: Norton, 1986), 136–155.

2. Peggy McIntosh's groundbreaking essay on white racial privilege came out a few years later and was, for me, like so many others, revelatory. Peggy McIntosh. "White Privilege and Male Privilege: A Personal Account of Coming to See Correspondences through Work in Women's Studies," Working Paper 189 (Wellesley, MA: Wellesley College, Center for Research on Women, 1988).

3. Toni Morrison, Taylor-Guthrie, Danille Kathleen. *Conversations with Toni Morrison* (Jackson: University Press of Mississippi, 1994), 195.

4. William Arnold, Sr., last will and testament, Perquimans County, North Carolina Will and Probate Records, 1762–1960, accessed June 4, 2016, from www.ancestry.com.

5. Edward Ball, *Slaves in the Family* (New York: Farrar, Straus and Giroux, 1998), 14.

6. Though colonial tension surrounded slavery for decades, the Revolutionary War highlighted the contradictions in white political consciousness. "To contend for liberty," wrote John Jay, one of the founding fathers, "and to deny that blessing to others involves an inconsistency not to be excused." Cited on "Race: A Project of the American Anthropological Association," accessed June 6, 2016, http://www.understandingrace.org/history/gov/paradox.html.

7. "Symons Creek Monthly Meeting, Pasquotank County, North Carolina, Births, Deaths, and Marriages," vol. 02, 1715–1866. *U.S. Quaker Meeting Records, 1681–1935,* accessed June 4, 2016, from www.ancestry.com.

8. "Sold at Publick Vendor, June 7, 1773," William Arnold Probate File, *Will Records, 1762–1960,* Perquimans County, NC. Clerk of the Superior Court, accessed June 4, 2016, from www.ancestry.com.

9. J. William Frost, "George Fox's Ambiguous Anti-Slavery Legacy," reprinted in 1991 on the Quakers and Slavery website, accessed June 6, 2016, http://trilogy.brynmawr.edu /speccoll/quakersandslavery/commentary/people/fox.php#foxattitudes.

10. Kenneth L. Carroll, "George Fox and Slavery," *Quaker History* 86, no. 2 (1997): 16–25, accessed June 6, 2016, http://www.jstor.org/stable/41947358.

11. John Woolman, *The Journal of John Woolman*, 56–58, accessed June 7, 2016, http:// www.ccel.org/w/woolman/journal/cache/journal.pdf.

12. Woolman, *The Journal of John Woolman*, 51–52.

13. Hiram H. Hilty, *Toward Freedom for All: North Carolina Quakers and Slavery* (Richmond, IN: Friends United Press, 1984), 22–24, accessed online June 7, 2016, https://archive.org. See also Kirsten Fischer, *Suspect Relations: Sex, Race, and Resistance in Colonial North Carolina* (Ithaca, NY: Cornell University Press, 2002).

14. "Symons Creek Monthly Meeting Minutes, Pasquotank County, North Carolina," *U.S. Quaker Meeting Records*, 1681–1935, accessed June 8, 2016, from ancestry.com (emphasis added).

15. Michael J. Crawford, *The Having of Negroes Is Become a Burden: The Quaker Struggle to Free Slaves in Revolutionary North Carolina* (Gainesville: University Press of Florida, 2010), 58–59.

16. Molly Oshatz, *Slavery and Sin: The Fight against Slavery and the Rise of Liberal Protestantism* (New York: Oxford University Press, 2012), 25.

17. Moses Bundy, Inventory of Personal Estate, Book B, July 9, 1782, Wayne County North Carolina. North Carolina Estate Files 1663–1979, online database and images accessed October 29, 2016, from www.familysearch.org.

18. "Communications: Anti-Slavery Meeting at Young's Prairie," *Signal of Liberty* (Ann Arbor, MI), July 3, 1843, accessed June 8, 2016, http://signalofliberty.aadl.org/signal ofliberty/SL_ 18430703-p1-04. Moses Bundy's granddaughter, Mary Brown Marmon, and her great-granddaughter, Mariam Marmon Lee, were founding members.

19. Debian Marty, "The Kentucky Raid: Lessons from Practical Abolitionism," the Borderlands III Underground Railroad Conference, Northern Kentucky University, Highland Heights, Kentucky, September 2004.

20. Stephen A. Crockett, Jr., "Ben Affleck Admits to Asking That Ancestor's Slave-Owning Past Be Hidden, Says He Was 'Embarrassed.'" *The Root*, 2015.

21. Debian Marty, "White Antiracist Rhetoric as Apologia: Wendell Berry's The Hidden Wound," in *Whiteness: The Communication of Social Identity*, eds. Thomas K. Nakayama and Judith N. Martin (Thousand Oaks, CA: Sage Publications, 1999) 51–68.

22. Wendell Berry, *The Hidden Wound* (1970; repr., San Francisco: North Point Press, 1989), 4.

23. Marty, *Apologia*, 52–53.

24. Berry, *The Hidden Wound*, 7.

25. Berry, *The Hidden Wound*, 8 (emphasis in the original).

26. Marty, *Apologia*, 58.

27. James Baldwin, "A Talk to Teachers," *Collected Essays*, edited by Toni Morrison. (New York: Library of America, 1998), 682.

28. Josina M. Makau and Debian L. Marty. *Dialogue and Deliberation*. (Long Grove, IL: Waveland Press, 2013).

29. Makau and Marty, *Dialogue and Deliberation*, 65.

30. Makau and Marty, *Dialogue and Deliberation*, 66.

31. Makau and Marty, *Dialogue and Deliberation*, 67.

16 ⇶ THE TERRETTS OF OAKLAND PLANTATION

An Essay of Atonement

DAVID TERRETT BEUMÉE

I N 2010, AT the age of eighty-five, my mother fell and broke her femur, requiring surgery and a contentious monthlong stay in a rehab facility. During that time, her live-in caregivers were reassigned, and an African woman, Mercy Cartwright, was their replacement, a gentle and loving Ghanaian mother with beautiful dark-brown skin.

I drove Mom home, her rehab completed and her ability to walk again somewhat secure. As I pulled into the driveway, Mercy was standing in front of the garage waiting to help Mom out of my car. I heard a gasp and glanced sideways to see Mom's shocked stare and open mouth as she realized who was greeting her. Mom pointed and shrieked, *"What is that?"*

"That's your new caregiver, Mom," I said as I watched her expression change to bitter disgust and dismay.

Mercy expertly helped Mom out of the car and into the house, and I witnessed Mom's panic-stricken terror at being handled by a woman of color. As the weeks passed, my wife and I became increasingly delighted at Mercy's skill and gentle demeanor, and I remained confident that Mom would respond to Mercy's excellent care. That was not to be. During our weekly visits, Mom's scathing, contemptuous manner toward Mercy became more than I could bear, and I called Mercy's employer. I explained our heartbreak at Mom's treatment of Mercy and asked to have her reassigned. There was silence on the phone and then an astonished voice said, "I can hardly believe what you have just said to me."

Weeks later, Mercy called me, saying, "You were so kind to me, thank you."

The affair broke my wife Barbara's heart, as she had successfully engaged the shy and capable Mercy Cartwright, whom we will never forget. This was the appalling level of racial malevolence of which my mother was capable.

As such, this is an essay of atonement for the sins of my ancestors, whose bigoted and racist attitudes toward their African American slaves were passed down to me, particularly through my mother Priscilla Dade Terrett (1925–2012). My name is David Terrett Beumée, and my middle (family) name Terrett was given to me by my mother in honor and proud recognition of the slave-holding tradition of antebellum Virginia. I once heard Mom say how difficult it was preparing and serving meals "without the help of servants." My mother spent decades of genealogical research looking back with tremendous satisfaction to the genteel antebellum Southern-belle existence that generations of our Virginia ancestors enjoyed. My advantage as a white was established in myriad ways early in colonial Virginia history and was passed onto my brother and me by way of generations of white privilege—more than a hundred and fifty years after Lincoln declared African American slaves "free."

As Mom's primary caregiver in the last two years of her life, I found myself trying to find subjects to discuss with a woman whose racial prejudice had severed our relationship. When the Terretts' family history of slave-owning became apparent, I confronted Mom about it, to which she shrugged her shoulders and said, "I wasn't there; I'm not responsible." At that moment I recognized that the story of Terrett slave-owning had been buried for generations, and I became determined to expose it.

Since that encounter, and after years of research and soul-searching, I am now comfortable with and confident in the facts. I may never know why I did not share my family's racism during my growing-up years, which happened in Billings, Montana in the fifties and sixties, but this I do know: unless people are willing to examine their attitudes about racism, such prejudice passes from generation to generation unrestricted, and it resurfaces indefinitely. If the conversation around racial justice in America is ever to change, stories of ancestral enslavement—such as the story of my ancestors that follows—must be brought to the light of day.

My sixth great-grandfather began a four-generation Terrett tradition of enslaving African Americans in the one hundred twenty years between 1741 and 1861. William Henry Terrett (1707–1758) was a twelve-year-old orphan brought to Virginia from London in 1720 by his uncle, to be apprenticed to a York River lawyer for twenty-two years. When William Henry was thirty-four, Col. Gov. Thomas Lord Fairfax granted him 982 acres of land in what is now western Alexandria, Virginia, instantly making him a wealthy landowner. In that same year, William Henry constructed, undoubtedly with slave labor, a grand octagonal mansion, his "dwelling plantation" south of the original grant of land that he inherited from his wife Margaret Pearson (1720–1796). William Henry added an additional 539 acres through more grants and purchases from neighbors.

"The plantation relied heavily on the labor of enslaved African Americans."[1] The cash crop of the day was tobacco for an increasingly addicted European citizenry, but finding sufficient manpower to raise such a labor-intensive crop was a problem. Deadly consequences had resulted from the attempt to enslave Native Americans, and white European indentured servants couldn't satisfy the number of workers needed. My ancestor was now a wealthy man who could afford to buy many slaves to work the tobacco fields of Oakland Plantation. Slaves were in abundant supply within a day's ride of the shore of the mighty Potomac River, and temptation to enslave human beings proved irresistible. There will never be an excuse for the actions of my ancestor; and yet, I must ask what I would have done in that situation, at that moment in history—after coming to Virginia as an orphan, serving a long apprenticeship, and suddenly being given great land wealth. It is yet another demanding pair of opposites to experience and try to accept within my psyche.

The tradition of Terrett enslavement created family wealth and white privilege that was passed down through time, through Mom and Dad's "Greatest Generation,"[2] onto me, racial prejudice included. Upon returning from
WWII, my father was offered college and law school tuition through the G. I.
Bill, yet the same benefits were not offered to African American veterans who
had fought in the same battles in Europe and the Pacific. Banks refused to
make loans for mortgages in black neighborhoods, and African American veterans faced vehement racism if they attempted to buy into suburban neighborhoods, including the 100 percent white neighborhood and city where I
was privileged to be born.

Dad was from central Montana (Lewistown) wheat-ranching stock, and
Mom grew up sixty miles from Miles City, Montana, on the Terrett JO cattle
ranch, but her values were Virginia genteel. Her people were descendants of
urbane antebellum Virginia slaveholders who became rugged Montana cattle
ranchers. The Terrett family moved from Alexandria, Virginia, to Garden
City, Missouri, in 1870, where the breadwinner of the family, my great-great-
grandfather William Wiseham Terrett (1847–1922) learned the cattle business. (His dad died fighting for the Confederate States Army in 1863.) In
1881, W. W. Terrett was sent to Montana to establish what would become the
JO cattle ranch, now in its fifth generation of Terrett-family ownership. My
grandfather, Colville Dulany Terrett, son of W. W. Terrett, toiled at the JO
Cattle Ranch nearly all of his working life. One of his daughters, my mother,
born in 1925, became a marvelous horse woman—a 110-pound athletic rider
who loved to rope and work cattle as a ranch hand. As I became familiar with
my mother in the last phase of her life, it became obvious that her years on
the ranch were the best of her life. The progression of racial prejudice follows
a direct line from W. W. Terrett, son of a slaveholder, through my grandparents, to my mother, and to me.

Grandmother and Grandfather Terrett were third cousins who shared the
same great-grandparents, John Hunter Terrett (1790–1831) and Julia (West)
Dade (1789–1865). Grandmother and Grandfather Terrett were kind, loving,
and generous, and at the same time held beliefs about African Americans,
and all people of color, that astonished me as a child. Because Grandfather's
dad and Grandmother's mother were both of Terrett-family ancestry, Mom
received her racist attitude from both her parents and never had any intention or desire to examine her racial bias. Mom's bigotry was a given, a part of
the atmosphere of growing up in my family. My mother and I didn't have

much of a relationship because of her bigotry, which I found disgraceful and unforgivable, and yet both my parents inevitably passed their racial prejudice onto me, which I must now reconcile. This contrast of loathing racial bigotry while unwittingly participating in racist attitudes constitutes yet another pair of opposites for which I pray for help to stand firmly in the middle, resorting neither to defensive violence on one hand or despair on the other. Lord, have mercy on us all.

My Terrett ancestors were among many southerners willing to fight to the death to preserve their way of life. The allegiance of my ancestor Colonel George Terrett (1807–1875) to the antebellum enslaving way of life was so passionate that after thirty-two years in the United States Marines, he switched sides upon the first hint of Virginia seceding from the Union to join the Provisional Army of Northern Virginia. It was the colonel's great-grandfather, my sixth great-grandfather William Henry Terrett (1707–1758), who founded the Oakland Plantation (1741) and initiated four generations of Terrett slave-owning.

William, Thornton, Israel, Eliza, and Emily were among thirty-seven slaves listed, along with dollar values, next to horses, cattle, and furniture in George Hunter Terrett's will (1778–1842), father of Col. George Terrett. This is irrefutable evidence that my ancestor was complicit within Virginia slave society in his belief in a hierarchy of human value, a hierarchy that placed African American slaves at the bottom and British American slave masters at the top. Two hundred seventy-five names appear in the four-generation Terrett slave chart, but many slaves were willed to succeeding generations of the Terrett family. This chart contains the names of one hundred African Americans enslaved by my Terrett ancestors.

After 1808 it became unlawful to purchase internationally embezzled slaves, so the practice of holding female slaves as breeding stock to bring new generations of slave boys and girls into the world became increasingly essential for the survival of my ancestors' way of life. "More common than forced pairings among slaves were forced sexual encounters between white men and black women. Potential sexual partners of enslaved women included the master, his sons, neighboring planters, visitors of the slaveholding family, traveling salesmen and hired workers."[3] Did this practice include my ancestors? Could they have really invited a traveling salesman or a neighbor to rape slave women for more "pickaninnies?" Racism and its history is so much larger an issue than I can handle as an individual. I seek my own

Colonel George Hunter Terrett (1807–1875). Courtesy of the Fairfax County Public Library photographic archive.

transformation as my best attempt to transform the world. I can't change the world, but I can change that little part of it that is me. Through personal analysis, I have become better equipped to accept "the task of being a carrier of evil."[4] This means I am always caught up in the drama of the opposites, attracted to the generosity of spirit my family has displayed while simultaneously repulsed by their bigotry and hatred of "the other." On the one hand,

Wedding picture of John Hunter Terrett and Virginia Hutton, March 17, 1853. Used by permission of the author.

Fairfax County Sct.   July Court 1843

Ordered that Allen Macrae, James Cloud, Richard
H. Clagett, Edward C. Fitzhugh, Orson Liday & Thomas Z. Smith, do Inventory and appraise all and singular the Estate of George H. Terrett deceased which shall be presented to them over by the Execut. and make
report to the Court, they being first duly sworn according to Law

A Copy
Teste
Mc Nhall CC

Pursuant to the annexed order of Court to us directed, we the
undersigned appraisers, having been first sworn for that purpose,
have inventoried and appraised, as below stated, all the personal
Estate of George H. Terrett dec'd which was presented to our view,
by Hannah B. Terrett his Executrix. In testimony whereof we have
hereunto set our hands this 25th day of August 1843
Subscribed and sworn to before   A Macrae
me this 25 day of August 1843   R H Clagett
Orson Liday J.P.   Orson Liday

35 Head of Cattle average value per head $6	210	00
1 Yoke of Oxen	30	00
36 Sheep @ $1.25 each	45	00
1 Dun colored mare	30	00
1 Black Horse	20	00
1 Blooded Mare	80	00
1 Grey Horse	40	00
1 Sorrel mare + colt	50	00
1 Ox cart	11	00
2 Horse Carts	35	00
1 Grain Fan	5	00
1 Sleigh	11	00
2 Harrows	10	00
Cart Gear	3	00
1 Carryall	10	00
8 Beds + furniture of 4 rooms	200	00
2 Sideboards	12	00
1 Sofa	15	00
1 Mahogany Arm chair	12	00
2 Ottomans	5	00
Carried over	832	00
1 Doz. chairs	12	00
1 Pair Brass Andirons, Fender, + Shovel + Tongs	15	00
2 Large Looking glasses	25	00
1 Eight day clock	30	00
1 Bookcase + Books	10	00
Silver Plate	35	00
1 Sett Blacksmiths Tools	20	00
	979	00
Slaves as follows.		
Jackson (aged)	00	00
John (aged)	00	00
Hanson (aged)	50	00
Mike	300	00
Trunsina	400	00

Will document of George Hunter Terrett (1778–1842).

Name	£	s
William	400	00
Thornton	400	00
Israel	350	00
Charles	300	00
Lewis	300	00
Aaron	250	00
George	200	00
William	175	00
Richard	200	00
John	250	00
Dennis	250	00
Edward	250	00
Thomas	100	00
Lavinia	250	00
Sam	250	00
Mary Ann	300	00
Maly	300	00
Arianna	250	00
Eliza	300	00
Amt carried forwd	6804	00
Martha (absconded)		
Eliza	300	00
Emily	150	00
Hannah	200	00
Lucretia	200	00
Julia	100	00
Maria	100	00
Susan	150	00
Bersheba	75	00
Mary Ann	75	00
Robert	100	00
Emma	100	00
Sally	75	00
(8379) Total	8379	

At a court held for the County of Fairfax the 18 day of Septr 1843
This inventory and appraisement
of the Estate of George H. Terrett and was this day returned and or
dered to be recorded

Teste
Jno Ball C.C.

In the name of God Amen. I James Wren of the
County of Fairfax and State of Virginia — being of sound mind
and sound and disposing memory — as ordain, and declare
this to be my Last Will and Testament — hereby revoking all others
heretofore made by me.
In the first place — I give to my dearly beloved wife Ann Wren
the whole of my Estate, real, personal, and mixed during her
natural Life — (saving, and excepting such bequests, or legacies,
as I may hereafter name) and at the death of my said wife
Ann. all my property is to be equally divided among my heirs—
I also desire and request that my said wife will carry on

Will document of George Hunter Terrett (1778–1842).

Terrett Family Tree, abbreviated from the original by Priscilla Dade Terrett.

William Terrett b. 1 Nov., 1705 m. Mary Arne.
Issue: William Henry Terrett,
baptized 4 May 1707
at All Hallows the Great Church, London, England.
He was orphaned. 17 December 1720 Wm Henry Terrett was
apprenticed from Christ's Hospital London to his Uncle Thomas Arne,
who brought Wm. Henry to Virginia to serve William Beverley in York
River, VA.

Colonel George Terrett was the third son of George Hunter Terrett
and Hannah Butler Ashton and is the subject of the Ralph Donnelly
article "George Hunter Terrett." He was a Mexican War hero and
resigned his commission with the Marines when Virginia seceded
in 1861 to join the Provisional Army of Northern Virginia as an officer
under Robert E. Lee.

Colonel George Terrett
b. 15 Oct. 1807 d. 27 Nov. 1875

Margaret Stuart
d. 1904

George Hunter Terrett
b. 18 March 1778 d. 1842
Hannah Butler Ashton
d. 1842

William Henry Terrett, Jr.
b. 2 Oct. 1785 d. 1860 m. 1801

Nancy Douglass Terrett
b. 31 May 1794 d. 1857
John (Chapman) Hunter Terrett
d. 1831
m. 1812

William Henry Terrett
b. 19 April 1707 London, Eng.
b. 1758 VA m. 1735
Margaret Pearson
b. 1720 d. 1796

Elizabeth Chapman
b. 1733 d. m. 1753
Dr. John Hunter
b. 1721 d. 1763

Amelia Hunter
b. 1756 d. 1833

Catherine Emily West
b. 1762
d. 1804
m. 1781

Capt. John West, Jr.
b. 1726 d. 1777
m. before 1755
Catherine Colville
b. d.

Townshend Dade Terrett
b. 1 Jan. 1854 d. Nov. 1925

John (Hunter) Terrett
b. 1824
d. 17 March 1864 - Civil War

Julia (West) Dade
b. 1789
d. 1865 (Civil War)

Verlinda (2nd Wife)
b. d. 1798
m. 1743

Col. Baldwin Dade (Jr.)
b. 1760 d. 1834

John Fay (or Fry) Smith
b. 1762 d. 1825 VA
m. 1788

Baldwin Dade
b. 13 Oct. 1716 d. 1783

Isaac Garner (Rev)

Julia Emeline Terrett
b. 1856
d. 1931
m. 6 September 1876

m. 17 March 1853

Rebecca Emeline Smith
b. 1806
d. 1864
m. 1823

Catherine Yost
b. 1769
d. 1807

Ann

Isaac Garner Hutton
b. 1790 England
d. 1858 VA

Elizabeth (Garner) Little
b. 1751 England d. 1833 VA
m. 1780
Rev. Jacob Hutton
b. 1742 Eng d. 1822 VA
(Wash DC)

Beatrice Overend
b. d. m. 1733
Charles Hutton
b. 1709 England
d. 17... England

Zola Rosalie Ferrell Blevans
b. 25 December 1895
d. Sept. 1989 CO

Rosalie Blevans, daughter by her
first marriage to Neil Blevans

Henry Lee Ferrell
b. 1850
d. 1935

Virginia Hutton
b. 1826 VA
d. 1907 MO

Baldwin Dade
b. 1716 d. 1783
m. 1743 second wife
Verlinda
d. 1798

Col. Baldwin Dade
b. 1760
d. 1834
m. 1781

Catherine Colville
m. 1714

Julia Rosalie Blevans
b. 30 Oct. 1918
d. 29 January 1979

Lee I Thompson

Priscilla Gantt Richards
b. 1846 VA
d. 1929 MT
m. 26 Feb. 1869

Elizabeth Cerington Paine
b. 1818
d. 1871
m. 1846

Catherine Emily West
b. about 1752
d. 1804

Capt. John West, Jr.
b. 1714 d. 1777
Dr. John Hunter
b. 1721 d. 1763

Linda Ann Thompson
b. 15 November 1947

Virginia Lee Terrett
b. 6 April 1924
d. 29 January 1996

William Wiseham Terrett
b. 1847 VA
d. 1922 MT

Alexander Hunter Terrett
b. 1818
d. 1863 in service of Conf.
States Army of America in VA

Julia (West) Dade
b. about 1789
d. 1865
m. 1812 Woodville Cottage near
Alexandria, VA

Amelia Hunter
b. 1756
d. 1833
m. 1775

William Terrett Koch
b. 6 Jan. 1948
James Robert Koch
b. 29 January 1996
Richard Lee Koch
b. 19 July 1949
Robert Koch
b. 10 March 2016
b. 7 Jan. 1954

Colville Dulany Terrett
b. 30 November 1881 MO
d. 13 October 1966 MT

John (Chapman) Hunter Terrett
b. 4 March 1790
d. 1831

Priscilla Dade Terrett
b. 29 November 1925
d. 5 February 2012
John Keith Beumée
b. 20 September 1951

Stephen Dulany Beumée
b. 18 April 1945
David Terrett Beumée
b. 20 September 1951

William Henry Terrett, Jr.
b. 1752
d. 6 April 1828

Elizabeth Chapman
b. 1733
Margaret Pearson
b. 1720 d. 1796
m. 1735

William Henry Terrett, Jr.
b. 1752
d. 6 April 1828

Capt. John West, Jr.
Dr. John Hunter
b. 1721 d. 1763

Amelia Hunter
b. 1753

William Henry Terrett
b. 1707 London, England
d. 1758 VA

my grandparents were loving people; on the other, they were bigots. On the one hand, my mother could be a generous and loving person; on the other, she once explained to me that children must have "a healthy fear of their parents." On one hand, I grew up in a family where bigotry was a given; on the other, these people are the only family I have.

As author Edward F. Edinger has said, "Consciousness requires a simultaneous experience of opposites and the acceptance of that experience. The greater the degree of this acceptance, the greater the consciousness."[5] Personal analysis has made it abundantly obvious, however, that both good and evil exist within me, and good and evil make up what is arguably the most powerful and terrifying pair of opposites that exists. To tackle this challenge is to balance the tension of the opposites simultaneously and to accept that both good and evil exist in me so that it no longer becomes crucial for me to project evil onto "the other"—whatever their skin color or whoever they may be. As Jung says, "For if you have to endure yourself, how will you be able to rend others also?"[6] As I continue to pursue the process of obtaining and preserving the integrity of my ego and becoming whole, and as I make amends for the racist language and attitudes that were created and maintained by generations of my enslaving ancestors, so the world is changed, one person at a time.

Researching and writing the story of my enslaving ancestors has been an immense help in transforming the racist attitudes instilled in me. I now understand the background of hatred that entered the collective consciousness of whites in America long ago, resulting in murderous vengeance being visited upon fellow African American citizens. Finding and exposing the truth of Southern slave-holding families like mine could lend insight and a place to begin reparative conversations between African and Caucasian Americans for a better path forward.

NOTES

1. "Appendix, Beauregard Corridor Stakeholder Group (BCSG)," Working Draft, January 23, 2012, p. 156, "B" Historical Context—Region and Neighborhood, para. C "Terrett Family."
2. "Greatest Generation" was the title of a book by Tom Brokaw about the generation that grew up during the Depression, went on to fight in WWII, and contributed to the war effort at home. It has come into common usage to describe this generation.
3. Marie Jenkins Schwartz, *Birthing a Slave: Motherhood and Medicine in the Antebellum South* (Cambridge: Harvard University Press, 2006).

4. Sylvia Brinton Perera, *The Scapegoat Complex: Toward a Mythology of Shadow and Guilt* (Toronto: Inner City, 1986).

5. Edward F. Edinger, *The Mystery of the Coniunctio: Alchemical Image of Individuation.* Toronto: Inner City Books 1994), 13.

6. C. G. Jung, *Mysterium Coniunctionis: An Inquiry into the Separation and Synthesis of Psychic Opposites in Alchemy* (Princeton: Princeton University Press, 1970).

17 ❧ NOT A WOUND TOO DEEP

KAREN STEWART-ROSS

M Y GRANDFATHER ALWAYS kept freshly picked cotton on the dashboard of his old 1970s Pontiac, and I always wondered why. Hans Edward Hill, or Granddaddy, as we affectionately called him, had been a well-known and respected government official—a Falls County negro agent—in my hometown of Marlin, a place located in the heart of Texas, once known for its mineral bathwater. Growing up, I was always referred to as "Mr. Hill's granddaughter."

A community leader, Grandaddy came from a strong farming family with roots in Georgia. The family owned a masonic lodge, and Grandaddy owned a grocery stand that everyone in the neighborhood called the Snack Center, a mineral bathhouse that was once part of a "colored" hospital complex, and several other properties. Grandaddy built solid, long-lasting relationships with all types of people and, according to my dad, was quite powerful, but not without his challenges. An agricultural guru and tax agent, he was one time called "boy" as he presented a solution in a government meeting about a water issue the town was having, but he didn't allow that or any similar moment to deter him from helping African American farmers with both their land and their money.

Perhaps a testament to this "power" and the excellent interpersonal skills he possessed was that during the Jim Crow era, Grandaddy was a key figure of the civil rights movement in our town, able to garner relationships with people of various ethnic backgrounds. For example, according to my mother, when he wasn't feeling well, he would often call Mr. Shelton, a dear friend and white local pharmacist, in the middle of the night to obtain medicine, and Mr. Shelton would open the establishment every time. His bathhouse catered to people of all racial backgrounds, and he converted old hospital rooms into hotel rooms for guests who wished to undergo his twenty-one-day mineral bath regiment. He also worked out partnerships with local African American-owned restaurants that wished to serve his guests. In what appears to have been a preplanned strategy, the local NAACP would often call on him to bail out civil rights protestors during sit-ins in the 1960s. Grandaddy understood the importance of land ownership and financial security for African Americans and was cognizant of the role race played in these issues. While he knew race was significant, however, he did not consider it a barrier. He would negotiate and establish relationships with anyone, regardless of ethnicity or economic status. I loved my grandfather dearly, went everywhere with him, ate the pecans he always kept in his house, and learned to deal with difficult people by observing his interactions. I was a "Granddaddy's Girl."

Granddaddy's father, Rev. James H. Hill, or Papa Hill as we called him, was a Methodist minister and carpenter who pastored several churches in the Central Texas area. He was a tall, light-brown, quiet man, who always wore a slight "knowing" smile. A peaceful man, Papa Hill could often be seen in a rocking chair on his front porch, dressed in overalls, slowly fanning flies and listening to the woes of passersby. And while Grandaddy had a great affection for pecans, Papa Hill loved peaches. There were several peach trees on his property, one tree separated from the rest directly behind the home he built. Every summer, Papa Hill would invite our neighbors to his home to pick from his peach trees—but never from the one that stood alone. That tree's refreshing peaches were a source of comfort during hot summers, and later—after both Papa Hill and Grandaddy died—it soothed some of our pain. Long after their deaths, that peach tree remained.

Throughout their lives and after their deaths, pecans and peach trees were almost sacred in our family, representing a historical tie to a country town called Rome, Georgia; while the cotton on Grandaddy's dashboard, as I was to learn later, represented the truth of enslavement and the African American experience that permeates my family's history.

Several years following both my grandfather's and great-grandfather's deaths, I decided to find that place in Georgia where the peaches and the pecans were plentiful, despite the presence of suffering. In December of 2015, I encountered a researcher—a supposed ally—whom I entrusted to help my family document land our ancestors once owned. But the researcher, who was white, felt that the land was insignificant despite ample physical evidence of our family's presence that had endured over 100 years. "There is nothing to see," he told me. His remarks were callous and cruel. They were also indicative of a larger issue that I have faced while uncovering family history and working toward healing—the inability of many white Americans to "see" and understand what we, as African Americans, are faced with while attempting to retrace the steps of our ancestors. This inability, or perhaps unwillingness, to look beyond perceived differences, and to either experience the pain or acknowledge the successes of formerly enslaved African Americans or their descendants, is a recurrent theme in my journey of uncovering my family's history.

That month, on the road to uncovering my ancestors' roots, I found myself in a little town called Lincolnton, North Carolina. Right outside of Charlotte on the south fork of the Catawba River, Lincolnton seemed innocent enough—quiet, slow, historical, and set in its ways. It reminded me of Marlin somewhat. But there were no pecans or peaches. All I noticed were the small shacks that seemed to pepper the backyards of houses lining the towns' long, winding back roads. At one point, I lost count of what had surely been slave quarters. I felt a coldness there—there was nowhere to "hang my hat" as we say in the South—I didn't belong there. I knew in my soul that horrible things had happened in that town—things involving my ancestors—and I did not sense any accountability for the abuse that they endured. There were many times I wanted to leave, as the anger, the sadness, the pain, and the blindness was often overwhelming. Yet, I couldn't leave. I needed to embark on the journey and I needed to do it alone. I had to.

Death certificates, probate records, census records, a Civil War diary, a DNA analysis, and so many other discoveries told the story. Papa Hill's great-grandparents and Grandaddy's great-great-grandparents, Jonas Cathey[1] and Delse (sometimes spelled Dilsey) Barry Cathey, were enslaved in Lincolnton and then forcibly taken to Rome, Georgia, in the mid-1830s. Jonas, also known as Joe, was born in Africa,[2] and his owners and (later Delse's) were John and Sarah McArver Cathey. The Catheys were Presbyterian missionaries and probably relocated to Rome to continue going about "God's business"—making sure, of course, to bring their enslaved with them. The area where they lived, once known as the Narrows, came to be known as Cathey Gap.[3] Delse was born in North Carolina and belonged to Sarah's stepfather Andrew "Andy" Barry and mother Elizabeth "Betsy" Lewis McArver Barry. After Andrew died in 1839, Elizabeth moved in with John and Sarah.[4] After Andrew's death, Delse became Elizabeth's property and, albeit unofficially, John and Sarah's.

Founded in 1834, Rome is often cited as one of the beginning points of the forced removal of the Cherokee and their ensuing trek to Oklahoma, known as the Trail of Tears. Positioned at the feet of the Appalachian Mountains in northwest Georgia where the Etowah, Oostanaula, and the Coosa rivers meet, Rome is about an hour and fifteen minutes from Atlanta and about forty minutes from Cherokee County, Alabama. It was in Rome that the Treaty of Echota was negotiated in 1835, promising the region's Cherokee inhabitants compensation if they relocated to Oklahoma.[5] Papa Hill was born in Rome as was his mother Joanna Cathey Hill Lewis and her father Lee, who was also enslaved by John and Sarah.[6] It is in Rome where I found peaches and pecans and stories of an indomitable spirit, but I also encountered cotton and narratives of pain.

The story of Lee's mother, Delse, my fourth great-grandmother, is perhaps one of the most troubling and perplexing that I have encountered in my family's history. Delse was a weaver for the Cathey family. Her mother was born in Africa. It was in her owner's will where it became clear to me that something was amiss. In the will, Delse's owner, Andrew, treats her differently from the other enslaved. He begins with Delse, as if to get the most difficult subject out of the way, perhaps a subject of many endless conversations. Unlike the other enslaved people mentioned in this probate document, Delse is pointedly referred to as the "mulatto girl." Elizabeth can do whatever she would like with Delse upon his death, Andrew states, on one condition—

that Elizabeth remain a widow for the rest of her life. This is in stark contrast to the conditions set forth for his other enslaved, particularly his "negro man" Charles and Charles's family: when Elizabeth dies or remarries, Charles and his family are to be liberated and given land.[7]

One part of our Cathey family's oral history said that Delse's husband was white. However, Delse's children stated in the 1880 Federal Census of the North Carolina District of Rome that their father had been born in Africa. But what about Delse's father? I think Andrew was Delse's father. Confirming Andrew's reference, Delse is listed as mulatto in the 1880 census and her mother is listed as being born in Africa. That means her father may have been white. That would explain the special attention given to Delse in Andrew's will—it was probably because she was his child, likely the product of a forced encounter with Delse's African mother. Perhaps Elizabeth had demanded that something be done about Delse, a reminder of Andrew's unfaithfulness, and in a final attempt to resolve the matter, Andrew acquiesced by giving Elizabeth free reign over Delse after his death. In essence, in circumstances that confound me, Delse's fate rested on Elizabeth's fidelity.

Did Andrew really believe that Elizabeth would remain a widow after his death? If Elizabeth remarried, how could Andrew control what would happen to Delse? I can't comprehend Andrew's true motives, but what is clear is there is something lurking underneath the surface of Andrew's desires. Unfortunately for Delse, Elizabeth did remain a widow until her death in 1866, and Delse was never set free.

Andrew's blindness to the pain he had caused our family, which often manifests itself in callousness, rears its head in Delse's story as does her resilience. First, there's the audacity to refer to another human being as property. Born in about 1813, Delse was a young woman at the time Andrew's will was written, and although enslaved, she was no one's property. There is also no reference to Delse's mother, and I wondered what happened to her. Was she sold? Did she die? Was she whipped to death in a fit of rage? Andrew didn't care about Delse's mother or the pain he had put her family—my family—through. Delse was simply the "mulatto girl," and he would become the subject of many whispers at family reunions for the next one hundred years.

In Jonas, one finds another story—that of resistance and mystery. Jonas is an interesting figure. He appears to have been not only Delse's husband but also the partner or former partner of Sara Ringer Cathey, who may have been enslaved with the Cathey family. Sara's fate is unknown as she does not appear in any census; however, we have learned that Delse's and Sara's children were very close. In fact, I recently had the opportunity to meet three of Jonas and Sara's descendants at a family gathering in Rome. A captivating figure, Jonas was also quite brave.

According to a Civil War diary penned by Nancy "Nannie" Cathey, a daughter of John and Sarah Cathey, in 1864, during the height of the Civil War, Jonas was threatened on two separate occasions by rebel scouts who found him with the gun of two "dead Yanks." In each instance, Nannie intervened. With both her mother Sarah and grandmother Elizabeth ill, Nancy had taken charge of the Cathey household during the Civil War, with the help of her uncle Isaac McArver. Whether it was for shoeing horses or creating a hidden escape route for the Cathey family and their enslaved, Jonas was relied on quite frequently. While it is reasonable to assume Jonas would be approached if he, an enslaved man, had guns, it is also tenable that despite his seeming loyalty, he may not have been a trusted man. On one occasion, Nannie asked her uncle Isaac to defend Jonas from the rebel scouts, and my sense tells me that Isaac may not have trusted Jonas as much as Nannie did, as it is unclear whether he ever came to Jonas's aid.

For the six months following the end of the Civil War, Jonas continued to work as a blacksmith for the Cathey family. In notes pertaining to the diary, one of Nannie's nieces expressed her admiration for Jonas's perseverance.[8] I often wonder if Jonas stayed out of need or obligation to Nannie. I've concluded that it was probably both.

In 1867, during the Reconstruction Era, Jonas, along with many of my relatives and their friends, registered to vote in Floyd County, Georgia.[9] Following enslavement, the family owned land, and many of their descendants became educated. Jonas died in 1869,[10] and Delse continued living in the North Carolina district surrounded by her family. In 1880, she is listed in the census as living with her son James "Wallace" Cathey. Two of her other children and their spouses are listed nearby: my third great-grandfather Lee and his wife Frances "Fannie" Shelton, and Susan "Susie" Cathey and her husband Sanford Freeman.[11] Jonas was also married to a woman named Sara Ringer of Alabama whose children were very close to their half-siblings. It is unclear what happened to Sara, but one can assume she passed away or was sold.

Delse's cause of death is unknown, but what is known is that her sons and daughter would not leave Rome until their mother's passing. In the mid-1890s, following Delse's presumed death, James Wallace married Fannie Shelton Cathey's sister Lula and moved to Chattooga, Georgia, and then, eventually, to Chattanooga, Tennessee. Papa Hill was named after him. Susie Cathey Freeman and her husband moved to the Flatwoods area of Rome. Lee and Fannie moved to Atlanta and eventually to Franklin, Texas, his descendants' homestead, which is about an hour from Marlin. Other Cathey siblings married, with some remaining in the Rome area and others moving to Memphis, Tennessee, and Detroit, Michigan. Each of these families would produce rich historical legacies.

On that cold afternoon in the winter of 2015, after conducting research in Lincolnton and Catawba, I decided to recalibrate before making the trip to Rome. Recalibrating is something I do quite often these days when I encounter information about my ancestors that is difficult to digest—evidence that involves reliving the horror my ancestors endured. While I will reach out to the white Cathey family that enslaved my own, what I feel is complex. In some respects, I feel this strange kinship to the people who saw no wrong in enslaving my ancestors—tearing them away from their family while they remained attached to theirs. Conversely, that realization makes me feel nothing but anger. It's not fair, this kinship I feel—a kinship toward people who treated my ancestors worse than animals. Admittedly, I want nothing to do with the descendants of my family's slaveowner, but to ask them why they did these things to our family. I often wonder what their response will be—will they embrace or reject me? What is certain is that despite their pain, my family continued to prosper and to believe that there was always something greater than the darkness—hope.

A few months ago, my mother revealed that in the 1920s, Granddaddy had fallen off the back of the family truck after a long day of picking cotton. The family took Granddaddy to the colored hospital complex on Island Street for treatment. One of the unfortunate byproducts of enslavement has been discrimination based on color or economic status within the African American community. For some time during and following enslavement, the lighter an African American's skin color or the higher his or her economic status, the better he or she was treated. Some would maintain that, in many respects, this practice continues today. However, despite being considered "mulatto," my grandfather was treated poorly because he was from a family of farmers and sharecroppers. So it was on that day that he vowed to eventually own the place. In the early 1940s, after he had graduated from Prairie View Normal and Industrial College, now known as Prairie View A & M University, and after he had married and begun a family, he heard about the death of the man who had owned the colored hospital complex. He quickly arranged a meeting with the man's widow and made her a deal she couldn't refuse. His mineral bathhouse remained in operation until the early 1970s.

I now know why Grandaddy kept cotton on that dusty dashboard. Soft and white, and appearing quite harmless, this offending plant is far from innocent; it is guilty of being witness to inconceivable terror. Yet it also symbolizes something else: aspiration. As such, that cotton served as a reminder to my grandfather that, regardless of any obstacle, anyone can rise when there is the presence of hope. As I have discovered through organizations such as Coming to the Table, despite the presence of struggle and pain, both now and in the past, there is a much larger truth, which is ever-present—that my ancestors, and perhaps yours, can forge through the darkness.

NOTES

1. Jonas had two last names—Rhine and Cathey. It appears Jonas was enslaved by someone with the last name of Rhine in North Carolina and then by the Catheys. He died as Jonas Rhine in 1869, and his wife, Delse, and their children continued to use the Rhine surname. But sometime before 1880, his survivors switched to Cathey.

2. The 1880 Census of North Carolina and Floyd, Georgia, Enumeration District 068, Roll 146, p. 244A.

3. See Diary Extract 1864 in the section "About the Diary of Miss Nannie Cathy," on the website Down Home in Alabama—Genealogy of Travis Hardin, http://gen.intelec.us/coosa/index.html.

4. The 1860 Census of North Carolina and Floyd, Georgia, Family History Library Film 803121, Roll M653_121jum, p. 261.

5. National Park Service, "Trail of Tears: Georgia," accessed May 15, 2018, https://www.nps.gov/trte/learn/historyculture/georgia.htm#CP_JUMP_2393662.

6. See Diary Extract 1864 in the section "About the Diary of Miss Nannie Cathy," on the website Down Home in Alabama—Genealogy of Travis Hardin, http://gen.intelec.us/coosa/index.html.

7. W. D. McCarver, *McCarvers in America* (McCarvers in America, 1996).

8. See the section "About the Diary of Miss Nannie Cathy," on the website Down Home in Alabama—Genealogy of Travis Hardin, http://gen.intelec.us/coosa/index.html.

9. Georgia, Returns of Qualified Voters and Reconstruction Oath Books, 1867–1869 (database online). Provo, UT: Ancestry.com Operations, Inc., 2012. https://www.ancestry.com/interactive/1857/32305_1220705227_0091-00275.

10. The 1869 Census of Floyd, Georgia, Subdivision 141. *Federal Mortality Census Schedules, 1850–1880, and Related Indexes, 1850–1880* (Washington, DC: National Archives and Records Administration), Archive Collection T655, Roll 9, p. 124A.

11. The 1880 Census of North Carolina and Floyd, Georgia, Enumeration District 068, Roll 146, p. 244A.

18 ⇥ TO SEE

The Blindness of Whiteness

SARA JENKINS

My experience ... has been so bitter, ... a cup that nobody should ever have had to drink. But what is bitter is the incomprehension of [my] *co-citizens.* —JAMES BALDWIN

THE IMAGES IN this chapter, from an exhibition titled *Sights Unseen* (Flood Gallery, Asheville, NC, February 2014), have lived in my mind ever since I first saw them. To me, they express all that is unacknowledged between black and white people. Barely visible in a sea of darkness, the faces appear largely inaccessible, while their gaze reflects a wary knowingness.

In Zen practice, a fundamental aim is to bring into awareness what is unseen, whatever obscures a clear view of reality, especially the fundamental reality of our interconnectedness. This is what I return to in my aim to see more clearly what separates us, black and white, and what connects us. I offer this exploration as a descendant of enslavers, who has just begun to glimpse the nature and extent of white privilege.

It was obvious to me even as a child—witnessing, for example, the stark contrast in housing conditions between the racially divided parts of town—

look and see (brother) and *look and see (sister)*. © Linda Larsen 2013, monoprints 5.5 × 6 inches (courtesy of the artist)

that enormous benefit came with simply being white. Only now, after many decades, have I begun to wonder, what did I *not* see?

My adult life began with teaching art history, but I soon realized that what interested me about art was a spiritual dimension, from the sacred calligraphy of Islamic art to Rembrandt's self-portraits, with their raw revelation of internal reality. Searching for what I meant by "spiritual" led me to Zen practice, and that in turn led to my awareness of unacknowledged sorrow and shame that cried out to be healed: the wound of white Southern racism.

Growing up in the 1940s and '50s in a small Southern town where roughly half the population was African American, I was aware of the paradoxical nature of that world: racially segregated, except in the intimate realm of white homes. As was common in middle-class households, many responsibilities in our domestic life were borne by an African American woman, Mrs. Mattie Cason. She and her husband were respected members of their community, parents of three children, and pillars of their church. Of course, we knew Mattie best in her role at our house, where she cooked, cleaned, and looked after my brother and me, along with any neighborhood children who were around. The discipline she administered could be lighthearted; often, she chased us through the house, laughing and snapping a damp dish towel at our bare legs as we shrieked with delight. But she was stern when necessary, settling quarrels by holding the wrists of the adversaries and demanding that they face each other, let go of their anger, apologize, and shake hands. To me, she embodied everything good—laughter, ease, warmth, compassion, and moral clarity. I loved her because of the qualities I saw in her and because I felt loved by her.

Once I was grown, there was no acknowledgement of the childhood bond I felt with Mattie, no word for it. This has left a hole in my life, along with confusion and fear. In that profoundly unequal relationship, did the inequality mean that what I experienced was less than true love, that the intimacy was false?

Mattie Cason and her family were much on my mind when I discovered Coming to the Table and the genealogy site OurBlackAncestry.com. The site provides data for African Americans searching for family history, including information from descendants of enslavers. When I entered information on the site about people who were enslaved by my family, I also added, impulsively, information about the Casons.

Many months later, I received an unsigned email saying only, "Looking for family." The Casons and I share no genealogical link, which is what people search for on that site. But I was touched: *Looking for family*. Yes, me too, sort of. So I responded to the email, asking where the family lived. After more months, I received a cryptic email from someone with the surname Cason, including a phone number with the area code of the county where I grew up. A call, however, elicited no results; the Cason family I knew was unknown to the person who had emailed me.

By then, I no longer expected the sort of emotional connection I'd envisioned. What was I really looking for? I began to suspect that a sort of nostalgia was at work, the longing to return to the safety, closeness, and all-around goodness I associated with Mattie Cason. A very incomplete picture, even— painful to admit—a stereotype. What was I missing?

An answer to this question came in the Just Like Family workshop led by Felicia Furman and Sharon Morgan at the 2014 CTTT national gathering. As I remember it, we began by each describing how we, as white children, experienced the relationship with the black women who provided childcare. Five or six of us in a row, white women of a certain age, offered almost identical descriptions. We were deeply attached to the women employed by our parents to care for us; more attached, in some ways, than to our biological mothers. I was astonished to hear others express the same conviction that our caregivers had been paragons of kindness, wisdom, fun, unconditional love, fortitude, and forbearance. But when we heard from black women whose mothers had been those caregivers, my eyes were opened to realities I had never considered:

- "When my mother worked all day for your family, she came home too tired to do more work, and we children were responsible for cooking and cleaning and looking after each other."
- "The strain of playing a role at your house meant my mother came home frustrated and irritable, so what we got was the dregs at the end of the day, not 'quality time.'"
- "Did you ever think when my mother spent holidays cooking for you that meant she wasn't home with us?"
- "My mother was so attached to a white child she cared for that she saved every little note and picture from him in this special box. He had no contact with her beyond childhood, but in the last weeks before she died, that box was her main treasure. I try not to be jealous."

Until I heard those stories, the ramifications of my family's relationship with the Cason family had been invisible to me. My view of our connection, I realized, was woefully incomplete—still the view of a child, unaware of her own privilege. To do her job, Mattie Cason had to know a great deal about me and my family, while I needed to know little about hers. This was the blindness of whiteness.

My second year in graduate school, I arrived late for registration and lived in a dormitory until I could find off-campus housing. There was only one place available: in the room with the only African American student. She and I were cordial, but we did not seek to truly know each other. I was focused on art history. She was older than I was, the first person of color seeking a PhD in her department. She studied hard—in fact, she was in the room studying every night. I never saw her around campus and don't recall her mentioning her social life. As a black friend of mine later commented, "She didn't have one."

At some level, I must have known it was hard being the only African American in her department at a large university. And in North Carolina in 1967, it was clear, if unspoken, that the single vacancy in the dorm existed because no white person was expected to room with a black person.

Looking back, I wondered, what did she and I talk about? What happened to her? Driven by a mixture of curiosity and remorse, I called the alumni office. Did I want to contact my former roommate? I was asked. I didn't know; I just wanted to find out whatever I could as I tried to fill another of those achingly empty holes.

I learned that she had completed her doctorate and spent her career as a professor at a historically black university in her hometown. She belonged to a Catholic church. She died in 2001, and a memorial scholarship for black students was established in her name. I wanted to call her university or her church—but to say what? To find out now what I neglected to find out about her fifty years ago? To repent for blithely going about my white life, not unaware of her situation but not daring to face it because of what that would reveal about me and my world?

In this instance, the personal loss I felt, so disproportionate to our brief acquaintance, was a clue that the "holes" in my life were about more than individuals. All those ways in which I've missed truly knowing black people coalesce into something larger: the loss of our whole human family that results when part of it remains unseen, unknown, unconsidered, unvalued. The invisibility of blackness.

Like others, no doubt, I naively assumed that passage of the 1964 Civil Rights Act meant the end of Jim Crow. Yet in the half-century since then, my world has in some ways become more segregated.

Some years ago, a mainstream church in the town where I live invited African American members to a regional service of repentance and reconciliation, which involved a formal apology for the church's role in slavery and racism. Two thousand people came to the large auditorium. As I walked down the aisle looking for a seat, I was dismayed to see that even here, people sat in self-segregated zones of black and white. The service was long, emotional, and moving, with singing, silent reflection, and tearful embraces at the end. Then, when I expected some sort of coming together—just taking time to speak with each other, exchange names—people returned to their separate groups.

A few years later, at the opening of a peace conference in the same auditorium, I took a seat near the front, next to an African American woman. We said hello and told each other our first names. I will call her Diane. Then, we each asked where the other was from. When she told me her answer, my face must have revealed that her place of residence held significance for me.

"That's where my father's family had a rice plantation before the Civil War," I said.

She asked my last name, and when I told her, she said, "I am a Jenkins, too."

I was flooded with emotion, but the program was starting, keeping us from talking further. But after sitting together during the conference, we met for dinner. We talked about our families and the place that was home to her, where, one way or another, our roots were probably intertwined. Diane said she knew all the white Jenkinses.

After the conference, we emailed occasionally, but fearing that I might be presuming too much about our encounter, I lacked the courage to continue our conversation on a more personal level. I made myself write down what was going on with me:

My fears:

- That she will perceive me first as a white person, the oppressor, descendant of enslavers, and I will be mistrusted, hated.

- That she will wonder if I am using her as a token black friend rather than genuinely wanting her friendship.

My hopes:

- That I can go to where she lives and meet her family and learn about them.
- That I can acknowledge what I felt from the first: that we are sisters.

But what did it mean to say *sisters*? Was there some unconscious connection to the scenario in which Mattie Cason was in the role of "mother" that casts Diane as "sister"? It didn't seem so to me, but it might well to others.

In any case, it was all about me. *Looking for family.*

Two Buddhist meditative practices help dispel the illusion that the universe revolves around oneself. The first, equalizing self and other, is introduced with this verse:

Strive at first to meditate upon the sameness of yourself and others.
In joy and sorrow, all are equal; thus be guardian of all, as of yourself.[1]

The process is to envision a person before you and reflect on what you have in common, especially the human wish to be happy and not to suffer, which makes the differences between you seem much less relevant. The second practice, exchanging self and other, builds on the first, in that you envision yourself *as* the other, and from that position see how you appear in their eyes and why they feel the way they do. Rather than try to describe the effect of this practice—which is intensely personal and, like gazing into another person's eyes, quite beyond words—let me just say that it is a powerful means of discovering what has been hidden from view. Seeing the essential sameness of another, and then seeing oneself as viewed by the other, pierces the illusion of our separateness.

Last year, I received a notice about an event recognizing the civil rights leadership of Diane's father, which was to take place in two days' time, three hundred miles away. I went, full of trepidation. Would Diane wonder why I traveled that distance for a ceremonial occasion honoring somebody I didn't know? Was I presuming a connection she might not wish to share? But Diane welcomed me graciously, introducing me to her family as "the other Jenkins

I've mentioned, whose roots are here." So there it was—a shared name, and no blame.

So deeply desired it was not to be blamed.

To examine what lies beneath my desires, fears, and assumptions, I turn to the Buddhist understanding of the self. Self seems so real in its constant urge for validation—the messages, internal and external, through which it is maintained: *I am this; I am not that.* But self is a construct, a phantasm. In exactly the same way, whiteness seems real, a given, until we examine how it is maintained. In the crucial matter of being *this, not that,* difference is everything, and separation is essential.

Later, when I sent a draft of this essay to Diane and received no response, I asked my friend Chimyo, an African American Zen priest, to help me look beyond my hurt. She pointed out that I didn't know what was going on with Diane, and that even with a shared intention to heal racial wounds, Diane and I might see things differently. If Diane did not want to connect with me, Chimyo asked, can I be at ease with that? Then she said something I found so helpful: fear, shame, remorse are impediments to healing, which happens only in the present. So, it's not about this essay, and it's not about Diane; it's about me, and the work to be done is right here.

I could easily have missed the *Sights Unseen* exhibition. I'd been unwell all winter when a friend called, urging me to go to the opening, which featured a panel discussion on the race-related content of the show. The gallery was in another town, I hadn't driven for weeks, and I doubted that I had the stamina. But my friend, knowing that I was writing a novel involving African American people, said, "I think this event will be important for you."

And so it was. The artist, a white woman, spoke about the African American figures appearing in her work, and the panel, including a black writer and a professor of African American literature, addressed the tricky territory of white artists portraying black people. That very subject had been heavy on my heart, and hearing it openly discussed lifted that weight.

But it was the images themselves that spoke most compellingly to me. All that is unseen, unspoken, unknown is starkly implied in the faces of the sister and brother in *Look and See.* And by sheer artistic magic, those images also revealed to me the underside of privilege, the damage to the psyche of those who benefit from the oppression of others.

I forgot about being sick. Instead, I felt the need to heal what had been harmed, most urgently the wounds born of the illusion of race.

Although I do not claim to understand all that James Baldwin intends in this passage, it seems to point toward what keeps us unknown to one another:

> The savage paradox of the American Negro's situation . . . is not simply the relationship of oppressed to oppressor, of master to slave, nor is it motivated merely by hatred; it is also, literally and morally, a *blood* relationship, perhaps the most profound reality of the American experience, and we cannot begin to unlock it until we accept how very much it contains of the force and anguish and terror of love.[2]

Dare I talk about love? What I experience (as opposed to what I worry about) among the black friends in my life now is much the same as what I experienced as a child from Mattie: kindness, wisdom, lightheartedness, forbearance. The more I look at how we have historically been together and apart, black and white, and how we are presently together and apart, the more I am humbled and inspired by the strengths that have enabled generations of African Americans to rise above the cruelty of their circumstances with a stunning nobility of spirit.

And still within me, the pattern plays again and again: wanting connection, fearing rejection, finding acceptance—then fearing "false intimacy."

I'm looking for family too. The family of forbearance, fortitude, fun, where I can see what has been unseen, speak what has been unspoken, even perhaps fill those holes in myself and begin at last to heal that wound. I am at the start of this journey, and I do not know where it will lead. But for now, as we work together side by side in facing the history of our connectedness, I can say that this work opens my heart. To mention love feels scary. But in a grown-up way that acknowledges complexity and paradox, it seems real.

NOTES

1. Shantideva, *The Way of the Bodhisattva*, rev. ed. (Shambhala: Padmakara Translation Group, 2006).
2. James Baldwin, *Notes of a Native Son* (Boston: Beacon Press, 1955).

PART IV TAKING ACTION

19 ❧ DIGGING UP THE WOODPILE

SHARON LESLIE MORGAN

AM ON a mission to find the names of my ancestors and reconstruct the stories of their lives so I can honor them. As I proceed, I hear my father's stern voice when he told me, "I'm not going to talk about that, because you want to go back to Africa and we're not African!" I remember my Uncle Louie explaining that history is "HIS-story"—a tale written by the victor—and my Uncle Irving calling what I do "digging up dead people." And I think about how my mother seemed to find relief in my relentless questions about our family history during the last two years of her life—finally revealing secrets that were disconcerting at best.

With reflections like these echoing in my head, I concluded early on in my mission that "No man is fit to be alive until he has something for which he would die." That is a quote from Rev. Vernon Johns, who preceded Rev. Dr. Martin Luther King, Jr. as the pastor at Dexter Avenue Baptist Church in Montgomery, Alabama. The thing for which I would be willing to die is the dignity of black people. I embrace my commitment through genealogy, an avocation that has obsessed me for most of my adult life.

Mine was a family like countless others of my generation—one with roots in the Deep South. My great-grandparents were enslaved. My grandfathers were renegades from Mississippi and Alabama. My father was born in Montgomery. My stepfather was an immigrant from McComb. My mixed-race mother was a first-generation Chicagoan.

Like six million others during the Great Migration, my family fled the terrors of the South to the "promised land" of the North, entertaining aspirations for a life that made real the principles of freedom, equality, and brotherhood as articulated in the American Bill of Rights.

Alex Haley's *Roots*, which aired on television in 1977, was a major turning point for me. As a twenty-five-year-old mother with a seven-year-old son, I was one of more than 100 million people who tuned their TV sets to ABC to watch one of the first, and still one of the few, programs to truthfully recount the real-life saga of an African American longing for his roots in Africa. Haley was the first black person who successfully traced his ancestry backward from the tobacco fields of Virginia, through the Middle Passage, to a West African village in the Gambia. His was a story that embodied extreme examples of horror and hope, along with an emotionally wrenching roller coaster of events that tied those reactions together.

My heart raced with fear as teenaged Mandinka warrior Kunta Kinte was chased through the bush by slave catchers. It trilled as he raised his "new born African" baby girl up to the skies of Virginia to "behold the only thing that is greater than yourself." I cried uncontrollably when his master forced him to accept "Toby" as his name and cut off his foot to stop him from running, and I cried again when his wife Bell wailed in anguish as their precious daughter Kizzy was sold away.

Roots was the story of *my* ancestors and the progeny of more than 500,000 people who were kidnapped from Africa and enslaved in the land of my birth. It helped make sense of the debacle of history that haunts me and the 40 million descendants of that historical trauma today. "A nigger in the woodpile" was the nineteenth-century version of "a skeleton in the closet." After viewing *Roots*, I embarked seriously on a mission to dig up the woodpile of American history and its effects upon my ancestors and, therefore, upon me.

My "Kunta Kinte" is my paternal great-grandfather Tom Leslie, born in 1845. He wasn't born in Africa, but he *was* born into slavery, as was his mother

Harriet. They endured servitude in "black belt" Lowndes County, Alabama. I have a document that places them firmly within the maws of moral turpitude when they were sold. Harriet's going price was $400. Tom was valued at $1,000. My father described Tom as a diminutive man in stature, and I have a photo that proves it. He generally wore black clothing and carried a shotgun, which he was not afraid to use. He claimed to be "Portuguese and Indian." Tom died in Alabama in 1938 at the age of ninety-three.

His wife Rhoda outlived him by many years. She passed away in Chicago at age hundred and four when I was three. I had no awareness of our relationship or its meaning until I was an adult and my father told me her story. He said she was thrown against a wall as a baby by the wife of her owner, who was her father. She did not die. She and her mother were sold away. A Leslie family member who knew Rhoda well described her as six feet tall and surely a Choctaw Indian. She attributed her good health at an advanced age to smoking one cigar, drinking one shot of brandy, and taking one aspirin each day. Her grandson Lonnie was the one dispatched to retrieve the items, and it was he who shared the memory.

The only reference I ever found for Tom's mother was the notation "Harriet Morass" on his Alabama death certificate. There were no dates or details, which leaves Harriet lost in a netherworld. The best I can determine (based on her surname) is that Harriet was likely enslaved by Dr. John Marrast, one of the largest slaveholders in Lowndes. I have no idea where the Leslie surname comes from, although DNA testing says Tom's sire was a Scotsman. I succeeded in finding a living descendant of the only white Leslie I found in Lowndes during the relevant time—James E. Leslie. He was a blacksmith who likely serviced local plantations, including the one owned by Dr. Marrast. Although he was in the right place at the right time with the right occupation and surname and he could easily have been Tom's father, his descendant's DNA did not match.

On my maternal side, there is Bettie Warfe, born in 1839. She was transported at the tender age of nine from Virginia to Mississippi where, over a thirty-eight-year period, she bore seventeen children with Robert Lewis Gavin—the nephew of her master. Not only was her personhood profoundly violated as a human being enmeshed in a system that denied her humanity, but her body was repeatedly violated in the act of producing children with a man she did not choose. In explaining the children that ensued from their relationship, she said in a court testimony, "I couldn't help it."

Tom and Rhoda Leslie were enslaved in Lowndes County, Alabama.
Rhoda was living when Morgan was a small child.

When Robert died in 1896, his relatives booted Bettie off their land when a court of law determined that Robert had been "a lifelong bachelor with no heirs." She was soon after indicted for "unlawful cohabitation" with the dead father of her children and convicted of running a "bawdy house" that sold the favors of her two youngest daughters.

In 1901, Bettie and five of her children applied before the Dawes Commission in Meridian, Mississippi for recognition as Mississippi Choctaw Indians. The transcripts of their testimonies were a goldmine of information. Bettie revealed that her father was a "Yankee" and that she was "raised up by a white lady and sold over here from Virginia." She identified her mother as Alsey Hughes and her grandmother as Elizabeth Owen, but said she had no idea where they were or what became of them.

Over the years, I tracked all of Bettie's children and found so many sad stories in their lives and outcomes that it rends my heart. Her daughter Ella (my great-grandmother) was raped by a white man in Cliftonville and bore a child—James Moses—who ended up living with my family in Chicago. Her son Owen moved from Mississippi to Oklahoma, where his family was terrorized by "night riders." They raped his wife and daughter in front of him and his sons. In 1912, he blew his brains out with a shotgun in Iowa. A newspaper reported "Receipt of a notice from the overseer of the poor to leave the county less he become a charge upon the county is given as the cause of his act." Daughter Bettie Pauline's eight children with a white man dispersed into the white community after moving to St. Louis, Missouri. Daughter Essie Mae had three children with a white man (her cousin) and died in 1911. Her children were raised in Chicago by her sister Pattie Pearl, who never had children of her own. Son William Henry's children passed for white and lived in Chicago where we knew one of his sons, a very angry man who did not surrender his identity as a person of color.

As I consider these personal family stories, I am forced to think *deeply* about the *millions* of foremothers and fathers who were subjugated in so many ways. Extant records prior to 1865 indicate that none of my great-grandparents had fathers, sisters, brothers, or children. I cannot believe that is true. Where are my lost family members? What am I to think about people who abandoned every vestige of morality and used religious belief to justify their behavior? Are they skeletons in the closet? Demons in the attic? Or are they to be considered family, with the loving intentions that term implies?

Bettie Warfe/Gavin was taken from her mother at the age of nine and transported from Virginia to Mississippi, where, over a period of thirty-eight years, she bore seventeen children with the nephew of her master.

After a lifetime of researching, I still have few definitive answers; merely a handful of stories that give unequivocal credence to my disgust over the malfeasance of an historic tableau that hangs on a chain of racial acrimony. Every detail takes me beyond the satisfaction of idle curiosity into a realm of sadness and horror. Defying my desire for scientific objectivity, my mind cannot fathom a system so horrific it depopulated the entire continent of Africa and circumscribed its self-development for centuries to come. African captives loaded on slave ships were reduced to the status of animals, even as their labor fueled America's heralded Manifest Destiny and the economic vitality of the entire western world. I remain unable to come to grips with the complicity of an entire community who sacrificed human compassion to the lure of personal wealth.

I now know the names of more than two dozen people in my ancestral family who were enslaved. I also know the names and stories of their descendants, at least one of whom was lynched in the wave of violence that swept post-reconstruction America under the reign of the Ku Klux Klan. Both grandfathers who migrated to Chicago experienced the Red Summer of 1919 when violence erupted across the nation in response to growing African American communities in the North. Multiple instances of miscegenation include the violation of the enslaved Bettie Warfe; my paternal grandfather's marriage to an Italian woman in 1922; and my maternal grandparents' interracial marriage in 1926. In the 1950s, my mother was fired from a job because the "white" woman they hired turned out, in fact, to be black. My uncle's dream of becoming a pharmacist was shut down because there was already a black pharmacist and dispensation could only be allowed for one. My white grandmother was disowned by her family when one of her children was born with brown skin. My parents were barred from buying property in Chicago because of "redlining."

Today, four hundred years after the "peculiar institution" of race-based slavery took hold in the American colonies, its residual effects continue to hold our nation in thrall. The pervasive issue of race—rooted in slavery—casts an ever-present pall. I cringe when people say, "Slavery ended so long ago; just get over it," because I am a living witness to its evidence. Slavery is not merely a vague memory, but something that touched my life in intimate ways. The scientific study of epigenetics tells me that slavery is a trauma encoded in my genes.

The cognitive dissonance that allowed America's founding fathers (most of whom were slaveholders) to envision and create a society that promised life, liberty, and the pursuit of happiness for all left us with a legacy that is anything but that. It is this paradox that must be addressed if we are ever to move forward to a truly egalitarian society that guarantees and protects the rights of *all*, regardless of race, creed, color, or sexual orientation.

Genealogy led me to Coming to the Table, a group that helps people reconcile the legacy of slavery by acknowledging the fact that slavery was a heinous crime against humanity and that it is at the root of where we are today. I was especially attracted to the thoughts of one of the founders, who said his goal was to convene "a big family reunion" where "... the sons of former slaves and the sons of former slaveowners will be able to sit together at the table of brotherhood."

That echo of the words of Rev. Dr. Martin Luther King, Jr., spoken in 1963, encapsulates the dream of Will Hairston, a contemporary scion of a family that enslaved more than ten thousand people over a two-hundred-year period on forty-two plantations in three states. I met Will when I attended a Coming to the Table event at Eastern Mennonite University in Harrisonburg, Virginia in 2008. What I experienced was life-changing. It led to encounters with Susan Hutchinson and Virginia Anderson, both descendants of Thomas Jefferson, the writer of America's Declaration of Independence; Shay Banks Young, a descendant of Sally Hemings, Jefferson's enslaved "concubine;" and Thomas Norman DeWolf, a descendant of the largest slave-trading family in American history, whose ancestors kidnapped and transported more than ten thousand people from Africa to plantations in Cuba and what is now the United States.

It is counterintuitive to think that being able to sit down with descendants of people who committed such atrocious acts against one's ancestors would be in any way productive. But, the reverse proved to be true. By confronting the past in consort with today's living witnesses, I have been able to come to terms with my anger and find a personal solution for how I might contribute to healing the antipathy of race in America.

Dr. Joy DeGruy's groundbreaking book *Post Traumatic Slave Syndrome: America's Legacy of Enduring Injury and Healing* "encourages African Americans to view their attitudes, assumptions, and behaviors through the lens of history and so gain a greater understanding of the impact centuries of slavery and oppression has had on African Americans. With this understanding we can explore the role our history has played in the evolution of our thoughts, feelings, and behaviors, both negative and positive. This exploration will help lay the foundation necessary to insure our well-being and the sustained health of future generations."[1]

The Iroquois Indians have a concept of seven-generation stewardship. It urges the current generation of humans to live and work for the benefit of seven generations (one hundred forty years) into the future. Note that the Iroquois Indian Confederacy provided the model for the U.S. constitution. My personal belief echoes their wisdom, anchored in a hope that my work will help fuel a change of paradigm in contemporary American society. My healing exercise is best embodied in the Our Black Ancestry website and Facebook group I created in 2007. Through these media, I share my knowledge of history, research resources, and techniques with a community of family historians, which is now 35,000 strong and growing.

I vividly recall Rev. King's oration at the March on Washington for Jobs and Freedom on the one hundredth anniversary of President Abraham Lincoln's Emancipation Proclamation. When he called for civil and economic rights for African Americans as well as an end to racism by saying, "I have a dream that my four little children will one day live in a nation where they will not be judged by the color of their skin, but by the content of their character," it reverberated over time into the present day. More than half a century later, King's dream remains an elusive goal yet to be fulfilled.

Two years after my first experience with Coming to the Table, Tom DeWolf and I embarked upon an experiment to live, in real time, a model for healing historical harms. Our endeavor was based on work promulgated by the STAR (Strategies for Trauma Awareness and Resilience) program at Eastern Mennonite University and refined by Coming to the Table. We ended up coauthoring *Gather at the Table: The Healing Journey of a Daughter of Slavery and a Son of the Slave Trade.*[2] A reviewer described our book as "a revelatory testament to the possibilities that open up when people commit to truth, justice and reconciliation."

It is by digging into the woodpile that we will become empowered to cast off the shackles of the legacy of slavery, the racism it engendered, and the animosity that continues to infect even our best intentions. We must dig into the woodpile to find what is suspicious or wrong and go about the work of setting things *right*!

NOTES

1. Joy DeGruy, *Post Traumatic Slave Syndrome: America's Legacy of Enduring Injury and Healing* (Oregon: Uptone Press, 2005).

2. Thomas Norman DeWolf and Sharon Leslie Morgan, *Gather at the Table: The Healing Journey of a Daughter of Slavery and a Son of the Slave Trade* (Boston: Beacon Press, 2012).

20 ❧ ON BEING INVOLVED

STEPHANIE HARP

*I*N THE AIR *over Little Rock, Arkansas. May 1998. Out the window is air travel's familiar cloud floor under an endless blue sky, with glimpses through to the ground. From so far up, nothing is recognizable. Deep breath. Deeper breath. I tell myself, "Don't get off the plane. Stay away."*

My last time in Little Rock was for my grandmother's funeral. My parents and I flew down from Virginia for a couple of days filled with family and friends offering too much food, fussing over the arrangements, debating how the funeral home had arranged her hair. A journey of necessity. Unlike now. This trip is by choice, to confront my family's deep, deep roots.

The plane's engine downshifts and I hear the doors retract beneath the landing gear. I can see that we're breaking through the clouds. Somehow I will need to be both open and thick-skinned to what I know and what I'll find. I'd rather stay in my seat for several hundred more miles, as though distance would make me more prepared. But I have to confront this past, have to do it here, and have to do it myself. No one else has my perspective: involved and removed, scared and exhilarated.

And the plane is descending into all of it.

In 1993, I lost my other grandmother, the one who'd been an anchor of my young life. Lacking siblings, I'd depended on the constancy of her presence as my parents moved me to ten addresses in four states from the time I was born until I entered high school. Born and raised in Little Rock, she had moved to live with or near us since I was two. A confidante and advisor, she taught me to love reading, writing, cooking, and friends.

When she died, I inherited her photographs and books, and several binders filled with her years of scribblings—diaries, mostly, seeds of the family stories she and others had told me throughout my childhood. Things she never could publish or even really write about, she'd often said, until everyone in them had died.

The day I flipped those pages, I was sitting in my cobbled-together attic office in a rented house in Maine. It was snowing and fifteen degrees as I read about chasing June bugs with her childhood friends in the alley behind their houses.

Learning to swing herself in an arc, with her leg hooked over the "acting bar" on a backyard swing set.

Playing Crack-the-Whip and breaking her collarbone.

Hiding in the house one night when she was eleven because, she wrote, the deputy sheriffs caught a black man who had killed a little white girl and hidden her body in a Presbyterian church.

Deputy sheriffs. I'd heard from everyone that "Pa was a deputy sheriff." He was my grandmother's father who died a few months before I was born. He'd carried a pearl-handled pistol, still rumored to be somewhere in the family. As a young man, he'd been dashing and daring. He and his wife would have cut quite the figures at speakeasies and at the dance parties they held in their tiny, shotgun house, when they pushed aside furniture to dance to jitterbug music on a wind-up Victrola. Everyone always sounded proud when they said he was a deputy sheriff.

He'd told his wife and daughters to stay inside the house that night and to keep the lights off because black men were rumored to be gathering all over town, ready to hunt down white females.

". . . they caught the man and 'lynched' him," my grandmother wrote. "Then brought him into town at Ninth and Broadway and burned the body."

I knew this story too: "The time they lynched a n——on Ninth Street." Always that exact phrase. As a child, the language had been so familiar that I hadn't questioned it.

"My Mother was so frightened because Daddy had been involved in this terrible happening and she was afraid they would try to get my sister and me."

What? Involved?

In that instant, I realized for the first time that "Pa was a deputy sheriff" and "The time they lynched a n———on Ninth Street" weren't separate stories at all. And that in all the times I'd heard these phrases, for years and years and from multiple family members, no one had ever told me the two were connected.

I picked up the phone. "How was Pa involved?" I asked family, in call after long-distance call. "What does that mean? What did he do?"

"He must have been there," I heard from three different relatives. "He was a deputy sheriff, you know."

That was my point. "Why didn't anyone tell me his connection to the lynching?" I demanded.

"You knew," they said. "You just forgot."

No.

I did not know. The language and the stories had been familiar for all those years, but I did not "just forget" that my great-grandfather may have committed an act of racist homicide. That's when I knew I'd hit a stone wall. They couldn't—or, more likely, wouldn't—talk about what he had or hadn't done, what he had or hadn't thought about the incident, or what anyone else had thought about it, either then or since.

"That's all there is to tell," they claimed.

Which told me plenty.

By 1993, I had already left the South of my own accord, had already moved as far into "Yankeeland" as I could, seeking escape from the modern-day legacies of the Confederacy.

If, as my family claimed, they truly didn't know—and didn't seem to care—whether or not we descended directly from a lyncher, either they were even more racist than I already thought, or they were afraid of what they'd find out. Neither scenario engendered sympathy from me. I was angry remembering how they'd insisted that, as a child, I be honest and polite and honor the commandments I heard in church every Sunday. "Do unto others as you would have others do unto you." "Thou shalt not kill."

Do as I say, not as I do.

That one vague word "involved" propelled me into research. From the psychologically safe distance of northern New England, I looked with widely opened eyes at the usual Southern litany of storytelling, food, friendliness, and faith that had filled my vagabond childhood but were now outweighed by what hid under that purposefully naïve veneer. I dove in with full force and, in 1998, enrolled in a master's program—"history as therapy," as I once described it to a friend—in an attempt to understand the legacy I carried from my white Southern family. Then I flew to Little Rock to research the lynching of a man named John Carter.

In April 1927, the Great Mississippi Valley Flood had roared down the Arkansas River and into Little Rock. In its panicked midst, an eleven-year-old white girl—the same age as my grandmother—disappeared during a rainstorm.[1] When the African American janitor of a prominent white church found her three weeks later in the belfry, bludgeoned to death, his teenage son was quickly arrested and indicted for rape and murder, based on circumstantial evidence and a questionable confession. The mayor appealed for calm, but that night, and for the next two, frenzied mobs gathered at the local jail and the state penitentiary, and drove convoys to nearby towns in search of both father and son, whom the police chief had sent away for their safety. The mayor assured the crowd that the teen would receive a death sentence when he was brought back and tried.

Three nights later, the city had quieted. The mayor left town and directed the police chief to do the same. But the next morning, May 4, word spread that a white woman and her teenage daughter had been confronted by an African American man on the outskirts of town. Confusion about whether he was helping or attacking them didn't matter to the police, sheriffs, deputies, and as many as fifteen hundred citizens who beat the woods for hours in search of him.

My grandmother's sister confirmed that Pa was among the searchers: "That's all I know," she told me, "is that they came and got him to go with them."

Late in the day, searchers found a man hiding in a tree, whom newspapers would later label as John Carter. The teenage daughter was brought to identify him. When she said he was the one, the mob hung him from a telephone pole, riddled him with bullets, and dragged his body into town in a procession of cars that stretched for twenty-six blocks.

"They were just all together dragging him down Ninth Street, all the ones that they called in," including Pa, my great-aunt told me. And again, she added, "That's all I know about it."

The mob stopped at the corner of Broadway and West Ninth Street, in the heart of Little Rock's thriving black business district, and rioted for three hours. They burned John Carter's body on a bonfire made of doors and furniture ripped from nearby buildings. With law enforcement hamstrung by the absence of the mayor and police chief, the governor called the National Guard, which dispersed the crowd.

Despite immediate public claims that local peace officers were negligent at best and complicit at worst, half a grand jury refused to issue indictments, others resigned in protest, and the matter of officers' involvement in John Carter's lynching was completely dropped.

Three weeks later, in a spectacle of a trial that featured hastily appointed attorneys and conflicting confessions, the janitor's son was convicted of murdering the little girl. The next month he died in the electric chair on his seventeenth birthday.[2]

Though commonly known in Little Rock and referenced in both scholarly and popular books and articles, the mob murder of John Carter rarely is discussed in public venues. The most in-depth academic treatment, to date, is my own chapter in a recent collection about lynchings in Arkansas.[3]

On my 1998 trip to Little Rock (and on a return trip two years later), I talked with more family members and long-time family friends. I tried to ask questions and react to answers as neutrally as possible. The blatant, vicious bigotry that erupted from some of them stopped my breath. After spouting stereotypes about crime, education, music, and families, one eighty-six-year-old white man actually told me, "Some of the best friends that I ever had were blacks." When he and his wife complained about black "demands," I asked if they thought anything within their lifetimes (both were born between 1910 and 1920) might have made black people feel like white people were holding them back.

"No," he said. And she agreed, "No, I really don't think so."

My grandmother's written memories had included this line: "In this Southern town there was lots of hatred toward the 'Colored' folks. I never could understand what it was all about." Her cousin told me, "If you got up to let [a black person] sit down on the bus, [white] people sneered at you, you know. But you did it anyway, if you wanted to. We've come a long way, but we're not in very good shape."

The folks I talked with in 1998 and 2000 didn't use the same language that I'd heard in the 1960s, '70s, and '80s when I was told the lynching story. But neither did I hear—from anyone—specific condemnation of the lynching or of Pa's role in it. He had not bravely stood up to a murderous mob, but neither had he taken a lead role in the violence. No one except me seemed curious about exactly what he'd done, nor did they seem to care.

I left Little Rock better informed but no less conflicted, and no closer to resolution than when I'd landed. I'd wanted them to condemn what had happened and condemn how they'd described it to me, wanted them to tell me they'd changed in the seventy intervening years since 1927. Instead, I flew home unable, still, to reconcile the family of my childhood with the rampant racism I now recognized.

Both the ambiguity of Pa's role in Carter's lynching and my family's blasé attitudes fueled my work. The master's degree afforded me greater knowledge of Southern history but not the grace to pardon my family for having neither heroes nor shame. "History as therapy" indeed.

For the next decade, my life was consumed by my young children. When I picked up my research again in 2012 and contacted the University of Arkansas at Little Rock's history department, they'd just heard from an out-of-state filmmaker who believed the murdered John Carter may have been his great-grandfather. I was stunned. I'd never come across a single mention of a wife or children. Like me, the filmmaker had no proof. But he wanted to go to Little Rock to see what he could find, and he wanted me to meet him there for an interview.

Together, we planned a public presentation at the Mosaic Templars Cultural Center, funded by the Arkansas Humanities Council. We found relatives of the executed teenage boy and the murdered little girl, who agreed to join us on stage. The only African American cultural center in the state, the building at the corner of Broadway and West Ninth Street is a replica of the original Mosaic Templars of America National Grand Temple, which stood there from 1913 until it was destroyed by fire in 2005.[4] An especially apt setting for our program, the original building had witnessed the hours-long riot that followed John Carter's lynching.

On a Friday night in February 2013, we watched as the auditorium filled. I introduced some historical context, the filmmaker showed a clip of his documentary-in-progress, and we all told our families' pieces of the complicated story.[5]

A niece of the teenager who'd been executed for murdering the little girl told us about her mother who, after her brother was lost to a racist justice system and her father vanished when the police chief sent him out of town, became an activist during the 1957 desegregation fight at Little Rock Central High School. A decade later, at an integrated Central High, the niece's sister became close friends with a white boy who later became a criminal defense attorney—he was the nephew of the murdered little girl. But they never knew about their shared connection to the 1927 events until that night in the auditorium. The sister was in the audience while the little girl's nephew sat on the stage and talked about the unjust legal system, especially in 1920s Arkansas. About the teen who was executed, he said, "Now, it wasn't as brutal, but he was lynched" too, and the nieces agreed.

For years, whenever John Carter's children, grandchildren, and great-grandchildren had asked his wife about him, she'd said, "He went to work and he never came home. So we don't know what happened." The man in the 1927 news photos labeled "John Carter" clearly was not the same person as the man in the picture his wife always kept on display. The family's John Carter had disappeared at around the same time, and the news said John Carter had been the victim. If he had been murdered on that county road, had the newspapers published a photo of someone else? Or was his name used to misidentify a different man? If so, why? And by whom? There were other John Carters in the area at the time. Did the mob kill one of them and, if so, what happened to the filmmaker's relative? The family had many questions.

We all did. Had the teenage boy really murdered the little girl, or had he been set up? Had the man on the road on the outskirts of town been helping or hurting the woman and her daughter? Had law enforcement seized that particular man or a different one? Had peace officers tried to stop the mob from killing him, or had they helped?

After our presentation, two history professors led a discussion, and we heard an outpouring of remembered pain and fear. One woman had been proud of her new high school diploma in 1979, but her mother was afraid the accomplishment would cause whites to take her away. Members of Bethel A.M.E. Church, a prominent congregation located on another Ninth and Broadway corner from 1866 to 1970, remembered a picture of the lynching that hung on a church wall. Growing up, one said, kids hadn't paid much attention to it, but its presence had seeped into their consciousness. Both panel and audience members described the lynching and riot with some details that were accurate and some that were not; my family wasn't the only one who inaccurately thought the lynched man was the accused killer of the little girl. In 1927, mob members knew John Carter hadn't killed her, but blatantly claimed him as their scapegoat.

Long after the scheduled close of the evening, our audience kept talking. We adjourned, and they stayed to talk more. The Mosaic Templars staff said the evening was transformative and that Little Rock had been hungry for this opportunity.

Before that first flight to Little Rock in 1998, I had packed my schedule with visits to family, friends, and research sites, carefully slotted into mornings, lunches, afternoons, and suppers. On a stack of maps, I'd traced my way to every significant place I could find in the family stories and newspaper accounts. On my second trip in 2000, and again in 2013, I did the same.

But schedules and maps couldn't have led me to this: The morning after our Mosaic Templars presentation, the filmmaker and I interviewed the two nieces of the executed teen. One said, "When I left there last night, it was like a wash. I just absolutely felt lighter. Today, instead of it being a different day, it's like a whole new world for me." Because her mother's brother was no longer lost in the public confusion about who had been lynched and why, she said, "I think we are all more at peace now than what we were." Talking had made the difference. "I am to the point that I think, in situations like this, everybody needs a panel," she said. "Get everybody a representative, and we just go sit and talk, because I've always felt that talking cures things. So it was good."

I cried when she said this, glad I'd gotten off the plane all those years ago. Grateful, even, that my family's conflicted past indirectly allowed me to witness this moment. I still hadn't forgiven my family. But she and her sister, at least, had found some peace for theirs. And that was a sort of therapy all its own.

NOTES

1. The following recounting of events is drawn from articles published in April to June of 1927 in the *Arkansas Democrat, Arkansas Gazette,* and the *Chicago Defender,* and from Marcet Haldeman-Julius, *The Story of a Lynching: An Exploration of Southern Psychology,* Little Blue Book 1260, ed. E. Haldeman-Julius (Girard, KS: Haldeman-Julius Publications, 1927), which first appeared as "The Story of a Lynching: An Exploration of Southern Psychology," *Haldeman-Julius Monthly* 6.3 (August 1927). The girl's age varied in different articles as eleven, twelve, or thirteen.

2. Newspaper reports (cited above) variously listed his age as sixteen, seventeen, and eighteen. According to his family, he was seventeen.

3. Some of the popular and scholarly references include Daisy Bates, *The Long Shadow of Little Rock* (Fayetteville, AR: University of Arkansas Press, 1987), 62; James Reed Eison, "Dead, But She Was In a Good Place, a Church," *Pulaski County Historical Review* 30 (Summer 1982), 30–42; Brian Greer, "Little Rock's Last Lynching was in 1927, but the Terrible Memories Linger," *Arkansas Times*, August 4, 2000; Stephanie Harp, "Stories of a Lynching: Accounts of John Carter, 1927," in *Bullets and Fire: Lynching and Authority in Arkansas, 1840–1950*, ed. Guy Lancaster (Fayetteville, AR: University of Arkansas Press, 2018), 195–221; Jay Jennings, *Carry the Rock: Race, Football, and the Soul of an American City* (New York: Rodale, 2010), 33–50, 126; Guy Lancaster, "Before John Carter: Lynching and Mob Violence in Pulaski County, 1882–1906," in *Bullets and Fire: Lynching and Authority in Arkansas, 1840–1950*, ed. Guy Lancaster (Fayetteville, AR: University of Arkansas Press, 2018), 167–193; Carlotta Walls LaNier with Lisa Frazier Page, *A Mighty Long Way: My Journey to Justice at Little Rock Central High School* (New York: One World Trade Paperbacks/Ballantine Books, 2010), 39; Todd E. Lewis, "Mob Justice in the 'American Congo': 'Judge Lynch' in Arkansas During the Decade After World War I," *Arkansas Historical Quarterly* 52, no. 2 (Summer 1993): 156–184; Edith McClinton, *Scars From A Lynching*, rev. ed., eds. Stacey James McAdoo and Christie Ellison-Thompson (n.p., 2000); Clifford E. Minton, *America's Black Trap*, adv. ed. (Gary, IN: Alpha Book Co., 2001), 91–93.

4. "About the Museum," Mosaic Templars Cultural Center, April 15, 2016, *http://www.mosaictemplarscenter.com/About/about-the-museum*.

5. "Project 1927," Mosaic Templars Cultural Center, February 15, 2013.

21 ⤳ CHANGING THE NARRATIVE

JOSEPH McGILL, JR.

As a self-proclaimed historian and preservationist who lives and works in Charleston, South Carolina, I am excited by old buildings—especially those classified as antebellum vintage. Through the buildings we preserve, we can interpret our history.

As an African American born and raised in South Carolina, I was short-changed by the history taught in our education system. This system touted a revisionist history, a history I could not take pride in. A history that painted enslavers as victims whose way of life was stolen from them by Northern aggressors during the Civil War. A history where Native Americans were the villains and enslaved people not only deserved but were also happy with their lot in life. A history with so much left untold.

It was not until the early 1990s, in my quest to become a Civil War reenactor, that I found out that the history taught to me was distorted, biased, and flat-out junk.

I was working at Fort Sumter at the time and, on a clear day, I could see Morris Island from my job site. Soon after, I discovered that the island was an important Civil War battle site. The 54th Massachusetts Volunteer Infantry, made up of black soldiers, both enslaved and free, fought valiantly there, suffering many casualties. They were the first African American regiment recruited in the North and the first black unit to lead a major attack. The 54th proved that when given the opportunity, black men would fight, and they were every bit as proud and courageous as white men. Because of their valor, President Lincoln committed to widely recruiting black soldiers. And in 1989, their story was depicted on the big screen in the movie *Glory*.

The 54th's story had been hidden for a century, and it could have remained that way indefinitely if not for the interest generated by the movie. The movie inspired me to do research on the 54th, and after reading the accounts of formerly enslaved people who had become Civil War soldiers, I discovered a history quite different than the one I'd previously known. It was a history that taught me that I was among a proud and resilient people. Now, in every way possible, and at every opportunity, I honor these people, even using a capital *A* whenever I write the word *Ancestor*.

This is what brought me into the hobby of being a Civil War reenactor. Fifty years ago, there was not a lot of scholarship that presented African Americans in a positive light in that war, but that started changing, and I wanted to be a part of that change. I wanted to show that African Americans didn't just sit idly by waiting for their freedom. They were actively involved in gaining their freedom. Becoming a reenactor was about honoring their accomplishments.

As a Civil War reenactor, I camped out overnight at Morris Island and at other historic battle sites like Olustee in Florida and Franklin in Tennessee. We slept as rough as the soldiers presumably did when fighting in the war, to make the experience more realistic.

I was not as extreme as some. I didn't use horsehair toothbrushes, march for miles to the battlefields, starve myself to look like an emaciated soldier, or go shoeless as many actual Civil War soldiers had to when supplies dwindled. One time at a battle site, I pulled out a roll of toilet paper and got shunned. Sometimes we mingled with the Confederate reenactors to get into their heads a bit. Some of them told us they wished the war had a different ending. That got a little scary. Otherwise, camaraderie around the campfire was meaningful and enriching, no matter how extreme my colleagues.

To me, the most important thing was to value the accuracy of the history, to wear the uniform properly, and to represent the 200,000 black Union soldiers—along with the many women who supported them—well.

Later, I decided I wanted to apply this same concept of reenactment to learn what it was like to live on the grounds of some historical sites, especially extant slave dwellings.

That I knew of, every antebellum site open to the public was once a place where people were enslaved. But whenever I visited one, I found the stories of the enslaved blatantly missing from the narrative presented. Few, if any, of these sites included any reference to the lives of the enslaved when they opened to the public. The buildings that could interpret the stories of the enslaved Ancestors are scarce, but they are still on the landscape. They now function as garages, storage spaces, rental property, pool houses, and offices. On rare occasions, buildings are maintained and opened to the general public for visitation. One such occasion was in 2010, when nearby Magnolia Plantation was renovating their slave cabins. So I asked them if I could sleep in one.

Between the brick-hard floor and the creaking branches brushing against the cabin, I didn't get much sleep that night. Being alone in a former slave cabin was a little spooky and uncomfortable, both physically and psychologically. There were family and friends who thought the idea of sleeping in extant slave dwellings was odd—and it was odd. I wondered that night what had possessed me to do such a thing. And then I remembered, it was the Ancestors. So I continued on. And while it took four sleepovers and a lot more padding for the wood floor, others began to join me.

After that, I acquired a list from the South Carolina State Historic Preservation Office of the historic places that still had slave quarters. I then began to seek permission from the property stewards to spend the night in them. When my overnight stays began to garner public attention, I leveraged that attention to educate the public on the need to preserve, interpret, maintain, and sustain extant slave dwellings.

I started the Slave Dwelling Project, in which I began making more regular overnight visits and publishing blog posts about my sleepovers. Soon, several news outlets, including National Public Radio (NPR), were covering my work. That's how Coming to the Table found me. I received an invitation in 2012 to attend the Coming to the Table National Gathering, held in Richmond, Virginia. At the gathering, I discovered that our missions ran parallel.

While the Slave Dwelling Project focuses on buildings that once housed the enslaved, Coming to the Table's focus is on the descendants of people who both enslaved and were enslaved. The mission of both organizations, however, is to uncover history and to effect systemic and institutional changes that more accurately and equitably tell our nation's story.

A few months after the gathering, three members from Coming to the Table joined me in a sleepover at the Bush Holley House in Greenwich, Connecticut. Several more members have joined me since. Linda Davis of Baltimore, Maryland, an avid ambassador of the Slave Dwelling Project, has accomplished almost ten sleepovers, and Prinny Anderson of Durham, North Carolina, who has done thirty-plus sleepovers, is now a board member of the project. Coming to the Table is one of only two national organizations with whom the Slave Dwelling Project has officially partnered. The other is the National Park Service's Network to Freedom.

Coming to the Table has especially assisted the Slave Dwelling Project when—despite archaeological and genealogical research that establishes ties between a particular family and an extant slave dwelling—the ensuing interactions between the descendants and the property owners proves challenging. With CTTT's continuing assistance, I hope more relationships can be established between the descendants of both the enslaved and enslavers through my work with and research of extant slave dwellings.

The Slave Dwelling Project thrives because of the vast portfolio of sites it works with, many of which are still content with feeding their visitors a sugar-coated and watered-down version of history. Unfortunately, some visitors are comfortable remaining in the dark about the true history of these sites, which presents another challenge all its own.

I'm in my fifties now and mostly retired from Civil War reenacting; however, I continue to don the uniform while conducting living history programs connected to the Slave Dwelling Project. It is important to me to continue to commemorate the 200,000 African American men who served the Union during the American Civil War, especially now that Civil War reenactments are decreasing—in part, because of the problematic symbolism of the Confederate flag. When Dylan Roof snuffed out the lives of nine people in Emanuel AME Church in my hometown in 2016, the largest reenactment was canceled in the wake of the tragedy. Because Roof's rantings were peppered with the Confederate flag, places began examining their relationship with it and removing it. Nonetheless, reenactments are a great educational opportunity, and now I fear they will be lost.

In the face of this downward trend, I hope that the Slave Dwelling Project will open up further educational opportunities. I hope that, through genealogical and archival research, descendants of the enslaved can discover and establish their ties to these extant properties. Our enslaved Ancestors built these antebellum buildings. They cut down the trees to provide the frameworks, made the bricks to create the walls, and provided the labor to give the structures life. Unfortunately, that I know of, African Americans do not own any of these buildings, so we must develop creative ways to gain access to these historic structures—if not through sleepovers, then through special tours, interviews, and research—even if such access is temporary. Through our efforts, it is my ultimate hope that every extant slave dwelling in the United States will be restored, interpreted, maintained, and sustained. For through the buildings we preserve, we can embrace our history.

22 ❧ TANGLED VINES

A Bloodline Shaped by Slavery

GRANT HAYTER-MENZIES

I HAVE SPENT most of the past fifteen years writing books about the lives of extraordinary but inexplicably unsung women. Comfortable being the offstage prompter, I had never remotely dreamed of writing about myself. Then I made a series of genealogical discoveries that pushed the boundaries of my own private and not particularly unique life, delivering information that demanded to be shared.

In my maternal Southern grandmother's ancestry, almost every branch of the family tree is rife with enslavement of African American people. But I found that her colonial New England ancestors were enslavers also, both of Africans and Native Americans. In fact, their involvement in enslavement started not long after the *Mayflower* arrived, which means they were involved in greater quantities and for a longer time than any of my Southern ancestors. One ancestral line even linked me to the DeWolfs, the largest slave-trading family in American history who, ironically, were based out of Rhode Island.

While slavery in the North, and slavery in my Northern ancestry, were a shock all their own to someone who had been taught nothing about this in school, there was another, greater shock in store. I thought I had established that my New England enslaver ancestry dated back no further than Boston in the mid-seventeenth century. Then I found that one slave-owning ancestor, Margaret Locke Willoughby, was a great-granddaughter of London merchant Thomas Lok.[1] In 1554, Thomas had invested in a journey captained by his brother, John Lok, to the west coast of Africa. The next year, John and Thomas sailed back up the Thames bearing in their ship's hold not just gold, spices, and ivory from Ghana, but also five human beings (carried off "perforce," as John wrote later), the first Africans ever seen in the Tudor capital.[2] Given that seven years later, in 1562, Capt. John Hawkins of Plymouth would pioneer the transatlantic slave trade, these men from Ghana would not be the last to have such an experience. In fact, Africans would swiftly become a crucial factor in English trade and fortune, and in West Indies and New England fortunes, too. After calculating that my family's involvement in slavery began somewhere around the return date of the Loks' voyage and ended in 1862 (when my third great-grandfather—a Southerner born into an enslaving family—joined the Union Army to help end the "peculiar institution" at cost of his life), I concluded that people of my direct and collateral bloodlines had been complicit in every aspect of slavery for three hundred years.

It is sobering to suddenly become aware of the weight of the deeper histories we carry inside our genes and our hearts. In writing about the lives of others, I have always actively sought out and told these deeper stories. Now I turned the microscope on myself. But I realized, too, that mine is not merely a story of a white family's several hundred years' involvement with slavery. For such a story is not as unique as many people (particularly those who don't think history from beyond last year is relevant) may prefer to believe. Black and Native American slavery underpins and supports the substructure of what we consider white-conceived North American civilization and culture. Whether your ancestors came here in 1620 or in 2015, you either benefit from slavery's legacy or suffer from the long reach of its crimes against humanity. Slavery helped fund our universities and build our public monuments; it stocked private fortunes that greased the wheels of industry, government, and international diplomacy; and we still feel the aftereffects of the great moral battle it exacted of us from 1861 to 1865. Thus, the story of slavery is the story of North America—my story and your story, whether you know it, whether you like it, or not.

What especially moved me to share my story was that it was not really about me or my family. It was, much more significantly, about the lost autonomy and robbed identity of people coopted by slavery. As do many descendants of enslavers, I ended up with documentation that named a great many of the people my ancestors enslaved. I could start with the five Ghanaians of 1555—Binne, George, Anthonie, and their two unnamed countrymen, who later returned to Ghana to be public relations men for the English. I could then move on to seventeenth-century Indian slaves John and Job, just two among whole villages of native people whom my New England ancestors bought, sold, worked, and traded. Then there were the African people held in bondage, whose experiences spanned from colonial New England to the antebellum South just before the Civil War—from Amparo, the elderly Atlantic Creole woman whom my eighteenth-century Connecticut forebears enslaved and listed under the inventory rubric "Creatures;" to Vinia, whose body, along with her children's, were rented out by my North Carolina ancestors; to Ginette and Warren in Louisiana, who, in 1864, purchased mementos from the auction of my deceased third great-grandfather's plantation just before they themselves were sold to pay the debts that had outlived the old man.

My purpose for knowing these names and being fortunate enough to unearth many others, I realized, was so that I could write them down to be read, so I could tell as much of the story behind each name as research and educated guesses made possible, and so I could put a human face on what was a truly inhuman institution. How to do this, where to start, eluded me.

It was at this point, for another reason entirely, that I reached out to Coming to the Table for help and guidance. I had tried to make contact with a descendant of Randall, a man enslaved by my Lambright ancestors in Mississippi in the early nineteenth century. I was entering uncharted waters and, should my linked descendant take my outstretched hand, I had no real message to deliver except to apologize—and that didn't seem enough, or appropriate, for acknowledging the history we both bear. Randall's descendant had decided not to take my hand, however, and though no reason was given, or needed, I could understand why. But as the one member of my family actively seeking to reconnect with descendants of those my ancestors enslaved, I was intensely haunted by my failure. I now think part of my problem was that, until I encountered CTTT, I operated in a vacuum.

Shortly before her death, my mother—my link to slavery—was my sole companion on this road. Between the two of us, we made up a matching duo of emotion and rage over the enormities of our ancestors. But emotion cannot make plans or strategy. And in March 2012, two events changed my life.

In Norwich, Connecticut, I was able to meet with descendants of Guy Drock (circa 1730–1787),[3] an African man enslaved by my eighth great-grandfather, Benajah Bushnell—the first time in over two hundred years, according to Norwich historian Dale Plummer, that descendants of these men had come together in the town that held our shared history.[4] Afterward, I drove down Interstate 95 to Greenwich, where I spent a night in the preserved slave quarters of the Bush-Holley House as part of the Slave Dwelling Project (SDP).

Founded by Joseph McGill, SDP aims to acknowledge and preserve extant, often neglected, slave quarters wherever they are known, whether in the Deep South or, as here, in the thick of colonial Congregationalist Connecticut.

I shared the space with Joe and two other CTTT members, Dionne Ford Kurtti and the Rev. David Pettee. Joe and Dionne are descendants of enslaved people (Dionne also descends from enslavers), while Dave descends from dozens of New England enslavers, including some we share. Out of this group, I was the only person whose ancestral complicity in slavery crossed so many categories at once: slaves from the North and South; African American cousins descended from white-on-black sexual exploitation; imperialists guilty of the generational eviction and extermination of native peoples for gain; and slaveholders guilty of selling, buying, and working slaves of both African and Native American descent.

Aware that I was bunking in a sacred space, I thought I might pass the night in a quiet slumber, as in a chapel. But for the first half hour, lying in the dark on the thin but ungiving boards, I experienced what I can only describe as a full-blown panic attack. It was not because of a spirit visitation; it was because of an intense awareness of what the space's former residents had endured. For a split second, I, who have never been a slave, felt I understood what life in that space had been like for slaves. I knew the lack of any privacy from the master and mistress. I knew the sense of being controlled, of being unable to change my situation. I knew what it was like to endure heat under the eaves in the summer and cold in the winter (or spring, as was the case with us) without a murmur. I knew I had to work every day because if I stopped, repercussions could involve not a warning letter from a supervisor but degrading threats to my dignity or personal safety. Despite my three friends in the room with me, I felt extraordinarily alone and extraordinarily out of place. I kept thinking of one of the most heartfelt and articulate of the fugitive slave narratives, published by Bostonian Benjamin Drew in 1856. How could my forebears, I said to myself, echoing escaped slave John Little, "who know they are abusing others all day, lie down and sleep quietly at night . . . when they know that men feel revengeful, and might burn their property, or even kill them?"

What John Little was asking was what I ask every time I look at the names of Juba and Rose, Ginette and Warren, Judy and Satin, and others enslaved by my ancestors: how *did* my people have the conscience to sleep at night? What right did I have to sleep in this space, which was made sacred by the work and lives of slaves? I sat up and pulled the several-page list of my ancestors' slaves, folded into a thick square, out of the pocket of my shirt, which was hanging on a nearby chair. In the dark, against the rhythmic breathing of my sleeping friends, I held the folded pages close to my face and whispered, "I remember you." When I lay back down, I finally began to drift off, as if the boards had been softened under me. Yet in that light-edged darkness that is the door between waking and sleep, I sensed the presence of a woman. It was Rose Jackson, a cloth wound around her head. The elderly slave nurse of the Hart family of Old Saybrook was renowned for her loyalty, refusing to leave them when she was freed. She was laid to rest at some distance from her white family in Cypress Cemetery. I had visited her grave the day before arriving in Greenwich and had read on the weathered surface of her marble marker the following words:

In memory of Rose Jackson

Born 26 November 1778, Died 18 October 1866

A colored woman who for nearly seventy years was a trusted and faithful servant in the family of Gen. William Hart and of his descendants to the fifth generation.

Faithful Ever In All Things

Rose Jackson had remained, even into her eighties, a person treated more like a child than an adult, yet she was leaned on whenever her white family—people less adultlike than children themselves—needed comforting. Still, she was consigned to her own corner for burial, far from the house where she had heard so much laughter by children who were not her own. Author Ann Petry, born into the very small African American community of Old Saybrook in 1908 and subjected to racial discrimination throughout her childhood there, wrote of her outrage that "Sister Rose" had been buried in "the 19th century equivalent of the back of the bus, not only segregated but standing, so to speak, the wrong way round."

> Every time I have ever looked at [Rose's grave] I think about that spiritual, "On that great gittin' up mornin' I'll be there." Well, come the Day of Judgment, I am sure that Sister Rose Jackson will be there with all the other risen souls but Sister Rose Jackson, a colored woman, will be standing alone and she will be facing the swamp. The other folk will be facing the Main Street of the town.[5]

This appeared, sadly, to be the case. But unless I was mistaken, it had seemed to me, as I touched the warm stone face of the marker that looked out to the cold Atlantic, that should Rose Jackson rise with the rest of the saved on the Day of Judgment, she would turn toward her white family, arm in arm with her sister Phillis, and walk to join them in eternal bliss. I was angry, as Ann Petry would have been, that she should have to do so, but Rose, "faithful ever in all things," would likely not have had it any other way. Danish author Karen Blixen wrote that for married couples, even in what may seem to be the most absurd and dysfunctional of circumstances, only they know what holds them together; it is an area of shared intimacy, of both pain and pleasure, that is not to be trespassed on by outsiders. So, too, with Rose and the Harts. Questioning her love for her white family, even when that same family buried her far from their own plot, was the same as robbing her of what little agency she'd had in her circumscribed world.

Under the rain-pattered eaves of the Bush-Holley House, I am sure I did see Rose Jackson, sitting in the darkness, watching over us four seekers of the peace that she had found long ago. "*Ashé*," I whispered. A kind of word-prayer that means power, command, or so be it, her very presence seemed to reply, "*Ashé*" in return.

Rose had also told me what I must do. After that night, I knew I had to write about the Guy Drocks, the Rose Jacksons, the Vinias and Ginettes and Amparos. And I knew that in writing about them, I had to write about me.

Overnight, in the slave quarters of the Bush-Holley House, I went from biographer to memoirist. And over the course of the next three years, buried in inventories and wills, family histories and census records, and those turgid volumes of what a New England cousin of mine calls "exercises in ancestor worship," the heavy history I carried came tumbling out onto the written page, penned interchangeably with anger and tears and wonder. And memories I had not revisited since childhood, shared by my mother, grandmother, great-grandmother, and more distant links of memory, came alive again, along with their voices and those of the long-dead people they'd told me about, whose actions had shaped our lives for generations afterward.

I thought again of my grandmother sitting with me, looking at an inventory of some of the human beings her Louisiana ancestors had owned: Judy, Ginette, Warren, Satin, Moses. Wondering about their descendants, she asked me, "Do you think you can find them, honey?"

It had taken me years to get this far, just as it would take more years still to locate within myself the necessary courage and the appropriate voice to tell their stories, along with stories of how my family's exploitation of them helped make me who I am—a writer whose entire life has been supported by books the enslaved were not taught to read. Slave labor made possible the leisure of learning afforded to their enslavers' families, and the deliberate absence of such learning among enslaved people complicated and thwarted the pathways of their descendants down through time. Looking at the inventories of human beings that filled my research files, I knew that for many descendants of the enslaved, these often paltry and degrading records were all that remained of ancestors they might otherwise know nothing about. Which brings us back to what CTTT did for me. When I explained to them my sense of failure at being unable to reunite with Randall's descendant, and when I feared doing or saying the wrong thing when I met the descendants of Guy Drock, CTTT shared with me a simple rule of thumb: "Just tell the truth" was their collective advice. "Because the truth will set you free." That sounds deceptively easy. I would not advise anyone to leap into it without sufficient preparation.

The truth can haunt us, and far less benignly than the presence of Rose Jackson did in the slave quarters of the Bush-Holley House. But truth, and freedom, are better for the soul than the prison of a lie.

I know this because I've walked the floors of that haunted house we all have in our family history. You don't know who you'll meet behind each closed door. But the doors must be opened. One of my maps into that old house has been that greatest of truth serums, DNA testing. Thanks to 23andMe, I've reached out to, and been contacted by, descendants of the enslaved with whom my white ancestors fathered children. This, too, is rife with irony: through this history, I am related to some of the brightest lights of the civil rights movement, from Daisy Gatson Bates of the Little Rock Nine; to the Rev. Samuel Berry McKinney of Seattle, who invited his friend and colleague Rev. Martin Luther King, Jr. for his only visit to the Pacific Northwest; to writer Ta-Nehisi Coates, who wrote with devastating truth, "Americans defy democracy in a way that allows for a dim awareness that they have, from time to time, stood in defiance of their God."[6] My ancestors stood in defiance of more than God. They defied the inalienable truth that all men are created equal.

The ancestral house I carry with me is held together by the tangled vines of interwoven relationships and interdependencies—vines that embrace even as they strangle. In my forthcoming book *The North Door: Echoes of Slavery in a New England Family*, which traces my journey into this long and complex history, I invite readers to join me as I open doors on successive floors and introduce enslaved and enslavers, along with themes that I began with at the top of this essay—how integral slavery is to every feature of our modern world, how widespread the ignorance (deliberate or otherwise) of that fact, and how critical our collective responsibility to carry out Dr. Martin Luther King, Jr.'s dream—that one day the sons of slaves and the sons of slaveowners will sit together at the table of brother- and sisterhood, joining hands, facing facts, opening hearts and minds to the histories within each one of us and to the consequences we live with today. Consequences that we can change for the better if we want to—if we, too, wish to be free.

NOTES

1. Col. Joseph L. Chester, "The Descent of Margaret Locke: Third Wife of Deputy Governor Francis Willoughby," *NEHGR* 35 (1881): 63.

2. Miranda Kaufmann, *Black Tudors: The Untold Story* (London: Oneworld Publications, 2017), 183, cites primary sources for both John Lok's 1554 voyage and that of his colleague William Towerson. Towerson landed in Ghana a year later to find the people questioning him about what had happened to the men taken away by Lok, who Towerson described in his account as having been removed from their village "perforce" or against their will. See also, Sujata Iyengar, *Shades of Difference: Mythologies of Skin Color in Early Modern England* (Philadelphia: University of Pennsylvania Press, 2005).

3. For information on Guy Drock's history and that of his descendants, see Grant Hayter-Menzies, "Slavery and Freedom in a Colonial Connecticut Town," *American Ancestors* 13, no. 3 (June 2012), 26 (New England Historic Genealogical Society, Boston, MA), which draws on Donald W. L. Roddy and Daryl Y. (Hooper) Holmes, now Daryl D'Angelo, "The Drock Story," 2nd ed., August 2005, 28 pp. (privately published by Donald Roddy; no longer available on line). Find the Drock story at www.roddy.net/images/2_The_Drock_Story_2nd_Edition_Web.pdf.

4. Benjamin Drew, *The Narratives of Fugitive Slaves in Canada* (Toronto: Coles Publishing Company, 1981).

5. Elisabeth Petry, *At Home Inside: A Daughter's Tribute to Ann Petry* (Jackson: University Press of Mississippi, 2009).

6. Ta-Nehisi Coates, *Between the World and Me* (New York: Spiegel & Grau, 2015).

23 ❧ A DREAM DEFERRED ALONG HOLMAN'S CREEK

SARAH KOHRS

"WHAT HAPPENS TO a dream deferred?" I was sixteen when I first read Langston Hughes' poem—one of many that lodged inside me like a grain of sand, turning opalescent over time. His words echoed in my mind while I brushed dirt from broken bone and pottery. It was a clear July morning in 1999. Wheel tractors whirred in another part of the field, which was being leveled for rice planting. The thick Arkansas heat pressed as close as skin, mimicking the urgency of our excavation. Fellow archaeology field-school students and I were working to remove Middle Woodland Period artifacts and burials before the farmers finished their leveling. We worked up until the day they flooded the field: water inundating the final resting places of Native Americans, whose own dreams were long lost to us. Sixteen years later, like most other mothers of young children, I found myself holding many dreams deferred, including my dream of becoming an archaeologist. It was then, in 2015, that I learned about the slave cemetery.

I sat in a restored woodshop near Quicksburg—a small town with a post office, an abandoned railroad, and a smattering of boarded businesses—a poster of Christ Pantocrater proffering a blessing on the wall to my left and a fire crackling in the wood stove to my right. It was Martin Luther King, Jr. weekend, and several other members of the community were gathered here at Corhaven, a spiritual retreat farm, for the workshop "Honoring the Forgotten." My husband was caring for our three sons while I attended. The aim of the workshop was to educate participants about Sam Moore's Slave Cemetery, a rediscovered graveyard near Holman's Creek in Shenandoah County, Virginia, and to begin the good work of caring for the site and making it a place of honor, remembrance, and healing.

I listened to local high schoolers talk about an English plantation that began in 1736 and continued in the hands of various slave-owning landholders until the American Civil War's end. Local historian, Nancy Stewart, relayed that, at one time, nearly 14 percent of the county's population had been enslaved African Americans. And DeLois Warr, a member of the community, gave an account of a social injustice she experienced at a local store during the civil rights era. All the while, I felt as if Jesus was staring intensely from that poster on the wall and the floor was falling out from underneath me. The plantation had been less than five miles from where I had first read Langston Hughes. In English class, I remember lamenting over Elie Weisel's account of the Holocaust in *Night*, listening to King's "I Have a Dream" speech as it mingled with the scratch of metal on vinyl, and examining my own incredulity over the treatment of slaves in the Deep South. The Deep South, it now turned out, was less than five miles away from my hometown.

I felt jaded. In my entire time growing up in Mount Jackson and attending Stonewall Jackson High School, not a single adult had ever told me that slave-owning plantations and iron forges were prolific in the Shenandoah Valley. I had been duped into believing that the valley consisted mostly of God-fearing German and Scots-Irish settlers who scraped together their living on small farms. They would never own slaves. They would never condone such a practice. They survived because of strong community, helping one another when they needed it most. Theirs was a community of barn-raising and haying, wakes and poundings—opportunities to band together during hardship, back-straining work, and times of transition. They fought in the American Civil War to protect their farms and families. It was a place for nostalgia and true home. And yet, was this a true home for the thousands of enslaved African Americans that lived here for over a hundred years before the American Civil War? Who were they? Where did they live? Did my family own slaves?

During the workshop, we shared our experiences and understanding of slavery, we prayed, we cried, we grew passionate about remembering and honoring enslaved people whose lives were steeped in a dignity that was not given to them by others. As we walked to the cemetery, Anglican minister and owner of Corhaven, Bill Haley, and I talked about the Native American purification ritual I had experienced during my time at that archaeological field school in Parkin, Arkansas. I was remembering out loud the waft of smoke feathered over my head to purify me from the work of removing burials from the salvage site.

"Would you be willing to help lead this good work, Sarah?" Bill asked. Our feet seemed to murmur through the weathered grass as we neared the fence line to the slave cemetery, which almost whispered of time forgotten and time to come.

I didn't answer at first—not because of any hesitation to help, but because there was so much to do. This was not a lightly-entered project; the cemetery was a tangible reality of immense meaning, steeped in both the emotional and physical scarring of a people and a community. Caring for a slave cemetery begins with an acknowledgement of the past—and people are not always willing to uncover the past when it has been silently swept under the rug for so many decades.

"Yes, I will help," I said. "I will do the best I can."

A place can get inside you, like a dream deferred, and become like a home. There's a bittersweetness to a place like the Corhaven Graveyard, which holds such sorrow and yet such true beauty too. Meandering along Holman's Creek not far from where the North Fork once changed its course, the graveyard has now become as familiar to me as home. The sounds of grazing cows, donkey haws, and cricket chirps whisper the continuance of life in the pasture. The rosy-bronze heads of grasses bob groundward as a slight breeze settles and rises. At the top of the knoll, oak and walnut trees tower overhead, and the tips of the pines show signs of death in some of their browned fronds. The trees form a thick canopy near the fence line—once threaded with 1881 square-rib barbed wire, its lance points mimicking wild thorns—where farmers piled stones from the field. In the woods, the land slopes sharply toward the creek, whose gentle waters babble.

Nestled there in that setting—amid the briars and moss, thick roots and new growth, and even a grapevine that grapples skyward—are depressions, most about two meters west to east. They line the fenced boundary of what once was a four-hundred-twenty-acre Fairfax grant,[1] which changed hands from the Holemans to the Huffmans, the Beales to the Moores—families noted in county will books and federal censuses as owning slaves. On March 27, 1984—one day before my fifth birthday—two local historians took the first documentation of the site, dubbed "Sam Moore's Slave Cemetery."[2] And on May 16, 2015, representatives from myriad nonprofit organizations, attendees from our spiritual retreat, and local citizens came together to take the first steps in preserving the site: removing undergrowth and clipping away a modern wire fence that cut directly through the graveyard. That day, while the Battle of New Market reenacted a Confederate victory one town away, we gathered to reenact a victory of compassion in Quicksburg—honoring the preciousness of life and the importance of nonviolent actions in relating with one another.

Soon after, I began recording details about the site. I will always remember kneeling down to make observations about the burials. Inundated with delicate details—the curve of the miniscule shells attached to the fieldstones, their rough edges often echoing the look of a knapped arrowhead; the smell of damp moss that grew in the shadows—I suddenly felt a connection, as with family. In her research of African American burial places, Lynn Rainville mentions, "[i]n antebellum slave graveyards we see this focus on family units rather than individuals in [the] unmarked but uniform stones."[3] While I photographed and mapped features in conjunction with the depressions, in order to create an archaeological record for future preservation, I came to know those stones intimately. Most of the depressions are large enough for an adult; three are child-sized. Some depressions have headstones and footstones, while others have one or the other, and many have no stones at all. Two fieldstones are obelisk-shaped; two tombstones are broken, manufactured bases. None of the stones show clear inscriptions. In a slave cemetery, inscriptions might divulge evidence of something the 1806 Virginia legislature declared illegal: teaching a slave to read or write. And from the time of the graveyard's use to its rediscovery, several large trees had disturbed some graves by forming substantial craters when they fell.

Virginia law protects cemeteries, including Native American mounds and graveyards for enslaved people. I find this ironic, considering the state's laws did not protect entire races and tribes of people during their lifetimes. Standing in Corhaven Graveyard, time and again, I remember most the weeping. The fading sun filters through the trees, the wind barely moves, Holman's Creek whispers below the knoll, and the sound of gentle weeping pierces the calm. My own weeping. The weeping of others who visit. Even, it seems, the weeping of those who once stood beside fresh graves and mourned their loss. Some of the trees surrounding the graveyard rise so high, they seem to touch the clouds. In that moment, surrounded by the presence of silence and rumination, I wonder about my role in preserving the graveyard. How could I go beyond protecting it to honoring the people buried there, both personally and communally? Those of us involved with the preservation were working toward a goal of dedicating the graveyard on April 30, 2016. That left sixteen months (from the time I learned about the slave cemetery to its dedication) for historical research, community connections, and preservation work. And there was still that task of grappling with the silence of not knowing my own familial connections with slavery.

My ancestors came to the Great Valley in the late 1700s and early 1800s. I imagine them in their horse-drawn wagons, nearing Signal Knob, as they trekked down the Great Wagon Road: eyes drawn to the mountains, to the roving river, to the inspiring skies that woke them with a newly painted sunrise every morning. Some of my ancestors began as indentured servants in Maryland and settled in the Valley early enough to interact with the Native Americans who once lived and hunted here; others were Revolutionary War patrons or Civil War soldiers; and many are family lines that seem to begin nowhere. I don't know if any of my mostly-German families were slaveowners—there's no record in the censuses, no family papers, no letters that show this—but, I also don't know what their thoughts were surrounding the idea of enslavement. It's as static as an unused radio frequency: that silence. It permeates my thoughts and I want to know: Was my family as appalled at the reality of slavery as I am? Did they attend or read about the lashings or the sales on the courthouse steps? What about the injustices that occurred long after the American Civil War? Were they accepting of practices and attitudes that discriminated against anyone who was different? Were they angry? Indifferent?

The book of Revelation reveals indifference to be worse than strong emotion, and that seems to scare me more than anything: the indifference, the silence, that seeped into the Shenandoah Valley while human beings were cuffed into coffles and sold on a block, flogged and raped, buried chronologically along a fence line with no names or dates and sometimes not even a headstone, as if they were not worth much more than the cattle in the fields. And yet, Virginia law allowed for manumissions of slaves. A slaveowner could legally free his slaves, and many did so through their wills or through emancipation papers. But, in Virginia, a slave freed privately after May 1, 1806, risked re-enslavement if he did not leave the state within one year. Were some of the people buried in Corhaven Graveyard emancipated or promised emancipation, but died before their earthly freedoms could be realized? In *Hidden History: African American Cemeteries in Central Virginia*, Rainville reminds us, "a cemetery is often the only record we have of the lost community it memorializes."[4] The only record we have. One without names, without faces, without voices to relay the injustices they endured in life.

I want revelation, and yet I dread it too. In the 1960s, when race persecution smoldered into the civil rights movement, the Shenandoah Valley was still rife with misanthropes for the African American race. The Harrisonburg, Virginia, public radio station WMRA[5] interviewed DeLois Warr, an African American whose family stayed in the Shenandoah Valley—even though her ancestors first entered the folds of the mountains as enslaved people. She recounts in ghastly detail how a storefront owner refused to allow her to stand under his awning while she waited for a bus, even though white children were huddled there, safe from the pouring rain. Injustice rings from America's cracked Liberty Bell.

While reading local historian Nancy Stewart's notebooks, compiled from a lifetime of researching county, state, and federal records concerning slavery in Shenandoah County, I came across an entry from 1878. An African American was found guilty for a crime; in the chancery papers, it states that he "graciously submitted to the old time punishment so familiar to that race—ten lashes with orders to return after the lapse of ten days and receive ten more, which, of course, he will do."[6] My jaw dropped. I was sitting in the Shenandoah County Circuit Court clerk's office, where hundreds of years of wills, deeds, and papers lent the air a musty stench. Overhead incandescents buzzed. Vinyl seats creaked as other visitors rose to find more thick books to peruse. Here I sat in a room filled with records that condemned our own government of directing malicious acts toward someone specifically because of their melanin count. I was appalled and ashamed as I rose to meet my young sons and husband for a cup of cocoa at the local coffee shop, just across the street from where public lashings occurred. The sickening slap of leather on bare skin seemed to echo still from the past.

What happens to a dream deferred? Three hundred years yields more than enough people to break the silence that surrounds the discrimination of an entire race. And yet, at family reunions, I still hear the defamation of anyone deemed as "other," including African Americans. Was it always thus? Certainly, I'm not the first one in my family in three hundred years to look for reconciliation, for the beauty in difference, for the common thread of human dignity we each hold. Certainly, someone else in my family would have relished the opportunity to help care for a slave cemetery forgotten along Holman's Creek. Certainly, indifference no longer settles on the sloping banks of the Shenandoah.

But this was just the beginning of my research. After delving into the history, looking for connections to better understand the Corhaven Graveyard, I learned more than I could have imagined about the people who once owned it. The land associated with the slave cemetery was first settled by Daniel Holeman. His son, Jacob Holeman, a commander during the Revolutionary War, was the largest slaveowner in the county when he died in 1783. The names of those he enslaved are preserved in the will and deed books of Shenandoah County: John, Nan, Lydia. Reuben and Doll. Sall, Jenny Boastwin, Old Nan. Jim and Ann. Mary and Sue. George and Winney. Jacob willed these enslaved people *and their descendants* to his sons and daughters. Through language in a will, Holeman was creating life sentences of slavery, not only for those he deemed as property, but also for any children born to them. Intentional enslavement in perpetuity. The reality of that revelation still haunts me. Only Toby, a mulatto boy, was promised freedom at twenty-one years of age. And the remaining named people, Tom, Old Jack, and Sam, a young negro boy, are part of the 1784 will but are not mentioned in 1796 when the sale of those enslaved persons became a reality. What happened to them?

History quiets until Abraham Hoffman buys the property and then sells it five years later, in July 1827, to James Madison Hite Beale. The 1820 census confirms that Hoffman had at least one male and one female slave. Beale served in the Virginia House of Delegates (1818–1819) and was elected to Congress (1833–1837 and 1849–1853). He added slave quarters to house those who built his manor house, Edge Hill. In 1846 (six years after Edge Hill Manor was finished), Samuel Moore, son of local plantation owner Aaron Moore, purchased Edge Hill Plantation, which he owned until his death in 1870.

Two of Samuel Moore's slaves are listed in the *VA Slave Births Index, 1853–1865* compiled by L. A. Morales and archived at the Library of Virginia in Richmond: Serena and her child Caroline, who was born on July 9, 1853.[7] According to the 1850 census, Moore owned nine slaves. By the end of the American Civil War, Samuel Moore's wife had written a letter to her brother decrying that only three African Americans were left to help them on the farm: "Margaret, Ferrel, and Caroline." What had happened to then twelve-year-old Caroline's mother Serena? Is she, perhaps, buried in the slave cemetery beside Holman's Creek? Will we ever know the names of other slaves associated with Beale and Moore, who were most likely buried here?

Holman's Creek. That trickling stream, whose placidity seeps into the graveyard. I imagine floods carrying flora along the riverbanks downstream. A North African perennial bulb, known as Star of Bethlehem, was found as far as Indiana by 1940 and was found, too, on the knoll of the graveyard along the west side of the boundary wall. Perhaps it had been planted by empathizing hands. Research in slave cemeteries often finds that organic memorials have been planted in association with the graves.[8] At the Corhaven Graveyard, white violets and grapevine are two plants associated with specific burials. As a Northern Shenandoah Valley master gardener, I worked with fellow master gardeners to plan a tribute garden outside the cemetery. The garden brings in plants such as yucca, typically associated with African American cemeteries, and native perennials such as tansy and feverfew, which would have been foraged by enslaved African Americans to use in plantation life. The landscaping and hardscaping, completed with generous donations of materials and time from numerous small businesses and individuals, includes benches handcrafted by students from the local technical school, a cairn sculpture to which visitors can add their own rock, a chalkboard for personal expression, and even the bell from a local one-room schoolhouse. All of these, together, allow visitors to remember the sacredness of the site, to contemplate the tragedy that befell those buried there, and to participate in the healing and hope that Corhaven Graveyard offers.

The expectation, though, is for continued action and healing. A site such as the Corhaven Graveyard is not set aside after it is preserved and opened to the public. A slave cemetery is an opening whereby heaven's light can shine more brightly into this world. It is a place whereby an individual, and even a community, can change for the better. It is a place where suffering gives meaning to peace. It is a place where we learn from the past to effect a transformed future that promotes true equality for all.

Through researching the families associated with the Corhaven Graveyard, I learned about Coming to the Table. The Shenandoah Valley CTTT chapter held a workshop highlighting research tools to help the descendants of African American slaves face the challenges of uncovering their genealogy. I attended the event to aid my research in the slave cemetery and discovered that Coming to the Table's approaches—uncovering history, making connections, working toward healing, and taking action—directly aligned with the work at the Corhaven Graveyard. Although tracing my own family's history, to ascertain what their opinions were on slavery or whether they even owned slaves, has not been fruitful, I have been following CTTT's approach to help find information about the historical Shenandoah Valley families whose lives were intimately entwined with those buried in the graveyard. Because of the lack of information surrounding those who were enslaved, research often has to begin with the family names of those who enslaved, people who were significant members of the community, as justices of the peace or representatives, while also owning slaves. The final goal is to learn as much about the identities and lives of the enslaved at rest in Corhaven Graveyard as possible, and especially to provide a place that promotes healing in the community.

What happens to a dream deferred? God has directed my life toward the restoration and dedication of the Corhaven Graveyard in ways I could never have foreseen. He took my passions in archaeology, philanthropy, and social justice and wove them into tools that could remind a community about the importance of helping others, especially those whose voices were muffled by the past. Silence and indifference have reigned far too long in the Shenandoah Valley. I believe that the best way forward is to acknowledge, to forgive, and to allow the peace that develops from forgiveness to change our own biases. *What happens to a dream deferred?* It is transformed.

NOTES

1. R. T. Clifton, *Barbs, Prongs, Points, Prickers, & Stickers: A Complete and Illustrated Catalogue of Antique Barbed Wire* (Norman: University of Oklahoma Press, 1970), 317.
2. J. F. Wine, *Life Along Holman's Creek* (Stephens City, VA: Commercial Press, 1982) 8–9.

3. D. Borden, *Tombstone Inscriptions of Shenandoah County and Bordering Counties,* vol. 8 (Ozark, MO: Yates Publishing Company), 1986), 96.

4. L. Rainville, *Hidden History: African American Cemeteries in Central Virginia* (Charlottesville: University of Virginia Press, 2014), 3.

5. M. Woodroof, "Integrating Mt. Jackson's Past" on *WMRA,* June 12, 2015, accessed March 1, 2016, http://wmra.org/post/integrating-mount-jacksons-past.

6. N. B. Stewart, *African Americans in Shenandoah County, Virginia Notebooks,* vol. IV, Book B, 181 (personal notebooks).

7. L. A. Morales, *VA Slave Births Index, 1853–1865: Volume 5, S–Z* (Alexandria Library, Heritage Books, 2007), 181.

8. Rainville, *Hidden History,* 62.

24 ⇥ A TALE OF TWO SISTERS

BETTY KILBY FISHER BALDWIN
AND PHOEBE KILBY

THIS IS THE tale of two Kilby families—one who owned land and one who was owned by it. Generations later, descendants Walter and James grew up on neighboring farms. Walter, descended from the land-owning Kilbys, left for the University of Virginia to become a medical doctor. He later set up his practice in Baltimore, where he raised his daughter Phoebe. James, descended from the second family, had only a fourth-grade education; he lived on the Finks farm with his family, working for virtual slave wages. Later, he moved to Front Royal, Virginia, where he became a laborer and farmer. His daughter was named Betty. Betty and Phoebe lived very different lives.

BETTY: I was born February 22, 1945, seven years before Phoebe. I grew up on a
    fifty-two-acre farm in Happy Creek, Virginia, on the wrong side of the tracks.

I played in the fields that were home to bears, bobcats, and snakes. One hot summer day, when I was about ten years old, I was playing in the field when I heard a great moaning sound. I moved in closer to see what it was. Something that looked like a bear was standing tall, with his hands pointing toward heaven. I heard weeping and the muffled words, "Lord, I stretch my hands to thee; no other help I know. If thy withdraw thyself from thee, where shall I go?" He fell to his knees and sobbed. Then I realized it wasn't a bear. It was my father, and I began to cry too. Not wanting to be seen, I ran back to the house and straight to my room to my secret hiding place. I later realized that this was the day "old man Dick Finks" had stolen my daddy's land.

In 1958, I was about to complete the seventh grade at Ressie Jeffries Colored Elementary school. My brothers were commuting twenty-five miles each way, five days a week, to Johnson Williams High School, the only one available to "colored children" in my county. It was time for Daddy to sign my form. I heard Daddy and Momma talking. Daddy, holding a legal-size document and my pupil placement form in one hand, slammed both on the table and said, "I won't! I won't send Betty or her brothers to Johnson Williams High School another year when the 1954 Brown decision outlawed segregated schools." Then he took my pupil placement form, scratched out Johnson Williams, wrote in Warren County High School (WCHS), and gave it to me to return to my teacher. Then I watched Daddy as he hid that legal document under the seat of his car. When he'd gone, I took it and went to my secret hiding place where I could read it without getting caught. As I read, I came to understand why education was so important to Daddy. He'd grown up on the Finks farm, where he'd been given a deed to twenty-four acres of land when he was seventeen. Years after my father came to own that land, my grandfather sued my father for the land, got the land, and then gave it back to Dick Finks. Even at thirteen, I understood how painful it must be to be betrayed by your father, and especially when it was in favor of Finks "the slave master." Daddy had said once, "If old man Dick Finks had let me go to school and get an education, he wouldn't have been able to get my land back. I must do everything in my power to make sure that my children get a quality education." The document was dated July 13, 1955. I now understood the significance of that hot summer day in the field when I was ten.

My father continued to try to get me into WCHS despite threats and intimidation. He became president of the local chapter of the National

Association of Colored People (NAACP), contacted the NAACP lawyer Oliver Hill, and together they filed a lawsuit to enforce the 1954 *Brown vs. Board of Education* decision in Front Royal, Virginia. The case became *Betty Ann Kilby, et al. vs. Warren County Board of Education*. Because the one high school in the county was for whites only, the judge ruled in favor of letting me and twenty-one other colored children, including my brothers, attend WCHS. However, the Virginia legislature had previously passed "Massive Resistance" laws, which allowed the governor to close the schools should any judge rule against segregating them. The governor invoked his powers and closed the school. This was the first school to close under Virginia's Massive Resistance laws. Thus, there was no education for us from September 1958 to February 18, 1959. The laws were ultimately deemed unconstitutional, and the higher court ruled again in my favor.

The night before WCHS was to open on an integrated basis, shots were fired at our home. I was washing dishes. Daddy yelled, "Gunfire, hit the floor!" I woke to Momma slapping my face and crying hysterically. Momma thought I'd been hit by the bullets. In actuality, I had been so scared that I passed out.

The next day, volunteers drove us children to school. We were dropped off in front of an angry mob of people who had gathered to further traumatize us. Police were on hand to hold back the crowd, but that did not keep us from being afraid. I began to recite, "The Lord is my Shepherd, yea though I walk through the valley of the shadow of death, I will fear no evil." I thought I was going to die that day.

Not a single white student came that February day in 1959, but in September they all returned. If I had died that day it would have been more humane than going through the isolation, name-calling, and spitballs, not to mention the inability to participate in normal teen and school activities, not even my school prom. But the worst was going through the rape. The rape almost destroyed me. Afterward, I began car-racing from Happy Creek Road to town; I had a death wish. I couldn't eat, couldn't sleep. I had a nervous breakdown and was put in the hospital. While hospitalized, I talked with a local minister who convinced me that God was keeping me for greater things in my life.

I didn't get that quality high school education, but many other black children would benefit from my sacrifice. When I was later tested in the workplace, my employer was amazed at the test results because some of the questions I missed were at the lower level, and yet I had correctly answered the

WSLS-TV News Film Collection, 1951—1971, University of Virginia Library.

higher-level questions. The tests clearly showed the gaps in academic skills typically learned in high school. But sixteen years after my high school graduation, I went to work for a company that offered a tuition-reimbursement program, through which I was able to attend Shenandoah College (now University). I earned a supervisor certificate, an associate's degree, a bachelor's degree, and an MBA. After sharing my story at the 2010 Shenandoah University commencement, I received an honorary doctorate degree. Through my continuing education and struggle, I had made my way up at work from the lowest level job to become the highest-ranking African American female in that Fortune 500 Company in 1986.

PHOEBE: I was born on May 3, 1952, and grew up in Baltimore City during a time of white flight and the gradual increase of the proportion of African Americans from a quarter to almost half of the population in 1970. But I did not notice any of this. I lived in a white neighborhood, attended a white church, and was sent to a white private school because my parents did not want me to attend the integrated Baltimore City schools. I picked up from my family that "colored people" were inferior, my father disparaging them almost daily. Later, my mother told me that I had once, at the age of four, called the maid Inez the "N-word."

As I grew up and witnessed the civil rights movement in the news and the distant fires of black neighborhoods burning during the Baltimore riots after the murder of Dr. Martin Luther King, Jr., I began to realize the unfairness of discrimination. My teachers helped open my eyes to the disparities by assigning me books like *Black Like Me* and the *Autobiography of Malcolm X*. The process continued in college when, in sociology class, we were assigned to write a paper using the research methods we had been taught; I chose to research the image of black people in children's books in the college library. But it was the environmental movement that called to me and where I spent my professional life.

Fast forward to 2003 when, as an environmental consultant to the City of Harrisonburg, Virginia, I visited Eastern Mennonite University and its Center for Justice and Peacebuilding (CJP). Inspired, I enrolled and obtained a graduate certificate in conflict transformation. A few years later, I took a job with CJP and discovered that it had just helped start a program called Coming to the Table (CTTT), which brings together the descendants of slaves and slaveowners to "sit down together at the table of brotherhood."

I began wondering whether my father's family, a family with deep roots in Virginia, had owned slaves. My father had never spoken about it. Census data easily confirmed my suspicion: in 1840, my great-great-grandfather, Leroy Kilby, had "owned" two slaves. But who were those slaves and where were their descendants today? Research of wills of a number of Kilby relatives identified a few names—Sarah, Juliet, Simon. Only one aunt of my father's generation was still alive to ask about this. Aunt Lucia was glad to help. She knew that the Kilbys had owned slaves, and when I told her the names I had found, she recognized one—Simon. Rummaging in an antiques-filled room of her pre-Civil War house, she located an old stoneware crock of my grandmother's. Out of it she pulled a note identifying the pot as "Uncle Simon's pickle jar."

Meanwhile, I had discovered online a book called *Wit, Will and Walls* by Betty Kilby Fisher (now Baldwin).[1] When I read it, I knew that Betty's and my families must be connected. Betty's father and my father had grown up on farms less than a mile apart. But how would I find out? Fearful, but inspired by the CTTT pioneers, I decided to send Betty an email.

Uncle Simon's pickle jar.

Dear Betty Kilby Fisher,

My name is Phoebe Kilby, and I am white. My father grew up in Rappahannock County, VA, near where your father grew up. I have been doing some research on my family and have also read your book. Having no definitive answers, I suspect that our families had some kind of relationship in the past. I admire very much your courage and the courage of your father and family during the civil rights era and since. It would be an honor to talk to you and meet you someday. I live about 25 miles from Front Royal. Through conversations, we both might find out a little more about our families' pasts.

Martin Luther King had "a dream that . . . the sons of former slaves and slave owners will be able to sit down together at the table of Brotherhood." Perhaps, we as daughters can contribute to fulfilling that dream.

But there was no response from Betty. After two weeks, I thought "Oh, she doesn't want to talk to someone like me." But my CTTT friends would not let me give up, saying, "Send a longer email telling more about yourself." I did. And my second email got an immediate response from Betty. She had been having email problems when I'd sent my initial message. She titled her response "Hello Cousin." I was both excited and touched.

BETTY: I knew that I was descended from slavery. When I looked in the mirror at this caramel-colored skin, not black, not white, I knew I had to be a product of slavery. When Phoebe's email arrived, I was busy promoting my book and speaking about my life. I missed Christmas with my family, so I had scheduled a family dinner for after the holidays. It felt only natural to invite Phoebe to the family dinner—and to the premier of the documentary film *Wit, Will & Walls*[2] that was to follow.

I didn't think about what I had done until I called my children to tell them that I had invited the slave-holding Kilbys to dinner and the premier. They thought I must have lost my mind. But I responded by saying that I was going around the country talking about love and forgiveness; I could not be a hypocrite. And besides, Phoebe had quoted Martin Luther King. I had met Reverend King when he'd come to Richmond. Back then, he was just another one of those preachers trying to help integrate the schools, but he was my hero.

The night of the dinner and premiere, Phoebe came and brought her sister. My brothers weren't so sure of Phoebe's motives. John asked me, "Where is my forty acres and a mule?" James told Phoebe, "Well, I've seen a lot of white folks come to the table, but they usually don't stick around." At the premier, when I spoke to the audience, I introduced Phoebe and her sister as my cousins. "Tonight we have the privilege to live Dr. King's dream," I said, "that . . . the sons of former slaves and slave owners will be able to sit down together at the table of brotherhood."

The crowd cheered.

PHOEBE: Soon after the film premier, I invited Betty to EMU to participate in a CTTT gathering. During the gathering, after walking the healing circles laid out by CJP's STAR program, Betty was overcome with emotion. She could not stop crying. One of the African American attendees requested that all of the African American participants take a break to speak with Betty privately.

BETTY: They began to pray until I calmed to a coherent frame of mind. As I walked the circle, I became that sixteen-, seventeen-year-old girl. I got stuck in the cycle. With every step, I relived the rape, the pain, the guilt, and I felt so ashamed. I panicked, worrying that I had buried all the anger, shame, guilt, and hurt I needed to face in order to move forward with life. When all the praying was done, I was able to face those demons, and real healing became possible.

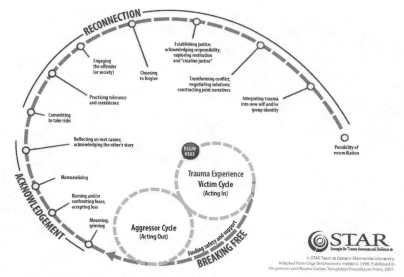

Breaking cycles of violence—building resilience.

When the African American attendees who were talking to Betty rejoined the group, they discussed what happens internally to participants who walk the healing circles. Phoebe and the other white people in the group talked about feeling helpless, sorrowful, and ashamed. Then the group continued to tell their stories, sharing tears, hugs, and much love and support.

PHOEBE: Not too long after I met Betty and her family, the fiftieth anniversary of Betty and her brothers integrating the high school was coming up. Betty's brother James had formed a group, the Historical Education Movement (HEM), to persuade the school board to celebrate this anniversary and to name the school after their father James Wilson Kilby. Living close to Front Royal and to James, I offered to help, and James accepted. HEM was able to get the school board to support the anniversary celebration but not to rename the school. The Town of Front Royal did name the street in front of the high school Kilby Drive, but that felt like a consolation prize. James and HEM decided they should not give up; more community engagement was needed. By this time, CTTT had some grant funding and agreed to support HEM in hosting a dialogue process called Our Shared History, involving HEM members, school system leaders, and blacks and whites who had attended the high school during

From left, Betty Kilby Fisher Baldwin, Phoebe Kilby, and James M. Kilby.

integration. The group met six times over six months to share stories about their integration period experiences and to develop ideas about how to honor that history. Betty joined the group, traveling from Texas when she could. At times, emotions were high, and agreement seemed elusive. One white person became angry at the suggestion that the Warren County School Board issue an apology, but Betty, the peacebuilder, stood up, reached out her arms, and hugged him. He calmed down. By the end, he had joined everyone in developing a list of recommendations, including the suggestion of an apology. The first item on the recommendation list was the erection of a Virginia state historical marker in front of the school honoring the work of James Wilson Kilby to integrate the school. The marker was installed on June 8, 2011, and paid for by the Warren County School Board.

Betty and I continued to build our relationship. We put together a presentation titled "A Common Grace." The name was inspired by a moment that James and I had one day while eating lunch together. He bowed his head

Unveiling of the Virginia historic marker in front of Warren County High School on
June 8, 2011.

and said grace, and it was the same prayer that I had heard my father say at
mealtime all throughout my childhood. This moment deepened the connection between me, James, and Betty as we worked together to honor the work
of their father. As a result, our family theme song became "Amazing Grace."

Not long after, I began talking more with a white cousin and found out
that he had started doing genealogy work also. After I told him about Betty,
he spoke to a cousin of hers who then agreed to have his DNA tested. On
July 1, 2016, Betty and I learned that we were indeed cousins. I was horrified
that an ancestor had violated a slave, but at the same time, I was happy to
call Betty true family. When Betty learned about the connection, it confirmed
what she had guessed all along but had found hard to accept. But Betty continued to say she loved me, and I continue to love her. "Hello, cousin" has
begun to feel more like "Hello, sister."

When I told Betty that I would like to make amends for the actions of my
ancestors, Betty responded, "You did not enslave anyone. You do not need
to do anything more than what you are doing now." But I just could not let

Virginia historic marker.

it go. I thought, "The Kilbys value education so much and want to make sure their grandchildren can go to college. Maybe a scholarship fund would be something they could accept." Betty liked that idea; this would not be for her, but instead, for the children—descendants of the people my family enslaved. The Kilby Family Endowed Scholarship Fund, housed at the POISE Foun-

Phoebe Kilby, Betty Kilby Fisher Baldwin, and Poise Foundation staff. By permission of the authors.

dation, is now up and running, and it has awarded its first scholarships to James's and Betty's grandsons.

BETTY AND PHOEBE: When challenged to live Dr. King's dream, we came to the table. Not only do we seek to live out King's dream of sons and daughters of former slaves and slaveowners coming to the table of brotherhood; we also seek his dream of creating the "beloved community"—a society founded on justice, equality, reconciliation and love for all. We strive to live, practice, and share the Coming to the Table approach of uncovering our linked histories, making connections to develop and deepen our relationships, working toward healing through honest sharing of our thoughts and experiences, and taking actions to heal from the wounds of racial inequality and injustice.

By coming to the table, we have truly become loving sisters.

NOTES

1. Betty Kilby Fisher, *Wit, Will and Walls* (Cultural Innovations Inc., 2002).
2. *Wit, Will, and Walls.* www.paulette@paulettefilms.com. https://www.loc.gov/folklife /civilrights/survey/view_collection.php?coll_id=1515).

AFTERWORD

What a Legacy of Slavery and Racism Has to Do with Me

JILL STRAUSS

WORKING ON *SLAVERY'S Descendants* inspired me to do genealogical research into my own conflicted German-Jewish history and heritage.[1] As a Jewish white woman, I have experienced sexism and anti-Semitism along with the privilege that comes from being a European American in the United States. These are complex, interconnected issues that run through my personal heritage and identity and the history of my country. In my research, I had my DNA analyzed, talked to older family members, and went to Michelfeld, Germany, the hometown of my paternal grandfather and ancestors going back to at least the 1600s. Not knowing what I would find, I brought friends with me for moral support and companionship. It was surprisingly emotional to walk the same streets my ancestors had for some three hundred years. To my amazement and joy, I was able to visit the still-standing home of my great-grandparents and the extant Jewish graveyard. I also developed relationships with the Germans doing the hard work of researching and documenting our shared past. Efforts by second- and third-generation Germans to acknowledge and make amends for an inherited legacy of wrongdoing is a model worth looking at as we in the United States find our own ways to address the legacies of slavery and the racism of the present. When I returned home, I talked to my relatives and friends again and then wrote about my trip and all that I discovered about myself and my ancestors. Reading the descendants' essays for this anthology showed me ways to understand and write about my own journey. I have now created my own narrative, which includes a past of forced displacement and migration; doing so, ironically, has created for me a sense of place and of new belonging.

The hope is that *Slavery's Descendants: Shared Legacies of Race and Reconciliation* will have a similar positive impact on anthology readers, regardless of background. For those who are similarly inspired to begin their own genealogical research, a section follows this one describing how to start the process, including ideas for interviewing across generations.

Many in the United States recognize the connections between slavery in the past and racism in the present, but they feel we need guidance to initiate and facilitate the pertinent conversations. From its inception, *Slavery's Descendants* has taken a multiple-perspective approach that aims to be a catalyst for different and deeper conversations about the legacy of slavery and racism in the U.S. It is meant to engender perspective-taking and empathy when readers consider the various narratives in their totality. It is a model for holding a multiplicity of voices and opinions in dialogue. Likewise, when we feel respected and heard, we find ourselves more open to hearing other viewpoints and considering the larger picture.

There are a variety of approaches to engaging in hard conversations over contested issues. An online search will result in various methodologies and provide suggestions for questions. To have the difficult conversations surrounding slavery and racism, CTTT uses the peacemaking circle process. A growing number of community-based groups and schools are using the circle process to build community and address wrongdoing. The circle process is an indigenous model that has been integrated with the contemporary practices of consensus-building, dialogue, and conflict resolution/transformation.

The use of a talking piece (any object that has special meaning to the facilitator and/or group) and a circle (in which discussion participants physically sit in a rounded formation) equalizes power relationships, allowing everyone to be heard through storytelling. The one who holds the talking piece has his or her turn to speak, while the others listen and support the speaker. What begins in dialogue has the potential to move to collective action for positive social change. In our conversations, we want to move beyond guilt, shame, and blame to imagine possibilities that could break open the many facets of our national story, acknowledge each other's respective truth(s), and heal. Perhaps we can even find a collective meaning in our shared legacy.

NOTE

1. A version of this text appears in "Writing the Wrongs of the Past: Descendants of Enslavers and the Enslaved Come to the Table," in *Listening to the Movement: Essays on New Growth in Restorative Justice*, edited by Ted Lewis and Carl Stauffer (Eugene, OR: Wipf and Stock Publishers, 2019).

POSTSCRIPT

From Branches to Roots

DIONNE FORD

AS EVIDENT IN many of this volume's stories, members often find their way to Coming to the Table after delving into their family histories. For African Americans or people in another group that have experienced group trauma, finding those histories can be difficult and disheartening. But it's not impossible. We're lucky to live in a time when many documents, which once required trips to archives or municipal-building basements to obtain, are now digitized and available online with the click of a few keys. We can now even harness DNA to retrieve an otherwise broken link in a family's roots, connecting us to our ancestors' geographic beginnings.

To get started researching your family tree, consider following the steps outlined in this section.

TALK TO YOUR FAMILY

Our elders are an incredible treasure trove of information. My grandfather's casual declaration one summer day, that his grandmother had worked for his grandfather on his plantation, ignited my curiosity like a match to kindle. In our brief conversation, I learned his mother's and grandfather's names, found out where they lived, and discovered that his grandfather had been a pecan farmer. Had he not told me this story, especially the name of his grandfather, I don't know that I would have ever been able to find information about my enslaved great-great-grandmothers.

You don't have to be a professional interviewer to get pertinent information from your family. The Oral History Association provides tips for getting started, and StoryCorps, the national organization that aims to collect America's stories, provides sample questions. Many genealogy books also provide sample interview questions, as do online sites like Genealogy.com. Print out a copy of the questions, and bring them and a recording device to the next holiday gathering, which is a great time to interview family members, especially elders. That's probably why, in 2004, Thanksgiving became National Family History Day.

BEGIN AT THE END

Documentation about the end of your ancestors' lives can give you a lot of information about how they lived. Gravestones often give the year of birth as well as death. Death certificates contain even more information, including parents' names and place of death, and funeral records can provide more detail still: if a person was sick for a long time or if they died suspiciously, for example. If you're close by, visit the cemetery where your ancestor was laid to rest. It doesn't have to be a somber affair. Bring a picnic along with your flowers. While you're there, check out the "neighborhood"—you may find more relatives buried nearby. If you don't live close enough to visit your relatives' final resting place, check out websites like FindAGrave. This volunteer-run site posts gravesite information from around the world, including pictures and tombstone inscriptions. If your relative's grave isn't already listed, you can request a picture of it from a local volunteer.

JOIN A COMMUNITY

Just about every town has genealogy groups that you can join. If your family is from the town you currently live in, the local historical society is likely a good place to explore. Working with other like-minded folk who are also looking to find their families can help you cross-pollinate ideas and lead you to fresh research avenues. Support and camaraderie is always a plus, especially if your family is connected to slavery, genocide, natural disasters, or other traumas. A plethora of online communities also offer genealogy support, guidance, and access to records.

FamilySearch, the genealogy organization operated by the Church of Jesus Christ of Latter Day Saints, offers a variety of free documents—everything from baptismal records to censuses—which can be accessed online. The USGenWeb sites include a myriad of documents, such as digitized family bibles, wills, and deeds, all collected by volunteers and organized by state. Take advantage of the oodles of virtual support-groups available too. Afrigeneas is for people interested in ancestors of African origin, and Our-BlackAncestry is a repository of sources and tools to help you find enslaved ancestors. Many researchers, beginners and experts alike, are taking to social media to document their genealogy journeys. GeneaBloggersTRIBE supports these researchers, sharing their families' stories on social media.

VISIT THE LIBRARY

Recognizing family-history research as a popular and fast-growing hobby, many libraries now have a genealogy department or someone on staff who can help with such fact-finding. At the local library in your ancestors' area, you'll likely find histories of the town that can shed light on your family. A quick web search should bring you to the appropriate library branch and contact information so that you can call or email with your query. If your ancestors spent a lot of their lives near a big university, their survivors might have donated their letters or commonplace books there ; their catalogs are usually available online.

HISTORIC NEWSPAPERS

After the town crier but before Twitter, there was such a thing as a newspaper. Some folks published anecdotes in their local papers the way people post on Facebook today. One branch of my tree had a running argument with another family that took place over many months, the quips published just about every week in their local paper. Religious and cultural newspapers, based on ethnicity, are also an incredible source for the family historian. Papers like the *Southwestern Christian Advocate* posted a Lost Friends column, in which formerly enslaved people could look for information about their families. The Historic New Orleans Collection hosts a searchable database of Lost Friends ads on their website. There are also subscription services to access historic newspapers, which are easily found through a web search.

SHARE YOUR STORY

Don't keep all of this research to yourself. Whether it's over pecan pie at the next holiday dinner or in a ballroom at an annual family reunion, share the story of your ancestors with the people in your family.

ACKNOWLEDGMENTS

The four-year process of taking *Slavery's Descendants* from idea to publication has been thrilling and nothing short of a group collaboration. We want to thank Coming to the Table for trusting us to usher these stories into the world as well as Eastern Mennonite University for their support of the program. The City University of New York (CUNY) Faculty Fellowship Publication Program supported Jill in early drafts of the anthology proposal. It was through that program that Jill and Dionne met Kim Guinta at Rutgers University Press; Kim shared our vision for this anthology and we are grateful to have her as our editor. Dionne's agent, Duvall Osteen at Aragi, Inc., provided invaluable insight on early drafts of the proposal. In addition, a PSC-CUNY Award, jointly funded by the Professional Staff Congress and the City University of New York offered a much-appreciated research and travel grant. We would also like to express gratitude to Furthermore: a program of the J. M. Kaplan Fund for their financial support.

Dionne's greatest debt is to her husband Dennis and to her daughters Devany and Desiree, for their unwavering support of this project. Jill thanks her parents, Ruth and Erich, for their support and love, and the rest of her family, friends, and colleagues for their enthusiasm over this book.

BIBLIOGRAPHY

Alexander, Michelle. *The New Jim Crow: Mass Incarceration in the Age of Colorblindness*. New York: The New Press, 2010.

Baldwin, James. *Notes of a Native Son*. Boston: Beacon Press, 1955.

Baldwin, James, and Margaret Mead. *A Rap on Race*. Philadelphia: J. B. Lippincott & Co., 1971.

Ball, Edward. *Slaves in the Family*. New York: Farrar, Straus and Giroux, 1998.

Baptist, Edward E. "'Cuffy,' 'Fancy Maids,' and 'One-Eyed Men': Rape, Commodification, and the Domestic Slave Trade in the United States." *American Historical Review* 106, no. 5 (2001): 1619–1650.

Baptist, Edward E. *The Half Has Never Been Told: Slavery and the Making of American Capitalism*. New York: Basic Books, 2014.

Berry, Wendell. *The Hidden Wound*. San Francisco: North Point Press, 1989. First published 1970.

Boler, Megan. "The Risks of Empathy: Interrogating Multiculturalism's Gaze." *Cultural Studies* 11, no. 2 (1997): 253–273.

Bonds, Anne, and Joshua Inwood. "Beyond White Privilege." *Progress in Human Geography* 40, no. 6 (2016): 715–733.

Branan, Karen. *The Family Tree: A Lynching in Georgia, a Legacy of Secrets, and My Search for the Truth*. New York: Atria Books, 2016.

Campbell, Benjamin P. *Richmond's Unhealed History*. Richmond: Brandylane Publishers, 2012.

Carroll, Kenneth L. "George Fox and Slavery." *Quaker History* 86, no. 2 (1997): 16–25.

Carten, Alma. "How the Legacy of Slavery Affects the Mental Health of Black Americans Today." http://theconversation.com/how-the-legacy-of-slavery-affects-the-mental-health-of-black-americans-today-44642.

Case, Kim A., Jonathan Iuzzini, and Morgan Hopkins. "Systems of Privilege: Intersections, Awareness, and Applications." *Journal of Social Issues* 68, no. 1 (2012): 1–10.

Coates, Ta-Nehisi. *Between the World and Me*. New York: Spiegel & Grau, 2015.

Coming to the Table, "Vision, Mission, Approach, Values & Facebook Community Guideline," https://comingtothetable.org/about-us/vision-mission-values/.

Crawford, Michael J. *The Having of Negroes Is Become a Burden: The Quaker Struggle to Free Slaves in Revolutionary North Carolina*. Gainesville: University Press of Florida, 2010.

DeGruy, Joy. *Post Traumatic Slave Syndrome: America's Legacy of Enduring Injury and Healing*. Oregon: Uptone Press, 2005.

DeWolf, Thomas Norman. *Inheriting the Trade: A Northern Family Confronts Its Legacy as the Largest Slave-Trading Dynasty in U.S. History*. Boston: Beacon Press, 2008.

DeWolf, Thomas Norman, and Sharon Leslie Morgan. *Gather at the Table: The Healing Journey of a Daughter of Slavery and a Son of the Slave Trade*. Boston: Beacon Press, 2012.

Drew, Benjamin. *The Narratives of Fugitive Slaves in Canada*. Toronto: Coles Publishing Company, 1981.

Edinger, Edward F. *The Mystery of the Coniunctio: Alchemical Image of Individuation*. Toronto: Inner City Books, 1994.

Fischer, Kirsten. *Suspect Relations: Sex, Race, and Resistance in Colonial North Carolina*. Ithaca, NY: Cornell University Press, 2002.

Gordon-Reed, Annette. *Thomas Jefferson and Sally Hemings; An American Controversy*. Charlottesville: University of Virginia Press, 1997.

Haldeman-Julius, Marcet. *The Story of a Lynching: An Exploration of Southern Psychology*. Girard: Haldeman-Julius Publications, 1927.

Hartman, Saidiya V. *Lose Your Mother: A Journey Along the Atlantic Slave Route*. New York: Farrar, Straus and Giroux, 2007.

Hartman, Saidiya V. "Venus in Two Acts." *Small Axe: A Caribbean Journal of Criticism* 12, no. 2 (2008): 1–14.

Hilty, Hiram H. *Toward Freedom for All: North Carolina Quakers and Slavery*. Richmond, IN: Friends United Press, 1984.

Hooker, David Anderson, and Amy Potter Czajkowski. *Transforming Historical Harms*. Harrisonburg: Eastern Mennonite University, 2012.

Howell, Isabel. "John Armfield, Slave-Trader." *Tennessee Historical Quarterly* 2, no. 1 (1943): 3–29.

Iyengar, Sujata. *Shades of Difference: Mythologies of Skin Color in Early Modern England*. Philadelphia: University of Pennsylvania Press, 2005.

Jacobs, Harriet A. *Incidents in the Life of a Slave Girl: Written by Herself*. Cambridge: Harvard University Press, 1987.

Jung, C. G. *Mysterium Coniunctionis: An Inquiry into the Separation and Synthesis of Psychic Opposites in Alchemy*. Princeton: Princeton University Press, 1970.

Junkin, William Sumner, and Minnie Wyatt Junkin. *The Henckel Genealogy, 1500–1960: Ancestry and Descendants of Anthony Jacob Henckel, 1668–1728, Pioneer Evangelical Lutheran Minister, Emigrant from the German Palatinate to America in 1717*. New Market, VA: Henckel Family Association, 1964.

Keen, Suzanne. "Life Writing and the Empathetic Circle." *Concentric: Literary and Cultural Studies* 42, no. 2 (2016): 9–26.

LaNier, Shannon, and Jane Feldman. *Jefferson's Children: The Story of One American Family*. New York: Random House, 2002.

Lazarus, Emma, and John Hollander. "The New Colossus." In *Emma Lazarus Selected Poems*. The Library of America, 2005.

Makau, Josina M., and Debian L. Marty. *Dialogue and Deliberation*. Long Grove, IL: Waveland Press, 2013.

Marty, Debian. "White Antiracist Rhetoric as Apologia: Wendell Berry's The Hidden Wound." In *Whiteness: The Communication of Social Identity*, edited by Thomas

K. Nakayama and Judith N. Martin, 51–68. Thousand Oaks: Sage Publications, 1999.

McIntosh, Peggy. "White Privilege and Male Privilege: A Personal Account of Coming to See Correspondences through Work in Women's Studies." Working Paper 189. Wellesley: Wellesley College, Center for Research on Women, 1988.

Morrison, Toni, and Danille Kathleen Taylor-Guthrie. *Conversations with Toni Morrison.* Jackson: University Press of Mississippi, 1994.

Nelson, Alondra. *The Social Life of DNA: Race, Reparations, and Reconciliation after the Genome.* Boston: Beacon Press, 2016.

Oshatz, Molly. *Slavery and Sin: The Fight against Slavery and the Rise of Liberal Protestantism.* New York: Oxford University Press, 2012.

Perera, Sylvia Brinton. *The Scapegoat Complex: Toward a Mythology of Shadow and Guilt.* Toronto: Inner City Books, 1986.

Petry, Elisabeth. *At Home Inside: A Daughter's Tribute to Ann Petry.* Jackson: University Press of Mississippi, 2009.

Philip, M. NourbeSe. *Zong!* Middletown, CT: Wesleyan University Press, 2008.

Pranis, Kay, Barry Stuart, and Mark Wedge. *Peacemaking Circles: From Crime to Community.* St. Paul: Living Justice Press, 2003.

Rangan, Pooja, and Rey Chow. "Race, Racism, and Postcoloniality." In *The Oxford Handbook of Postcolonial Studies*, edited by Graham Huggan. New York: Oxford Handbooks Online, 2013. http://www.oxfordhandbooks.com/view/10.1093/oxfordhb/9780199588251.001.0001/oxfordhb-9780199588251.

Ratcliffe, Matthew. "Phenomenology as a Form of Empathy." *Inquiry* 55, no. 5 (2012): 473–495.

Reisigl, Martin, and Ruth Wodak. *Discourse and Discrimination: Rhetorics of Racism and Antisemitism.* London: Routledge, 2001.

Rich, Adrienne Cecile. *Blood, Bread, and Poetry: Selected Prose, 1979–1985.* New York: Norton, 1986

Roberts, Ida M. Corley. *Rising Above It All: A Tribute to the Rowan Slaves of Federal Hill.* Louisville: Harmony House Publishers, 1994.

Sasanov, Catherine. *Had Slaves*, Dallas: Firewheel Editions, 2010.

Schwartz, Marie Jenkins. *Birthing a Slave: Motherhood and Medicine in the Antebellum South.* Cambridge: Harvard University Press, 2006.

Seixas, Peter C. *Theorizing Historical Consciousness.* Toronto: University of Toronto Press, 2004.

Shantideva. *The Way of the Bodhisattva*, rev. ed. Shambhala: Padmakara Translation Group, 2006.

Sizemore, Bill. *Uncle George and Me: Two Southern Families Confront a Shared Legacy of Slavery.* Richmond, VA: Brandylane Publishers, Inc., 2018.

Stevenson, Brenda E. *Life in Black and White: Family and Community in the Slave South.* New York: Oxford University Press, 1997.

Strauss, Jill. "Writing the Wrongs of the Past: Descendants of Enslavers and the Enslaved Come to the Table." In *Listening to the Movement: Essays on New Growth in Restorative Justice*, edited by Ted Lewis and Carl Stauffer. Eugene: Wipf & Stock Publishers, 2019.

Trouillot, Michel-Rolph. *Silencing the Past: Power and the Production of History.* Boston: Beacon Press, 1995.

West, Cornel. *Race Matters.* Boston: Beacon Press, 1993.

Wiencek, Henry. *The Hairstons: An American Family in Black and White.* New York: St. Martin's Press, 1999.

Wilkerson, Isabel. *The Warmth of Other Suns: The Epic Story of America's Great Migration.* New York: Random House, 2010.

NOTES ON CONTRIBUTORS

DAVID TERRETT BEUMÉE grew up in Billings, Montana, in a cattle-ranching and wheat-farming family. David began research into four generations of his enslaving ancestors after hearing an interview with Katrina Browne on *Democracy Now*, and has begun a regional CTTT chapter in the Denver metro area. David earned a bachelor's in art from the Montana State School of Art in 1979 and has been a full-time potter since 1983. He is the founder of the nonprofit organization East Boulder County Artists, which hosts a yearly studio tour in the eastern Boulder County cities of Lafayette, Louisville, Longmont, and Erie. David is currently exploring watercolor monoprinting after forty-two years at the potter's wheel.

KAREN BRANAN is the author of *The Family Tree: A Lynching in Georgia, A Legacy of Secrets and My Search for the Truth*. A veteran journalist, she has written for newspapers, magazines, television, and the stage for over fifty years. Her work has appeared in *The Guardian, Life, Mother Jones, Ms., Christian Science Monitor, Ladies' Home Journal, Good Housekeeping, Today's Health, Learning, Parents,* the *Minneapolis Star Tribune*, and the *Atlanta Journal-Constitution*, as well as on PBS, CBS, ABC, CBC, BBC, and CNN.

ANTOINETTE BROUSSARD is a writer, researcher, and public speaker whose work centers on documenting her ancestral roots. She is the author of *African American Holiday Traditions: Celebrating with Passion, Style, and Grace*. Her work has appeared in the *African American National Biography* (edited by Dr. Henry Louis Gates, Jr.), the *Columbia Magazine* (the Washington State Historical Society's journal), *Harlem of the West, The Baobab Tree* (a journal of the African American Genealogical Society of Northern California, Inc.), and BlackPast.org (a reference guide to African American history). She was a student in English literature and black studies at San Francisco State University, and she has an MFA in creative writing from Saint Mary's College. She's also a graduate of the Protocol School of Washington, DC, in contemporary business and social etiquette. Her twelve years of genealogical research are the inspiration for her forthcoming memoir

Sweetwater: History Meets Personal Journey. She has a website at www
.antoinettebroussard.com.

THOMAS NORMAN DeWOLF serves as executive director for Coming to the
Table, where he has been involved since the first gathering at Eastern Mennonite University in 2006. Tom is the author of *Inheriting the Trade,* a coauthor (with Sharon Leslie Morgan) of *Gather at the Table,* and a coauthor (with
Jodie Geddes) of *The Little Book of Racial Healing.* He is featured in the Emmy-
nominated PBS documentary *Traces of the Trade.* Tom is a public speaker
and workshop leader at universities, corporations, and conferences throughout the United States. The African American Jazz Caucus awarded Tom the
2012 Spirit of Freedom Award for Social Justice. Tom and his wife Lindi live
in Oregon. He has a website at www.tomdewolf.com.

FABRICE GUERRIER is a writer, poet, and entrepreneur and former president
of the board of Coming to the Table, the youngest person to hold the position. He is the cofounder and chief executive officer of Syllble Studios,
Inc. (pronounced *syllable*), a collaborative storytelling startup that organizes
peer-to-peer online production houses to publish original fiction stories
and books of collaborative writing. He coauthored *The Wall* (a futuristic
sci-fi novella) and *Syllble: Collection of Collaboratively Written Short Stories.*
He is a 2018 Shafik Gabr fellow, a Seth Godin AltMBA alumni, and a senior
fellow at Humanity in Action. He was named the 2016 PEN Haiti fellow at
the PEN American Center. Previously, he founded The LEEHG Institute
(a social venture) and has worked on issues of justice and reconciliation
in postwar communities in Sierra Leone. He holds an MA in conflict transformation from Eastern Mennonite University's Center for Justice and
Peacebuilding and a BS in international affairs and leadership studies from
Florida State University. He is fluent in French, Haitian Creole, and English.
His writing has appeared in *The PEN America Blog, Public Pool, Blavity,* and
Moko: Caribbean Arts and Letters.

STEPHANIE HARP is a writer and historian raised in Arkansas, Pennsylvania,
and Virginia, with family roots in Arkansas and Louisiana. She holds an MA
in history from the University of Maine. In 2013, she organized and led Project 1927 at the Mosaic Templars Cultural Center in Little Rock, supported
by an Arkansas Humanities Council grant. She has presented at Without
Sanctuary: A Conference on Lynching in the American South (put on by the

Center for the Study of the New South, 2012), at Roads to Salvation (by the Arkansas Historical Association, 2000), and at various conferences and events throughout Maine. For over thirty years, she has worked in journalism, creative writing, arts administration, and education. She has received grants from the Maine Arts Commission, and her writing has appeared in periodicals in Arkansas, Maine, and Virginia as well as on the radio, on stage, and online. She contributed "Stories of a Lynching: Accounts of John Carter, 1927" to *Bullets and Fire: Lynching and Authority in Arkansas, 1840–1950* (2018).

EILEEN JACKSON, PHD, RN, was raised within the Catholic cultural milieu in the 1940s and 1950s by Irish Catholic immigrants. She has been an award-winning young scientist, a nun, an elementary school teacher, and a nurse. While still a nun, she marched with Caesar Chavez on the march from Delano to Sacramento and worked with the migrant women in Morgan Hill, California. While in nursing school, she worked in home health at the Robert Taylor Homes and organized a Service Employees International Union (SEIU) chapter with the nursing staff at Miles Square Health Center in Chicago. In Chicago, she earned her BA in biology and her BS in nursing. She then returned to California where she served as a union organizer for the California Nurses' Association, and as president-elect and then president of the San Francisco region. She served as a lobbyist for the nurses' association and for the Association of Long Term Care Ombudsmen. She writes a blog at www.careislikewater.blogspot.com.

SARA JENKINS is the author of *This Side of Nirvana: Memoirs of a Spiritually Challenged Buddhist* and *Hello at Last: Embracing the Koan of Friendship & Meditation.* She is also the editor of *Lift Every Voice! African American History in Haywood County, North Carolina.* She lives in Lake Junaluska, North Carolina, on the edge of the Great Smoky Mountains.

BETTY KILBY FISHER BALDWIN, MBA, helped integrate the public schools in Warren County, Virginia, as the plaintiff in the case *Betty Ann Kilby vs. Warren County Board of Education.* She tells her story in her book *Wit, Will, and Walls.* Her research on Warren County's history has appeared in the booklet *Freedom Road* and in the Shenandoah Valley Historical Review. She is a historical and motivational speaker and leads workshops and dialogues on racial reconciliation. Betty earned an associate degree in business management from Lord Fairfax Community College, a bachelor's degree in business administration from Shenandoah University, an MBA from NOVA University, and an honorary doctor of humane letters degree from Shenandoah. She currently serves on the board of managers for Coming to the Table.

PHOEBE KILBY, former president of Coming to the Table, retired in 2014 having worked for eight years for the Center for Justice and Peacebuilding, the initial sponsor of CTTT. She has researched her family's history of slaveholding and was able to trace those enslaved persons to the modern-day Kilbys. With their concurrence, she established the Kilby Family Endowed Scholarship Fund as a form of reparation, which is described on her website and blog, A Common Grace at a commongrace.org. In 2014, she wrote the booklet *Forgiveness and Reconciliation* for the Center for Justice and Peacebuilding at Eastern Mennonite University. She holds a BS in botany and a master's degree in environmental management, both from Duke University. She also has a graduate certificate in conflict transformation from Eastern Mennonite University.

SARAH KOHRS is an author and artist. She has poetry published in *Adelaide Literary Magazine, Claudius Speaks, Colere, Crosswinds Poetry Journal, Evangel, From the Depths Gone Lawn, Horn & Ivory, Poetry from the Valley of Virginia, Raven Chronicles, Scintilla,* and the *Virginia Literary Journal.* Her photography is featured in *3Elements, Blueline Literary Magazine, Claudius Speaks, Columbia College Literary Review, Esthetic Apostle, In Layman's Terms, Mt. Hope, Ponder Review, Raven Chronicles,* and the *Virginia Literary Journal.* Sarah manages *The Sow's Ear Poetry Review* and directs Corhaven Graveyard, a preserved slave cemetery from the 1800s. SENK received a BA, with majors in archaeology and classical languages from the College of Wooster, and holds a Virginia State teaching license, endorsed in Latin and the visual arts. She lives in Shenandoah Valley, Virginia, where she homeschools her three sons. Find her online at www.senkohrs.com.

SHANNON LaNIER is a television cohost for *Arise Entertainment 360*, on BET's sister station, Centric, and a correspondent for *Black Enterprise* magazine's "Black Enterprise Business Report" and "Our World with Black Enterprise." He coauthored the book *Jefferson's Children: The Story of One American Family* with photojournalist Jane Feldman, which received a Best Books Award from the American Library Association. The Kent State University grad is an active member of his church, of Alpha Phi Alpha Fraternity Inc., and of the National Association of Black Journalists. Most importantly, he makes time for his wife and college sweetheart Chandra and their three children.

TAMMARRAH LEE is a third-generation African American New Englander and second-generation native of Boston, Massachusetts. She is a state-licensed, certified social worker and a certified teacher. An avid researcher of African American history and culture, Tammarrah has retraced her hidden maternal ancestral roots back to the early 1800s in both Halifax, Virginia and Halifax, Nova Scotia. Three generations on her grandmother's side were enslaved in Virginia; three generations on her grandfather's side were members of the African Refugees of the War of 1812 and resided in Nova Scotia. Her ultimate goal is to connect with long-lost relatives and to organize the first long-overdue family reunion.

DEBIAN MARTY is professor of communication ethics at California State University, Monterey Bay. Her research is in communication ethics, with an emphasis in dialogue and deliberation. She is coauthor of *Cooperative Argumentation: A Model for Deliberative Community* and *Dialogue and Deliberation* and she has written a number of articles and essays on the nineteenth century abolitionist movement, including "One More River to Cross: The Crosswhites' Escape from Slavery" in *A Fluid Frontier: Freedom, Slavery and the Underground Railroad in the Detroit River Borderland* (edited by V. Tucker and K. S. Frost).

JOSEPH MCGILL, JR. is a history consultant for Magnolia Plantation, a docent at the Old Slave Mart Museum in Charleston, South Carolina and the founder of The Slave Dwelling Project. Formerly, McGill was a field officer for the National Trust for Historic Preservation and served as the executive director of the African American Museum in Cedar Rapids, Iowa. He was also the director of history and culture at Penn Center in St. Helena Island, South Carolina, and was a park ranger for the National Park Service's Fort Sumter National Monument in Charleston, South Carolina. He is the founder of Company I, the 54th Massachusetts Reenactment Regiment in Charleston, South Carolina. The 54th Massachusetts volunteer infantry was the regiment portrayed in the award-winning movie *Glory*. He's featured in the book *Confederates in the Attic* by Tony Horwitz and is a member of the South Carolina Humanities Council Speakers' Bureau. A South Carolina native,

McGill served in the United States Air Force and holds a BA from South Carolina State University.

GRANT HAYTER-MENZIES specializes in producing biographies of extraordinary women, including stage and screen stars Charlotte Greenwood and Billie Burke; the Chinese-American author Princess Der Ling; the diarist Sarah Pike Conger; the wife of the American ambassador to China and friend to the controversial Empress Dowager Cixi of China, Pauline Benton; the American-born master of Chinese shadow theater; and Lillian Carter, the mother of President Jimmy Carter. In 2015, Grant published *From Stray Dog to World War I Hero: The Paris Terrier Who Joined the First Division*. His most recent book, *The Lost War Horses of Cairo: The Passion of Dorothy Brooke*, was published to acclaim in the US and UK. Grant's next book, *Woo, The Monkey Who Inspired Emily Carr: A Biography* will be published in March 2019. *The North Door: Echoes of Slavery in a New England Family*, his memoir of his ancestors' three centuries of complicity in the transatlantic slave trade, will be published in the summer of 2019. Grant lives in Victoria, British Columbia, Canada.

SHARON LESLIE MORGAN is a writer and genealogist. She retired in 2010 after a long career as a marketing communications consultant, a field she helped establish in the United States and for which she was awarded the D. Parke Gibson Legend Award from the Public Relations Society of America. She has lived abroad in Jamaica, South Africa, and France. In 2007, she founded Our Black Ancestry, an online community devoted to African American genealogy. She is the coauthor, with Thomas Norman DeWolf, of *Gather at the Table: The Healing Journey of a Daughter of Slavery and a Son of the Slave Trade*. Her first book, *My Daddy Is A Cool Dude,* was nominated for a Caldecott Medal. She is also the author of *Paris in a Pot: Living a Dream in the City of Light* and coauthor of *Real Women Cook: Building Healthy Communities with Recipes that Stir the Soul.*

R. GREGORY NOKES is a journalist and author, who has written three nonfiction histories of the West, the award-winning *Massacred for Gold: The Chinese in Hells Canyon* and *Breaking Chains: Slavery on Trial in the Oregon Territory,* and his new book, *The Troubled Life of Peter Burnett: Oregon Pioneer and First Governor of California*. Nokes has forty years' experience as a reporter and foreign correspondent, traveling the world for The Associated Press and The Oregonian and contributing as an author to *The Media and Foreign Policy* and numerous other publications. Nokes did his undergraduate work at Willamette University in Oregon, and attended Harvard University as a Nieman Fellow in 1971–1972. He lives in West Linn, Oregon with his wife Candise.

ELISA D. PEARMAIN, MA, LMHC, is the award-winning author of two collections of world tales—*Doorways to the Soul: 52 Wisdom Tales from around the World* and *Once Upon a Time: Storytelling to Teach Character and Prevent Bullying*. She has been telling stories professionally since 1986 and recorded an award-winning double CD of stories and commentary called *Forgiveness: Telling our Stories in New Ways in 2013*. Elisa's interest in the healing power of stories led her to a master's degree in counseling in 1998. She now divides her time between private therapy practice, storytelling, writing, and being on the board of the Healing Story Alliance. Elisa's interest in understanding and applying the forgiveness process led her to CTTT in 2015.

CATHERINE SASANOV is the author of the poetry collections *Had Slaves, All the Blood Tethers* and *Traditions of Bread and Violence*. She also authored the libretto for *Las horas de Belén: A Book of Hours,* a theater work commissioned by Mabou Mines. She is a National Endowment for the Arts fellowship recipient, and has held residencies at the Blue Mountain Center, the MacDowell Colony, the Millay Colony, and the Sundance Theater Lab. As a Charlotte and Robert J. Baron Creative Artist fellow at the American Antiquarian Society, she recently conducted research for her book in progress, *Mark^d Y (Archives and Invocations)*. Poems from the manuscript, as well as Sasanov's essay "In Search of the Woman Mark^d Y," can be read in online journals at common-place.org, pooryorickjournal.com, and calibanonline.com.

BILL SIZEMORE is retired after a forty-three-year career in journalism, most of it spent as a reporter and editor at *The Virginian-Pilot* in Norfolk. He was also a weekly newspaper editor and publisher. He is the recipient of more than twenty-five awards for excellence in journalism from the Virginia Press Association and was a finalist for the 2007 Pulitzer Prize in explanatory reporting. A native Virginian, he has written the book *Uncle George and Me: Two Southern Families Confront a Shared Legacy of Slavery* about his slave-owning ancestors, their slaves, and those slaves' descendants. He lives in Williamsburg, Virginia.

LESLIE STAINTON is the author of *Lorca: A Dream of Life* and *Staging Ground: An American Theater and Its Ghosts,* and she is at work on a book about her slaveholding ancestors. Her writing has appeared in the *New York Times*, the *Washington Post*, *American Poetry Review*, *Brevity*, *Crab Orchard Review*, *River Teeth*, and *Memoir*, among others. Learn more at lesliestain ton.com.

KAREN STEWART-ROSS is a multimedia artist working on her first two books, *The Blues Within: The Biography of Edwin Goodwin "Buster" Pickens*™ (a biography of her uncle) and a currently unnamed book about a historic Georgia town founded by her ancestor's family over 140 years ago. A writer and educator, Stewart-Ross is motivated by the untold story and produces radio-show topics to inspire other women and girls in regions like the Sudan and Haiti to live boldly.

LUCIAN K. TRUSCOTT IV is the son of Anne Harloe and Lucian K. Truscott III. He was born just after World War II in occupied Japan and grew up as an army brat. He graduated from West Point in 1969, served in the army as an officer, and he has been a writer ever since. He has written five novels and journalism for numerous publications such as *Esquire*, the *New Yorker*, and *Rolling Stone*. He was a staff writer for the *Village Voice* for five years. He has three children and currently lives in Sag Harbor, New York, where he writes a column for the online magazine *Salon*.

A. B. WESTRICK is the author of *Brotherhood*, the story of a European American boy who befriends an African American teacher and comes to question the racial prejudices he has been taught. *Brotherhood* made the American Library Association's 2014 list of Best Fiction for Young Adults and won numerous awards (Jefferson Cup, Jane Addams honor, Housatonic, and Notable Trade Book). A graduate of Stanford University and Yale Divinity School, Westrick received an MFA in writing from the Vermont College of Fine Arts in 2011. She teaches in the low-residency MFA program in writing at Western Connecticut State University and blogs monthly at ABWestrick .com. She and her family live near Richmond, Virginia.

RODNEY G. WILLIAMS is a writer, marketing consultant, chef, and genealogist. In 2011 he published *Memorable Mornings*, a coffee-table cookbook focused on breakfast and brunch entertaining, and his work has appeared on the websites One for the Table and Narratively, and in two anthologies. After leaving his career as a healthcare financing and actuarial junior executive, he went on to build a $2 million hospitality brand, with two locations. His forthcoming memoir tackles the intersection of race, history, and the criminal justice system through the lens of an African American male "with promise," who wrestles with the high expectations that accompany being born in the cradle of the civil rights movement.

THE EDITORS

DIONNE FORD is the author of the forthcoming memoir *Finding Josephine*. Her work has appeared in the *New York Times, More, LitHub, Rumpus,* and *Ebony* and has won awards from the National Association of Black Journalists and the Newswomens' Club of New York. She holds an MFA in creative writing from New York University and received a 2018 creative writing fellowship from the National Endowment for the Arts. Dionne joined CTTT in 2010 and served as board vice president from 2013 to 2014.

JILL STRAUSS, PHD, teaches conflict resolution at the Borough of Manhattan Community College, City University of New York. She earned her doctorate from Ulster University, Northern Ireland, and she is a Fulbright scholar. Her publications include "Writing the Wrongs of the Past: Descendants of Enslavers and the Enslaved Come to the Table" in *Listening to the Movement: Essays on New Growth in Restorative Justice* and "The Art of Acknowledgment: Re-Imagining Relationships in Northern Ireland" in *Reparation for Victims of Crimes against Humanity: The Healing Role of Reparation.*

INDEX

Page numbers in *italics* represent photographs.